MILLENNIUM

Towards Tomorrow's Society

Francis Kinsman

W H ALLEN

© Francis Kinsman

Set in Meridien by Phoenix Photosetting, Chatham
Printed and bound in Great Britain by
Mackays of Chatham PLC, Chatham, Kent
For the publishers, W.H. Allen & Co Plc
Sekforde House, 175/9 St. John Street, London EC1V 4LL

ISBN 0 49103744 9

TO

JACK, EM AND JOHN

THE BEST THAT HAS BEEN AND THE BEST THAT IS TO COME

CONTENTS

PREFACE AND ACKNOWLEDGEMENTS

At the time this is published there will be exactly ten years to go before the year 2000. Nobody is giving much thought to this as yet, but soon the magic of round numbers will assert itself as people begin to focus on the date as a milestone of tremendous significance. The magnetism surrounding our new millennium (ignoring the pedants who insist that it will actually begin on New Year's Day 2001) will create a source of energy that can be directed towards the lasting benefit of humankind if we so wish.

The first millennium in 1000 AD attracted many adherents to the belief that it would mark the Second Coming, and the failure of this forecast has since imbued the word with overtones of naive optimism. About the portents of the year 2000 we must be very much more guarded, but the purpose of this book is to present an analysis of today's society and then to show how selected parts of it can form the synthesis of a chosen tomorrow – a self-fulfilling prophecy that translates the optimistic ideal into the optimum real.

To do this I have drawn on the worlds of politics, economics, current affairs, and particularly of business which I expect to play a key role in these developments. I have also plundered the disciplines of philosophy, physics, biology, psychology and especially of social research. Some of the authorities whom I have cited might be surprised or even shocked to find themselves sharing the same side of an argument with others in such alien fields. I therefore cheerfully accept the responsibility for collating the data from these strange bedfellows in the quest for whole and unifying principles.

In the process, I have become convinced that over the next twenty years or so we have it in our power to construct a truly convivial future for our species – convivial in the root sense of living harmoniously and interdependently with each other and the planet that bears us. Whether we take this opportunity or not is another matter, but it is there for the taking nonetheless. My task in these pages has therefore been to introduce the arguments behind this claim. My future intention is to chronicle the progressive changes and pioneering initiatives that are now being made in many fields, so that those who feel like building the millennium will have an owner's manual for guidance – a set of user instructions for The Whole Thing.

I have many to thank for their support and contributions to date. First come all the friends who share my vision and with whom I have endlessly discussed and shaped these ideas and concepts. Among such a wealth of kindred spirits it is invidious to single out particular benefactors, but *primi inter pares* must be Edward Posey, Liz Hosken, Eileen Conn and Susan Balfour. I also owe a great debt to Barbara Somers and Ian Gordon-Brown of the Centre for Transpersonal Psychology for introducing me to the marvels of the human psyche. A cornerstone of the book is the theoretical and practical work of Taylor Nelson Group Ltd/Applied Futures Ltd on the dynamics of social change, and my deep gratitude goes to Christine MacNulty for her permission to refer to this.

I have also made frequent recourse to published data and comment, both in books and journals and in the national media. Attributions to the authors have been given where possible in the Appendix of Notes and References, but it is not inconceivable that the odd *bon mot*, picked up and squirrelled away over the years, may have escaped the net. If so, I hope that the originators will accept my apologies; I am as grateful to them as to those I have listed by name.

Finally on the production side I have to thank David Machin and Chris Holifield, both late of The Bodley Head, for all their counsel and encouragement; Carole Henley, Anne Porter and Gilly Cannon for their help in the early stages of the text; and Judy Smith for both her technical and her abundant human skills.

Francis Kinsman
Bath
May 1989

1

INTRODUCTION AND FUGUE

The Example of Business

The National Westminster Bank lends out over 1,000 staff members to work for charity. Two dozen of GEC's young management tigers lie on the floor together in meditation and then swop drawings of their daydreams. Marks & Spencer combines with its personnel to raise £4m. together for local community causes. And peering out over the Thames from his Millbank office, ICI's then Chairman, Sir John Harvey-Jones, muses 'we must love our employees more' . . .

Something Else Is Going On.

This Something Else is the very beginning of a dramatic metamorphosis – of business, and indeed of everything else as well. The traditional carapace is splitting open and a new and fascinating creature is struggling to get out. Impelled by a unique combination of technological and social pressures, we are finding ourselves in totally unfamiliar territory, from whence there is no return to those comfortable yesterdays. The old order changeth and the new to which it giveth place hath not been gracious enough to disclose itself clearly as yet. Nobody can escape its implications, though, however strong may be the wish to do so.

The story begins in a business context, although it is by no means a uniquely business story. It also concerns people who may consider themselves nothing to do with business. But business embraces us all in one capacity or another, and a general change in attitude within business will have the most galvanic effects upon us all. Business is now a global force. Multinational corporations are now turning over annual sums as large as the GNP of many national states. As Arthur K. Watson, then President of IBM, put it even as long ago as 1969 –

> 'Providence was not whimsical when it chose
> business to bring the world together. People
> care about business; they may never agree
> about religion or ideology but there is a
> logic to business, and through it we may see
> this quarrelsome, troubled world brought
> together.'

These words are carved into the wall of the IBM European Training Centre at La Hulpe, Belgium. Watson was speaking as the leader of a multi-national organisation in the context of international world harmony. Cynics may dispute the role of multinationals in bringing about international world harmony, but they cannot deny their key position as industrial diplomats, for good or ill.

Now, however, these industrial diplomats must modify their previous immunity. The planners, the schemers, the wheelers and the dealers are just beginning to come to terms with a fundamental shift in values that is occurring all over the world and is quite different to their previous conceptions of it. In some places, Great Britain being very much at the forefront of them, this movement is developing more rapidly than elsewhere; but though frequently camouflaged by other events which are superimposed upon it, it can be shown to be both universal and inexorable. By the time the new century dawns, this true millennium will have visibly dawned with it. Social change is on the menu and woe betide anyone who isn't hungry. Praise be, some in business are already, as the following examples show.

Four Straws in the Wind

*   National Westminster Bank plc

Our first success story relates to the 1973 foundation of National Westminster Enterprises Ltd.[1] These were early days for this sort of thing, but it was then that NatWest suddenly woke up to a very unpleasant staff problem. It had recruited a large number of young men in the pre-war boom of the late 1930s, most of whom had rejoined it after being demobbed and then stayed put for the whole of their working lives.

In consequence there was an excess of about 150 managers and assistant managers hanging over the internal labour market. These people were admirable – loyal, hard-working, trustworthy and efficient in what they were asked to do – but there were simply too many of them. Thus 150 people in their late forties and early fifties were permanently stuck in positions where there was no chance of progress for the rest of their careers. They were also standing in the path of the increasingly disgruntled younger generation, which could not be promoted over their heads without an uproar.

In such circumstances, a lot of managements would have considered redundancy provisions, but it was not the NatWest philosophy to administer a kick in the teeth to employees who had served it well for the whole of their careers. After all, under other conditions they would have been able to fulfil far more for their employer than it was now possible to demand of them. So the management eventually came up with another solution – a separate company within the Bank's structure to which the 150 were seconded. They were paid their same salaries and guaranteed all the periodical increases that their scales provided for, with holiday, sick leave, pension and other benefits remaining totally unaffected. They were, in other words, still part of the bank as such, but were moved completely away from actual banking duties; because the purpose of this particular subsidiary was to provide its own manpower free for charitable work.

NatWest Enterprises was thus not a profit centre, it was deliberately conceived as a loss centre; and it found hundreds of charities and worthy causes longing to lay their hands on just what it had on offer, namely professional advisers of financial experience, administrative and organisational ability, scrupulous trustworthiness and capable of hard and dedicated commitment. And free of cost. Such was the response, indeed, that the individuals concerned were able to pick and choose from the thousands of charities that came forward, so as precisely to suit their own personal interests and geographical requirements.

The experiment was a success. The charities were delighted with their new helpers. The seconded men found a major purpose in life at last, being transferred to fulfilling work of their own choice while remaining employed within the same group. The rest of the staff were relieved to see movement in the personnel log-jam, and proud that their bank was the one that had conjured up the scheme.

Since 1973 over 1,000 secondees have been through this process. It has cost NatWest a not inconsiderable sum of money, even though the redundancy alternative would have been expensive anyway; but in human terms, how infinitely less valuable. Instead, there has been full utilization

[3]

of the most valuable of all resources – good human material – to the benefit of all concerned. Since then, many many large organizations have embarked on similar secondment schemes – not least under the umbrella of Business in the Community, of which more later – contributing roundly to the sum total of human effectiveness in the form of useful life after, and nowadays often even during, formally productive employment.

*   GEC plc

The second reference relates to a senior management course held at GEC's training establishment at Dunchurch. Here, every year, 24 from among the company's *jeunesse d'orée* are thrown together for a three-week course in order to broaden their horizons and generally grind them into a pulp. As an exercise in helping them to get in touch with their creative processes the writer, with two colleagues, took them on a 24-hour 'Inward Bound' journey into the recesses of their psyches – as a contrast to the 'Outward Bound' element of the course which took place a week later and constituted a more physical journey up and down mountain-sides, potholes, and white-water rivers. It was a moot point among them which was the more traumatic experience. 'Inward Bound' was an attempt to introduce these logical, numerate, eminently sensible engineers to the junglier, irrational parts of their very own minds.

It is an established neuro-physiological fact that the brain's two hemispheres, besides being responsible for the motor and sensory functions of the opposite sides of the body, also control different aspects of mental behaviour. The left side of the brain is responsible for intellectual activity – for the precise logical, analytical and scientific side of our characters, and in particular the use of words and numbers. Straight-down-the-middle-of-the-road GEC requirements, in fact. The right brain, in daunting contrast, is concerned with the more emotional, intuitive and artistic aspects of our natures, with symbols and images, with dreams and with visions. But for the creative imagination to function at its most effective, both sides of the brain must be in use and in balance; representing in a sense a combination of the masculine and feminine sides of human nature, both of which are needed to conceive together the fully creative thought.

So it was that by means of a guided daydream technique, the three of us were trying to help these high-flying engineers – all men – to discover, accept and redeem the less familiar 'feminine' side of their mental processes through meditation and letting go – abandoning the logic for the symbolic, and exploring this different but equally important reality by first muffling the surface clamour of their more familiar left brains. Using a

[4]

effective and rich any more. Dr. Johnson said that nothing
so needs a philosophy as does business, and this is what
it boils down to. The whole essence of business in society
must be rethought through, and ringingly restated in human
terms.'

This quotation comes from another interview conducted with a senior
member of the British business establishment — Sir Peter Parker, ex-
Chairman of British Rail, and past president of the British Institute of
Management. As Chairman of Mitsubishi UK, Sir Peter also sees the
underlying philosophy of human awareness as a way in which one of the
basic principles of Japanese success can be grafted onto the British
commercial and industrial culture. His strong endorsement of the arguments put forward so far came in 1983 during the gathering of data for a
book 'The New Agenda' that has already been mentioned.

In the course of this research, 30 of the most forward-looking of
Britain's leaders of industry and commerce were interviewed. The results
were an elaboration of their answers to a single question: 'what do you
imagine will be the most important social issues facing British management in 1990?' These managers, besides being at the top of their
respective trees, were mostly in their late 40s or 50s, and thus already had
to be answering this question accurately for themselves if they were to
avoid the pitfalls of the future and end their careers at a peak. Those
who were above this age group were of a cast of mind likely to keep them
involved in public life after their retirement, and still greatly concerned
with its problems. Finally, they were all selected as seeming to demonstrate particular characteristics of imagination and sensitivity.

The fact that the points they made were quoted without attribution
gave them the confidence to speak their minds — indeed, they emulated
the PG Wodehouse character who spilled the beans with a firm and steady
hand. Spades, in other words, were resoundingly identified as such. The
answers to the single question about social change exploded into a rich
variety of opinions covering, *inter alia*, aspects of unemployment; the
place of business in the community; pensions; employee relations; the
third world and the environment; consumerism; changing patterns of
class, work, training and education; the role of women and young people;
organisational structure and management style.

It was a mosaic where many elements of common ground were shared
by certainly most, if not all, the individuals concerned. The most fundamental and important principle that emerged was so compact as to be

able to be written on the back of a postage stamp – People Matter Most. Encouraged by their anonymity, these business leaders revealed their true feelings in remarkably warm, human and unequivocal terms. As one high-ranking City figure put it –

> 'Up till now, there has been a complete difference between the way individuals relate to their colleagues in business and the way that they relate to their friends and family. In the latter area, kindness and tolerance are not regarded as sentimental and wet, but as essential in helping to make the relationship or group actually work. Now, the difference between the two sets of attitudes is beginning to narrow, thank God, and that may be the answer to tomorrow's looming problems.'

This enlightened theme was echoed consistently throughout the exercise, and led to feelings of elation and excitement. When these were shared with Sir John, he responded, 'do you really mean to tell me there are other nutters like me out there?'. Could this even be the possible birth of a vibrant new business philosophy, one conjectured – not new in absolute terms since it was simply the embodiment of all that was best of the old, but new in the context of being so significantly supported by an important group of the country's most influential business people. Heady stuff.

Once the book was written, copies were sent by its sponsors to all the 30 participants who were also invited to a dinner. The purpose of this was to discuss the results of the survey and plan some combined action that could be taken to encourage the new movement that it all seemed to herald. Fond dream. For the writer, the party was a disaster seeded third after Belshazzar's and Macbeth's. The fourteen who attended abandoned the genuinely enlightened approach that characterised their original inter-views, and opted instead for an exercise in verbal arm-wrestling – with a few exceptions who were quickly swept aside. Their statements as guests reflected a totally different cast of mind compared to their statements as interviewees – a reversion to the schoolboy urge to be seen as the toughest kid on the block when all the other kids are around.

The male-orientated culture of business life is as deep-rooted as a verruca, and to have expected an instant cure was naïve. Many years experience in consultancy, interviewing and lecturing within the British business community has confirmed how tenacious are the old founda-tions of yesterday's business practice and, by natural extension, of tomor-row's business problems.

[10]

The New Initiative

However, the examples cited earlier do show that at least some in the business world, and indeed some at the very top of it, are already marching to the beat of a different drum. It will soon be apparent that the beat of this drum is in rhythm with Something Else even more profound; and that inexorably all business people, indeed all people of any persuasion, must eventually resonate with whatever the rhythm of that Something Else may be. Technological but above all social change will necessitate reactions a good deal more sensitive than a mere knee-jerk from those who intend to survive at all, whether organisations or individuals – in business, in politics, or in the world as a whole. This is the theory whose evidence we are now going to explore, define and extend into a vision of the future.

When the theory finally hardens into self-evident reality over the passage of time, we must expect to see an absolute change in society; because business, as noted, touches every single member of society in all its multifarious activities – whether they be employees, consumers, pensioners, suppliers, associates or the great public at large – all the different kinds of People who Matter Most. Meanwhile, the profit motive is somewhere there behind this new aspect of business behaviour, as with every other. In our climate of social and technological change, very different demands are being subtly and increasingly placed upon business, and it is responding to them. There are now tangible rewards for instances of imaginative humanity; and corresponding punishments for the restrictive, traditionalist, blinkered and unbalanced ethos that characterised past practice and which is still, alas, largely prevalent today.

In this country the phenomenon has been overlaid with another and much more obvious manifestation – the Thatcherite approach of competitive assertiveness. We will see, however, the manner in which these two strands of contemporary thought are intertwined, and how gradually at first, and then ever more rapidly, it will become apparent that it is profitable to love thy neighbour. As shown, four of the biggest companies in the country are sending out the message already, in their different ways. But this particular penny is now beginning to drop universally, and once it has done so there are going to be an awful lot of happy neighbours about.

2

THE RULE OF THREE

No Longer Two Nations

Ever since Disraeli's[1] famous reference to 'Two Nations', politicians of all hues have been sounding off about the need for Britain to de-polarise, and about how under their own wise helmsmanships this integration would miraculously take place. They will have deep problems if they genuinely do believe their scripts. So individualistic are the British that it is not so much a matter of two nations, as two-to-the-power-of nations. But though generalisation is dangerous, it is revealing to consider the present and future state of the country on the basis of it being comprised not of two nations at all, but three. This at a stroke makes incongruous our legacy of confrontational politics, and releases us to the possibility of a far more productive future, once we recognise that three into two won't go.

The first of our real nations is 'Caring Britain'. Most of the story so far has been an attempt to show that some business institutions are just beginning to recognise the profit-related value of revealing their human sides, embarrassing though this may be to them, given the traditional macho business culture. But who are they trying to please, at such a cost to their patriarchal egos? In the time-honoured phrase, is there a market?

They can see very well that a great many people are more and more concerned with human values. Social research shows clearly that there is a gathering concern for the environment, for mutual help, and for the beautifulness of the small. Qualitatively there are many signs that the British are a caring people – one need look no further than the public response to Telethon or African famine to prove that. And, on a micro-scale, all these quiet, local, individual, person-to-person networking movements are growing and growing. An army of unsung men and women is forming itself up to battle with outside events – house groups, neighbourhood groups, issue groups, self-help groups, therapy groups – where individuals have joined to create closer and more mutually supportive relationships than are possible in larger gatherings. 'Caring Britain' embraces today's drive towards social consciousness, empathy with others, and a desire for more genuine personal interaction on the small scale.

In stark contrast, there is also 'Cabaret Britain'. More and more people want to enjoy themselves *now*, it seems, regardless of what the future might hold. Deferred pleasure is boring – grasshoppers are in and ants are out among today's glittering social insects. The good time, the new experience, the big bang, the short cut and to hell with the consequences; that is the rote for an increasing number of people, who make the automatic assumption that jam today can probably be ladled on to help swallow down tomorrow's mouldy bread. It is a colour supplement world for them, casual and carefree; feckless and reckless; escapist and fatalist, according to one's own philosophical interpretation. But whatever the interpretation, the reality is there and no mistake.

Finally, the third world is the Third World – or at any rate that portion of it that exists within these shores. As is glaringly shown by the research described in the following pages, there is an increasing sense of defensive class identification within the more disadvantaged social groups, among whom social inequality is still perceived as the dominating principle of human existence in the late 20th century, just as it has been for them and their like for the past 19 centuries before this. This is 'Combustible Britain', the tinder-dry country where social discrimination, racial, sexual and age discrimination are seen at their sharpest, where the howl of the underdog baying at the moon is most frequently heard. But within this psychological group, there are also those who see themselves as tribal chieftains forever sitting on top of their feudal piles. In their views of the world, many of the great and the good have more in common with the small and the awkward than either of them might imagine.

Clearly, there is a degree of overlap among these three nations, the Caring, the Cabaret and the Combustible. Some individuals are both caring and angry, and even the most hedonistic of us are struck by social needs when they are brought to our attention. The overall picture is cloudy, dappled even. There is certainly an identifiable 'People Matter Most' mode of thought, but concern about unemployment leaches gradually away as social consciences succumb to the effects of compassion fatigue; people may be primarily concerned with the present, but so are they dimly thinking about the future; class restriction and economic disadvantage are constantly and vividly real to the 'have nots', but some-times also drift across the minds of the 'haves'.

In strict truth then, we are not talking about one nation, not two, not even three, but many. However, let us take up the useful trefoil analysis, which because of its imbalanced nature, now foreshadows a period of inherent instability – with division, coalition, and turbulence awaiting us, derived from this basically tri-partite fragmentation. Its divisions cut across age, sex, class and geographical difference and introduce a wholly different grouping concept of social analysis – according to the underlying values that give rise to visibly evident lifestyles and patterns of behaviour.

The Theoretical Groundwork

It is this 3-part split that characterises the seminal Taylor Nelson/SRI International analysis, not only applying to the British Isles and the USA, but to the whole of human society – most evidently, however, in the nations of the Western developed world.

This philosophical breakthrough occurred in the 1970s when SRI International, an offshoot of the Californian Stanford Research Institute, was developing various social scenarios for the future and examined 16 different working models of the psyche – to see if overall societal behaviour in any way mirrored these theories of individual motivation. Their chief researcher Arnold Mitchell found that one particular development model, based on a hypothesis of the psychologist Abraham Maslow, answered the problem particularly neatly; and furthermore his colleague Christine MacNulty discovered that it also mirrored the European empirical social research work led by the Taylor Nelson Group[2] in Britain.

Maslow,[3] a follower of Carl Jung and a founder of the humanistic psychology movement, postulated the existence of what he described as the Hierarchy of Needs. Analysing human psychological development, he suggested that once the basic requirements of food, clothes, warmth, shelter and sex are satisfied, an individual will turn his aim to belonging to a group of other like-minded souls for mutual comfort and protection. When this urge is also satisfied, he concentrates on staking out his position in that group by means of material display and achievement. However, there is a limit to the charms of materialism, and the previously materialist individual may then find herself asking disquieting questions – like, if she has four television sets already does she actually need a fifth in the loo; and furthermore, how can it be that in spite of all these trappings of success she is still not particularly at ease with life.

At this stage she or he – let us not stereotype the gender – may also be beset by frantic psychological itches like 'what is it all for?', 'what does it all mean?', and 'who am I anyway?', that keep popping up in unscratch-able places and at unscratchable moments. What he now wants above all is to explore and develop himself internally; to be taken seriously as a human being; and to have his personal opinions accepted as mattering to the rest of the world.

The individual has thus moved from focusing on survival as her most important consideration, via the world of group belonging, then to mater-ial success as a touchstone, and finally for the time being to what Maslow called self-actualisation. Ultimately she may come to self-realisation, the state of enlightenment and peaceful adjustment with creation that is experienced by only a few. This final state of mind represents no great opportunity to the business and political worlds at present, and can thus be shelved for a while; in contrast, self-actualisation certainly now does present an opportunity, as we shall see, albeit one that is extremely difficult for would be opportunists to grasp unless they are part of the parade already.

Maslow argued that the earthier needs lower down at the bottom end of the scale had first to be satisfied to an optimum degree before the restless human spirit began searching round for some other form of satisfaction. However, he also suggested that some immature individuals become stuck in a relatively primitive stage of personal development, like Mexican axolotls, unable to move further up the ladder because they suffer from a psychological block that inclines them to *maximise* rather than to *optimise* the physicalities of security, or belonging, or material success, depending on the particular stage they have reached. There are more axolotls around than one might imagine. We will meet them later on.

The Lessons of the Past

SRI jacked up this whole concept a stage further and presented it to their clients in social, rather than individual terms, labelled the Values and Lifestyles System, and set forth in Arnold Mitchell's[4] book 'The Nine

American Life-styles'. They first argued that the history of mankind showed a similar spectrum of collective needs, according to the stages of civilisation that had been reached. Thus the primitive hunter-gatherer's most urgent need was for survival. However, by Neolithic times, the move had developed for an easier life-style than vaguely roaming all over the country for food. With the planting of crops and the husbandry of animals, the resultant agricultural revolution made it possible for human beings to settle down in one place.

Then, in order to protect themselves against thieving marauders from outside who might make off with their stores of food, people found they needed to band together into tribal villages of a size sufficient to deter external attack. The members of a nomadic or an agricultural society were thus sustenance driven in nature, motivated by the need to survive, and then also to belong to a supportive group. Life is simple in this state – on both the plus side and the minus side – and there is little if any social mobility. The feudal peasant mentality decrees that the rich man in his castle, the poor man at his gate, God made them high or lowly, and ordered their estate. And anyone who claims otherwise is probably in for the rack and the thumbscrew.

In this feudal past, the underlings were dependent upon their liege lords. The Divine Right of Kings filtered down the scale to the lesser important nobility and squirearchy. In return for paternalistic support from above, the nobs received subjugated support from below in the form of labour, taxes, and assistance in defence. However, the whole philosophical engine was fuelled by the belief that provision came from on high in a series of inter-connected steps leading from God downwards. The Renaissance put paid to all that, and with all its emphasis on self-help the resultant Industrial Revolution ushered in an era of independence. Humankind had in a sense outgrown the bonds of childhood and arrived at a rather disturbed adolescence, during which, as a fairly horrible know-all, it began to throw its weight about like nobody's business.

Thomas S. Kuhn[5] in his book 'The Structure of Scientific Revolutions' described how a revolution occurs in a science when one scientific paradigm (a model of how things should be done) breaks down and another replaces it, bringing with it a whole new order of scientists. The same is true of politics, of economics, and indeed of society itself. Thus though human development appears to be cumulative, piling fact upon fact in the vast storehouse of experience, it is actually a much more stormy affair. There are periods of intense struggle between competing paradigms which have few or no common points of reference. Ultimately they are resolved and fuse together to create a new paradigm which holds sway in its turn, pending the birth of an alternative rival. This process has also been noted by the philosophers Hegel and Popper, whose theories are referred to later.

So with the Industrial Revolution everything changed – again both for plus and for minus. No longer was anybody's estate ordered indefinitely. By dint of diligence, cleverness and skill, a man could rise rapidly in the social pecking order; but equally as rapidly fall down to the dregs of it through bad luck or bad management. There thus emerges a society where it is of primary importance to demonstrate very precisely where you are in comparison with your peer group. Ostentatious show not only to keep up with but to outstrip the Joneses becomes the order of the day. And in the initial scramble for positions on the inside track, classic gentility gives way to glitzy vulgarity, characterised by the move from the Georgian to the Victorian taste.

The industrial age, then, has proved itself to be one of materialism, of conspicuous consumption, of the worship of achievement and success. This is the moment when the protestant work ethic holds sway – where the creation of even more wealth by those who have a good share of it already is part of the Divine Plan, while those who never had it in the first place are reckoned to be punished for their idleness by God in a holy alliance with their employers. Competition is the keynote and 'win/lose' games head the programme; though their effects are mitigated by the fact that because competition generates economic growth, the final scramble for slices of the pie is made somewhat less painful, since for a while at least, the pie itself keeps expanding.

These transitions from one era to another are never smooth, as history shows. One of the last major battles between the hunting and the agricultural cultures occurred in the development of the American west, though similar clashes are still visible today in the Amazon jungle. Eventually, however, the emergent paradigm becomes wholly preponderant, in spite of resistance from the old guard. One can see this in today's Western agriculture, which is now essentially an industry. However, the current pace of the evolutionary process now makes this overall process even more traumatic. The last such development took 350 years to come to flower, from roughly 1400 to 1750. While the total long term change was profound, any particular individual with a life expectancy then of no more than half a century would have found it hard to detect. A man died within the broad state of life into which he had been born.

The social values of the pre-Renaissance world were moral, spiritual, authoritarian, governed by divine laws and orientated towards eternity. During the Renaissance this agrarian view of the world was abandoned, and the industrial view was established and perfected. The earth came to be seen as an insignificant side-show in a random process, even humankind itself seeming like software, programmed in a mysterious way which it has since struggled to formulate intellectually by the experimental examination of its environment. At the same time the purpose of human life became the immediate satisfaction of desires; and today's social paradigm though still moral, is – in contrast to the old – materialistic, scientific, governed by physical laws and orientated towards the here and now.

The Social Paradigm Shift[6]

What had happened between these two entirely different ages and what is happening to us at this moment, was a rare example of a social paradigm shift. The social paradigm has been defined as 'a commonly held frame of reference, comprising a constellation of attitudes, values, beliefs and experiences which are shared by individual members of society. This provides a yardstick that enables (people) to communicate effectively with one another and to arrive at closely similar judgements in any given situation'. Longhand, in other words, for the way things are, have been and ever will be, one hopes. But when society moves from one set of values to another – such as from the hunting to the agricultural, the agricultural to the industrial or as now, the industrial to the post-industrial – this so-called paradigm shift takes place, a socially driven phenomenon in four broad stages:

*   A few innovators feel they have satisfied the needs which preoccupy the majority of the society and turn their attention to the satisfaction of other needs higher in the Maslow hierarchy.

*   A new set of values is thus created, which in time forms the basis of the new paradigm. Concurrently, a new life-style is developed (based on technology in the latter paradigm shift and information in the current one) which derives from these new values.

*   This new life-style provides employment for large numbers of

people who work in and rely on the emerging paradigm, but who may well continue to hold the values of the previous one, even though an increasing proportion adopt the new way of thought. This is an inevitable basis for social conflict.

* Gradually, as the more appropriate life-style satisfies their newly recognised needs, more people turn to it and the new paradigm becomes the accepted form. However, a hard core continues to fight it, and just as it becomes acceptable an outer ring of social architects begins to prepare the blueprint for the next devlopment.

This concept is based upon the premise that the needs which an individual works to satisfy also determine his beliefs and motives, which in turn determine attitudes and life-styles and, ultimately behaviour – at home, at work, at play, in development, in markets and in politics.

In and after the seventeenth century wealthy European gentlemen, whose leisurely investigations of nature became the fundamentals of the physical sciences, were the initiators of the industrial paradigm. The technology and economics of this emerged in the eighteenth century as the Industrial Revolution, and provided employment for millions who still held the basic values and philosophy of the agrarian paradigm, but who worked in industry because it met their needs better than did the agriculture of the time. At present we are involved in a shift from the industrial to the so-called post-industrial, and what is even more painful for us is that this is occurring with considerably greater rapidity than did the change from agriculture to industry.

Our situation today is quite different from that of the newly emerging industrial revolutionary. This current paradigm shift may take as little as 100 years, and for us the change is not only noticeable, it is breathtaking. If we expect to live within three different generations, given a life expectancy of say 80 years we are actually living three totally different lives. Some will accept this and take advantage of it. Many others who cling to their old views are resisting and will resist it to the death. There may be nothing so powerful as an idea whose time has come, but there is nothing so frustrating as an idea whose time is being denied by the vested interests of the old-fangled.

In 'The Age Of Unreason',[7] Professor Charles Handy points out that for those in charge continuity is comfort, and predictability ensures that they can continue in control. Discontinuous change requires discontinuous thinking, and if the new way of things is genuinely different and not just a theoretical improvement on the same old story, we all need to look at life in a wholly new way. But this brings out the problem that such upside-down thinking has never been popular with the powerful upholders of continuity and the status quo. Handy illustrates the dangers of this with the story of a frog which, if put in cold water, 'will not bestir itself if that water is heated up slowly and gradually, and will in the end let itself be boiled alive, too comfortable with continuity to realise that continuous change at some point becomes discontinuous and demands a change in behaviour.'

The life of a product is said to go through six distinct stages – invention, innovation, development, maturity, saturation and decline. The curve of its market impact against time is sigmoid or S-shaped with two flattened sections at each end and a band of high acceleration in between. An idea may well have the same kind of life history, in which case we are now on the brink of an extraordinary and innovative phase, approaching a millennium where the new is about to burst out all over, if only we will permit it. The radical has already become the avant garde, and will soon be common knowledge.

Frustrating though it may be for the pioneers to go through these extended labour pains, it is important to realise that there is a strong tendency for people to label things selectively in accordance with their own individual situations. This may lead them to adopt what one might call a subjective conjugation, as in 'I am developed; you are in the process of growth; he is going to have to change.' Indeed, we are all prisoners of our own experience, and frequently, a new philosophical idea of this magnitude is so overwhelming that it is a matter of all or nothing. Either you accept it or you don't – either you see it or you don't. As Marilyn Ferguson[8] puts it, 'it is like one of those children's puzzle pictures where objects are disguised in the landscape. Until you have had that shock of recognition and actually discovered the toothbrush in the tree for yourself, it is no use everybody else telling you how extraordinary it is that you cannot see it there.'

Ultimately, however, the idea gains such momentum that there comes a moment where it splits society into two implacable camps – those who know and those who don't want to know. This is the nature of the paradigm shift and will be a constant theme of this text.

The Lessons of the Future

Have we, as a species, perhaps been through our childhood and adolescent phases, and now stand on the brink of adulthood?[9] We have passed through the period when the emphasis was on the body and its physical capability, and are now possibly coming to the end of the time when like school-children the emphasis has had to be on the education of our collective intellect. Now maybe it is time to begin transferring at least part of our attention to the emotions and the spirit – more so than we have done in the past, at any rate. These could be the lessons we have yet to learn.

The industrial is giving way to what is generally described as the post-industrial; but better perhaps, as the 'trans-industrial' – a term which implies the transfer and transformation of industry rather than its demise. It is at this point in human history, the cusp between two ages, where we find ourselves standing right now. We can hardly fail to see that much of our traditional industry is withering away, but as yet we are unclear about quite what is going to take its place. With the transfer of old-style technology from the developed western world to the newly developing countries of the Pacific rim, not only Japan but particularly also the 'four tigers', Singapore, Hong Kong, Taiwan and South Korea, we dimly perceive that we in our turn will have to transform our thinking and generate new activities in substitution for the now threadbare parts of our social and industrial fabric.

In the new trans-industrial world, clearly industry of some kind will still soldier on in the developed Western nations, just as agriculture still does even after the passing of the agricultural era as such. However, the number of people employed in the primary industries of agriculture, fishing and forestry shrank startlingly with the flowering of the industrial revolution, and now amounts to a mere 9% of the British workforce. In just such a way, the number of people employed in the secondary sector of traditional smoke-stack industry is also rapidly declining and will continue to do so at a runaway pace with the advent of the trans-industrial culture. Here in this country it now stands at around 26%, but is forecast to diminish to single percentage figures by the year 2000. We will continue to need these sectors but as the number of people employed in them contracts, so with it will the old influence of their characteristic philosophies as, in blunt terms, their voting power also declines.

It is as yet unclear whether our best future strategy in the face of this evolution will be to expand activities in the tertiary 'sunrise industry' sector – the worlds of electronics, bio-genetics and high-tech whiz-kiddery; or in the quarternary service sector – information, education, knowledge and health-based. Possibly the ultimate cocktail will be a mixture of both with more than a dash of leisure thrown in for good measure. However what is evident is that a new breed of person is now in the process of carving out the philosophy of the trans-industrial age even before it has arrived in material form.

Just as thinkers and scientists such as Luther, Calvin, Newton and Descartes unconsciously designed the foundations of what was to become the industrial age, so the new pioneers are already working on the blueprint for the trans-industrial without even knowing it. The movement embraces not only those who are the accepted opinion leaders of the new, but also a great mass of everyday people experiencing an inexorable discomfort with old values and a thirst for different ones – and acting accordingly, even though with faltering and uncertain steps as yet.

Senator Edward Kennedy[10] once declared that 'those who forget the past are condemned to repeat it, but those who anticipate the future are free to shape it'. There is quite a lot of quiet shaping going on right now, but establishment heads are mainly kept below parapets for the time being, as we have seen. The here and now is never a comfortable place to be in, particularly for the great and good, but at a time of such intensified change it becomes a cosmic roller-coaster ride and everyone has an excuse to feel sick. The situation is complicated by the fact of social faulting.

Just as the impact of time on geology creates geological faults, so social faults are derived from the fact that the physical and undeniable facts of society are out of phase with the leaders of thought on the one hand and the laggards of thought on the other. Today, we can find in the same bus queue the representatives of all three of the major psychological categories represented by the pre-industrial, industrial and trans-industrial eras, even though the first has now passed and the third is yet to come. They see each other, they don't know each other but they hate each other; can they ever understand each other?

The ebbing and flowing of general public opinion between these bundles of values, the mind sets of these three major social categories, has already begun as each struggles for dominance. The immediate future thus promises to be a period of temporary but intense turbulence. Ultimately trans-industrial values must predominate as the influences of the industrial age gradually weaken, but before that we are likely to face years, maybe decades of uncertainty. However, the secret for any successful society, any successful organisation or any successful human being is to become whole, by reconciling the warring elements within it, him or her till they reach a state of interdependence. By accepting fully that for the time being each part must have its place and each its accredited value, it is possible to redeem them all so that they all contribute positively to this ultimate wholeness.

That is the big millennial picture, but back in the here and now our situation is complicated by the fact that unlike in past philosophical battles where two participants have hammered away at each other – rich and poor, church and state, king and parliament, capital and labour – now there are three elements in approximate balance with each other, not two. Understanding the ground rules for a gainfully developing relationship between the three is the nub of the problem facing us all today. We are thrown together into this snake-pit and any intelligent person who wishes to survive must become very well aware of its serpentine realities. None more, however, than the business person who has to make a profit and the politician who has to get elected. And once they know, rest assured that we will all know too.

Three Worlds under the Microscope

Let us then examine in more detail the three different worlds inhabited by the three different psychological types, which SRI, developing its theory along the lines described, termed 'sustenance driven', 'outer directed' and 'inner directed'. The populations of western industrial societies divide themselves into these three broad groups, whose attitudes are sufficiently at variance with each other for them to be regarded as having three quite different approaches to life. The groups are characterised by their attitudes, rather than by any social or economic status – indeed members of each are found at every social and economic level, and within any categorisation of age or gender.

* **Sustenance driven**
The prime motivation for sustenance driven people is the need for security. Their concern is with just getting by from day to day and with belonging cosily to a supportive group of their peers. Although one particular sub-set, the 'survivors', tends to be economically disadvantaged and working class, its members being – not surprisingly – primarily

concerned about physical survival, this is by no means always the case. Many of them are comfortably well off, the 'belongers' for whom the driving force of survival entails holding on to their comfortable positions in life. They tend to be conservative, clannish, set in their ways and resistant to change. Even when they are economically able to do otherwise they are inclined to live narrow, confined and class-conscious lives. They are the left-over philosophical products of the agricultural era – the top, middle and bottom of the feudal heap.

*   Outer directed

The outer directeds are the flower of the mature industrial society, whose motivation is the search for esteem and status. The criteria by which they measure their success are to be found outside themselves – in the eyes of those who are watching their performance. They want to marry the right person, to live in the right part of town, to have the right job, to drive the right car, and to send their children to the right schools. They are concerned about appearance and behaviour, and particularly that their children should be 'a credit to the family'. It goes without saying that most of these people are materialistic – except in those circles where anti-materialism per se confers status – and they constantly seek to improve their position in financial and social terms through conspicuous achievement and conspicuous consumption. Outer directeds are often well, though conventionally, educated and mostly intelligent, with a reasonably broad intellectual horizon. They are generally supporters and maintainers of the status quo, though they can eventually change their tune if they perceive that there might be a social advantage in so doing.

*   Inner directed

Inner directeds are the children of the dawning trans-industrial age, and their psychological motivation is what Maslow termed self-actualisation. They are largely unconcerned about the opinion of them held by the world at large, since the criteria for their success and the norms for their behaviour are deep inside themselves. This does not imply that they are withdrawn or reclusive, however – indeed the inner directed individual usually has a wide range of interests, a sound grasp of current events and a high tolerance of other people's activities. In general, these people tend to be less materialistic and more concerned with ethics than the other two types. Developmental, emotional and spiritual satisfaction mean more to them than does material achievement. Their values, opinions and belief systems are based on personal growth, self-fulfilment, freedom of individual self-expression, sensibility, and the quality of life and of the environment. The others call them wimps.

As an illustration of these differences, we can conveniently consider how members of the three groups spend their money. To the inner directeds, money represents the means of doing things that interest them – neither a source of ostentation nor the way of acquiring security or maintaining it. Their earnings are dependent on the kind of work they want to do, rather than the kind of work they do being dependent on how much they want to earn. Their expenditure philosophy is selective and relates to their individual interests. In contrast, the outer directeds spend for show and the sustenance driven for security or out of habit. The broad spending patterns exhibited by the different social value groups are shown below.

* *The Home* Inner directeds' expenditure on the home is often aimed at enhancing their other activities, for example, the building of extensions to contain them. They will go in for functional DIY, refurbishing and conservation, and may well spend money on double-glazing, solar panels, heat pumps, etc., in this respect. Outer directeds spend as much as they can possibly afford on the house as their most conspicuous asset – it will be in the best location within their price range, and could contain a wealth of ostentatious DIY, barbecue pits, swimming pools, patio furniture, red leather three piece suites; and, for the rich ones, burglar alarms to protect it all. Among the survivors, DIY is undertaken for added value purposes – insulation is important but inexpensive. The home is a castle of security and a source of comfort for all sustenance driven, and this group's spending is supremely functional.

* *Consumer durables* Once again, inner directeds will be attracted to anything which enhances their other activities, either by saving time or money so that they can concentrate on them the better. Self-employed inner directeds are likely to use information technology business machinery, for example. Outer directeds are hooked on consumer durables and for them the newer and shinier the better. For the down-market sustenance driven spending is often on escapist items such as video cassette recorders and audio equipment. These, and other substantial durables such as cars tend to be bought second-hand, however.

* *Food* The health conscious inner directeds consume wholefoods and organic produce and tend to eat less meat. They also experiment with different kinds of cuisine and in particular with ethnic foods. They smoke less and drink more wine than the average. Outer directeds are great diners out and are always searching for the latest fashionable restaurant. When they are entertaining at home, both food and drink tend to be exotic and in excess. The survivors 'graze' on fast foods and convenience foods at frequent intervals, and the belongers in particular are very traditionalist in their tastes. Working class sustenance driven show a higher than average consumption of beer and cigarettes.

* *Services* Both inner directed men and fulfilled housewives use services as time-savers in order to enable them to carry on with their other interests. They tend to create networks covering a wide range of services based on professional/personal relationships. Outer directeds are more likely to use in-house gadgets than the corresponding service – unless it is of a showy nature like a kissogram or a specimen rose delivery. Sustenance driven tend to exchange services on a mutual help basis within their community – say, a car oil change swopped for two nights of babysitting. They frequently use public transport and car sharing as modes of travel.

* *Education* The inner directed considers that education is for life and has a broad spectrum of individualistic interests. Educational self-expression in children is encouraged and if private education is embarked upon it is to acquire higher standards. Educational toys, especially computer learning programmes, are often found in inner directed homes. Outer directeds consider that private education is for status and that adult education is to 'help you get on'. Survivors exhibit no education planning – education for them is a one-off experience, and the sooner finished and done with the better.

Three into One

The core values of the three major psychological categories reflect where each of them is looking for fulfilment. The sustenance driven looks nervously beneath himself to ensure that the fragile support that is all he can rely on from the world is still actually there. The outer directed is looking all around, though sometimes out of the corner of her eye, to gauge the signals that denote the esteem in which she is held by everybody else. The inner directed, though courteously tolerant of the rest of the world, is looking within for the fruits of self-actualisation and ultimately those of self-realisation and wholeness.

The behaviour of society as a whole is comprised of the aggregate of millions of individuals' lifestyles and attitudes, but these in turn are motivated by the deep sets of values that have been categorised above. It is therefore not enough to track the surface data of social behaviour simply, say, by collecting official statistics such as are published annually in the official publication 'Social Trends',[11] and then extrapolating them into a possible future.

Collectively, we may be becoming taller, larger and more intelligent; living longer but more frequently alone, as single households; acting more criminally; getting (gradually) better educated; approaching a relative dearth of young women; and consuming more baked beans and more champagne, but there is more to visible social trends than this. Because behaviour is ultimately motivated by these deep value systems, it is quite possible for different people each to do the same thing, but for fundamentally different reasons. Thus if you were to ask an individual from the three archetypal groups why she was eating less food these days, the sustenance driven would reply 'because food is getting too expensive', the outer directed 'because I want to look good in my new bikini when I go on holiday next month', and the inner directed 'because I feel healthier that way'.

Of course, one objection frequently met in advancing this analysis is the protest that people are not clones and cannot be slotted neatly into a mere three pigeon-holes. Maslow himself, upon whose theory the whole concept is based, fully appreciated that people slip from one mode to the other in their lives as they are dealing with different aspects of them. Even the most rarified self-actualised man will think along strictly belonger lines when considering the provision of life assurance for his family, and even the hardest-nosed materialist occasionally lapses into higher and kindlier thoughts.

Nevertheless one, or very occasionally two, of these three philosophical modes tend to be uppermost in any one person's mind and characterise his/her normal behaviour patterns. So society as a whole, or any particular subdivision of it, exhibits a preponderance of one or the other – but in gradually changing proportions over the passage of time. In broad terms, this progression shows a gradual shift from the sustenance driven to the outer directed, and from the outer directed to the inner directed, as individual after individual painfully climbs the steps of Maslow's hier-archical ladder; and as those who are stuck on a particular rung die off and fall off, giving place to the more upwardly mobile younger generation that follows.

Maslow originally perceived his ladder as a 'nested hierarchy', whereby all levels as they progress upward still also contain the levels lower down, like Russian dolls. Hence those who have reached the higher planes have a greater ability to understand what is going on in the minds of the rest, and can communicate downwards more easily than these others can commu-nicate upwards. This, however, smacks of intellectual snobbery and class division; perhaps a more attractive interpretation is that all of us possess the entire ladder within ourselves even though the higher rungs[12] of it may be invisible to us as yet. Nevertheless, if any man's death diminishes me, any man's life augments me – and it is the true realisation of every man's and every woman's potential that is the very nature of interdepen-dence, the very flavour of the new millennium itself.

3

THE NATURE OF INNER DIRECTEDNESS

Introducing Interdependence

What we have to learn is how to be less dependent on librium and more on equilibrium. The fact of the matter is that there are no Big Daddies any more. Our society has already moved from a position of dependency to one of independence, a move that has been so rapid that a number of us are still feeling dizzy as a result. However this relocation was something that had to happen. Dependency is the characteristic of the agrarian age, of fiefdom, tenancy, master-and-servant and a rigid class relationship. It depends on an absolute reliance upon the state – upon 'them' – to provide inevitable support.

It largely gave way during the industrial age to independence and a freeing up of class levels, a new philosophy which, with its emphasis on material self improvement, competition and the struggle for growth, ushered in an era which in spite of its many good qualities was also tainted with selfishness and the ritual kicking of the under-dog. Under-dogs have a habit of forming into packs, however, and the process has brought with it at the end of the industrial era an angry, snapping quarrel of confrontation politics, which we are now experiencing as the forces of self-interest, self-assertion, success and market dominance meet those of self-interest, self-destruction, failure and restrictive practice.

Alas, these are tired, old, self-important, self-indulgent arguments whose protagonists have nothing to do with the new reality of things any more. We are changing, like it or not, from having lived in an era of dependency through one of independence towards another where the name of the game is interdependence, a federation of free people working together to achieve a common aim. Interdependence is the watchword of the trans-industrial tomorrow and the millennial philosophy. Its nature will become gradually apparent as this story unfolds, but its true significance may not be visible until the very end of it.

An International Comparison

Even so, lucky us. We in Britain are further along in this evolutionary process than most. Here we have now reached the stage where the three characteristic types are in approximate balance, 29% being sustenance driven, 35% outer directed and 36% inner directed. This split compares interestingly with those in other countries. Every year the members of RISC, the International Research Institute for Social Change, of which SRI was the US partner and the Taylor Nelson Group the British, undertake a representative survey of the populations of their 19 different member countries. This social research was pioneered independently by Taylor Nelson in the early 1970s and as mentioned, its empirical findings, based on an elaborate questionnaire about participants' social behaviour, attitudes, opinions, and beliefs, strikingly support the theoretical work carried out by SRI on the Maslow hierarchy. What this combination therefore amounts to is an intellectually persuasive tool for comparing the evolution of social values country by country and year on year.

The truth, however, is as yet largely unappreciated by either business people or politicians – who could use it to the most advantage. It contains too many uncomfortably sharp edges to be widely acceptable – even though necessity is creeping up, and nowhere more rapidly than in these islands. This was revealed in Taylor Nelson's contribution to the National Economic Development Office's publication 'IT Futures . . . It Can Work',[1] a forecast of the country's future use of information technology.

Britain in fact comes out as further ahead in its social development than any other country in Europe except the Netherlands, which already claims 42% of inner directeds but where their growth in numbers is now slowing down. Comparative charts for the different countries reveal that Scandinavia, as one might expect from its high standard of living and radical social framework, has a relatively low proportion of sustenance driven people and a substantial number of both outer and inner directeds.

However, in contrast France and Italy, still with strongly agrarian cultures, exhibit the reverse – few inner directeds and a large proportion primarily driven by the principles of sustenance, survival and belonging.

Germany has more outer directeds than any European country, bringing it almost into equivalence with Japan in this respect. Finally, the United States contains a substantial block of outer directeds, too, though these are geographically concentrated outside the New England states and the West Coast. Thus, the three countries which have seemed to constitute the so-called locomotives of the world economy are nationally characterised by a drive for outer directedness and an inviolate emphasis on material success.

The members of RISC are primarily involved with the developed world, as it is only here that the symptoms of trans-industrialism are beginning to exhibit themselves. If one took profiles of Eastern bloc or Third World countries however, they would be likely to show very large numbers of sustenance driven, a few outer directeds and precious few inner directeds for the time being; but this picture changes rapidly with economic and social development.

Even within developed countries, national differences are often differentiated region by region, northern and southern Italy being an immediate case in point. In the United States, too, considerable differentiation is apparent, with the West Coast and New England having an inner directed population almost double the national average – whereas this sinks to half, down into single figures, in the 'moral majority' heartlands of middle America, dedicated either to standing pat or sitting pretty. It is the conventional wisdom that to spot a new trend one should look at California. Although many of its ideas travel badly and fail to take root when transplanted elsewhere, this is one place in the world where change is generated. But in fact, as the data indicates, new social trends have as much or even more chance of germinating in the Netherlands – or here in this country, to everyone's surprise.

One interesting phenomenon, which relates to social research into these three major categories across Europe, is the writer's experience in lecturing to the IBM European Management Training Centre just outside Brussels. Here representatives of the organisation's middle management from all over the Continent convened for various courses, and for a period of about 18 months there was a contract to speak to them on a dozen or so occasions on the subject of social change.

At that stage the writer had not yet come across the work of RISC, but was pursuing a similar line of enquiry on his own behalf. The presentation was therefore theoretical and anecdotal rather than having the stamp of authority provided by these black and white figures, but the response to them divided neatly along the national lines indicated by the RISC results.

The Dutch were particularly enthusiastic, as were the Scandinavians. British managers were split – half of them accepting and half firmly rejecting the thesis. Most of the French, Belgians and particularly the Spanish and Italians suspected that all this fancy stuff could be in some way a devious threat to their masculinity, while the Germans shrugged it aside with the classic German put-down – 'in our country we do things differently'.

It was, then, encouraging a couple of years later to find completely parallel evidence from RISC which explained so precisely why managers from these different nations reacted in their different ways. The message to IBM had been essentially an inner directed one, and as such unaccept-able to the outer directed and belonger orientated members of these audiences.

From British Disease to British Pregnancy

As stated, it is here in Britain that the inner directeds are now growing fastest of all throughout the world. This country demonstrates a discer-nable shift from sustenance orientation to outer directedness and from outer directedness to inner directedness, as the principle of Maslow's theory applies itself. So what has so often been characterised in the past as 'the British disease' is in fact more of a British pregnancy, a painful process of gestation of something new and different that will turn out to be far more appropriate for tackling the actualities of millennial trans-industrial life when they finally reveal themselves. In this country we are in fact leading the van, then, but our role as pioneers often proves laborious. Although we hold this wild card of a rapidly growing and increasingly powerful inner directed element, our national poker hand has also been characterised by another and highly damaging inheritance in which we are largely unique, namely the historically high proportion of belonger ABs in the British establishment.

Our class system makes for a safe feudal society, just as it does for Japan; but instead of the mainspring of this feudalism being group achievement and an economic conquest almost military in its ruthlessness, our British feudalism is primarily orientated towards the maintenance of a comfort-able status quo. The British establishment is change averse, its main aim being to keep things bobbing along more or less as they are until

retirement, after which somebody else can sort out the mess. The successful American businessman who makes five million starts planning to turn
it into 50 million; the successful British businessman who makes five
million starts planning to turn it into a Georgian manor house on the Test.
Ostentatious success is ungentlemanly and suspect per se; acceptable
success entails joining the same old clubs rather than founding new ones.

Further, with so much of British management and governance being
driven by these pre-industrial, sustenance driven, feudally belonger attitudes, there is another serious drawback to the British psychological mix.
It is an unfortunate fact that whereas those in the upper reaches of
Maslow's hierarchy are able to understand the motivations of those lower
down the scale without embracing them, to those in a less involved
psychological state the new thinkers might just as well come from not
only another planet, but another galaxy. An inner directed can
comprehend why it is that a belonger behaves as he does, while to the
belonger, the avid materialism of the outer directed will be distasteful, and
the laid-back individualism of the inner directed will be both mindless and
deeply threatening to members of the other two groups, poisoning what
they still see as the very core of their organisation and/or their perception
of society.

The Seeds of Conflict

The three archetypal categories therefore live in an uneasy relationship
with each other, their fundamental motivations being so profoundly
different. There are major points of conflict between them about the way
they see the world. But now that we have three constituent elements,
rather than two as so often in the past, life is rendered more complex by
the fact that they subconsciously form different coalitions on each of the
different points at issue.

Turbulence is therefore to be expected in future, in any event, since it is
rare for changes which are brought about by a shift in people's values to
occur comfortably – particularly so because institutions are almost
inevitably slower to respond to change than are individuals. Some insight
into the probable nature of the confrontations that are likely to beset us is
given below. The potential battlegrounds outlined here comprise an
incomplete listing of the issues around which conflict will develop during

the coming years. But at any rate, it is a start. The resolution of those conflicts and of the resultant upheaval which we are already observing in today's society will be the task of our 21st Century pioneers, for whom it is to be hoped that the following analysis will provide some help.

*   Autonomy v. Conformity

The smooth operation of a great many of our social institutions depends upon the willingness of their membership to conform. Autonomous action can cause horrendous problems for them. However, what they may see as disruptive and independent behaviour is becoming increasingly common; and with a growing sense of autonomy one can expect continuing conflict within organisations such as women's institute branches, trade unions, political parties, and even businesses, as their inner directed members act according to their own understanding in preference to following the party line. The NUM/UDM split arising from the 1984 miners' strike is an excellent example of this in a union context.

*   Materialism v. Non-materialism

This confrontation derives from the fact that many members of the sustenance driven groups are committed to the Protestant work ethic, while also being deeply concerned about unemployment. They think of their employment in terms of producing goods − 'Britain, workshop of the world', and all that byegone industrial jingoism. The non-materialistic lifestyle of the inner directeds, which places more emphasis on low personal consumption and the conservation of resources, is in direct conflict both with the high industrial output needed to ensure high employment for sustenance driven groups and with the competitive thrust that characterises the outer directeds. This will certainly raise the political heat in due course, and may ultimately lead to open violence around communities which are seen to have an assertively low consumption lifestyle.

However, it would certainly be wrong to think that inner directeds are antagonistic to money per se. In this respect, they are neither limp wimps nor hermits. They are often exceptionally hard working and may acquire a great deal of wealth in the process, but neither for its own sake nor in order to demonstrate how much of it they have managed to pile up. What they want money for is essentially to be able to pursue their own interests, which may or may not be expensive − cost being a factor which is not particularly significant to them − but which do require time. Money to the inner directed is a means to freedom, self-fulfilment, and the release of time for other things, not a goal in its own right. There is a strongly practical edge to all this idealism, though an unfamiliar one it may be to many others.

* New Solutions v. Doctrinaire Response

This conflict will occur most obviously between and within the political parties, but it may also constitute a source of trouble in industrial and commercial organisations. It has already caused the Labour party split and the subsequent rejigging of the two centre parties, for what that is worth in the long run. The issue of unemployment serves as a better general example, however. Pressure from the sustenance driven for more publicly created jobs to make work is at present countered strongly by the arguments for sound economic policy from the outer directeds, with a classic confrontation between dependency and independence.

But, when a new and more inner directed political philosophy does finally emerge, there will be acute political dichotomy between the real solutions it provides and the time-honoured doctrines of both left and right. Prominent personalities will have identified themselves with outdated modes of thought by then, and with arguments neither side of which is any longer appropriate. It will be difficult if not impossible for any of them to release themselves from the tyranny of their old scripts; as a result they will vigorously fight their corners.

Moreover, there is now a growing demand for work to be more fulfilling and more meaningful in content. This suggests that the sort of infrastructure jobs that can most easily be created by government action will be considered less and less attractive in future – and in a more general way indicates how emerging attitudes will take the sting out of the traditional doctrinaire debate, at the same time creating a whole range of new points at issue. More of this in due course.

* Trans-nationalism v. Localism

This contention emerges periodically in connection with the nature of British membership of the EEC, and with other upheavals among the various members of the Community. The outer signs of conflict will probably continue to be technical economic ones – import quotas, tariffs and so forth – but the driving motive of all concerned will be to enable the individual citizens of each country and indeed each region, to maintain their lifestyles in the manner of their choice. In this connection the sustenance driven groups may be joined by some inner, and maybe even some outer directeds who have particular single-issue axes to grind.

On the other hand, the vision of most inner directeds tends to embrace a world view unrestricted by mere national boundaries. 'Thinking globally and acting locally' is their motto, and their loyalty to what they see as the crumbling concept of the nation state is diminished. This echoes another and longer-running source of dispute – big is best v. small is beautiful. Those who opt for size and national interest are mostly drawn from the ranks of the outer directed and the sustenance driven, while inner directeds have more frequently discarded these traditional attitudes, and are more concerned with small-scale and local issues – but also with their ultimate adaptation in a global context.

* Achievers v. Askers

Sustenance driven attitudes contain many elements derived from the highly structured class system in which they developed. Among these is the notion that certain things should be arranged for the workers by the powers that be – in particular that they have a 'right to work' and should be provided with a job. The gentry had a responsibility to organise things while the workers did the work – 'it is the duty of the wealthy man to give employment to the artisan', intoned Belloc[2] in his cautionary tale of Lord Finchley, who electrocuted himself trying to mend a fuse.

In the 20th century the efforts to remove the more objectionable aspects of the class system have transferred this organising function from the gentry to the state, which is therefore now expected by the sustenance driven to manage things so that the working man has not only an automatic and attractive job, but a house, a car, a happy wife and two children. The outer-directed Tory right wing has been bold enough to suggest that perhaps the working man might get on his bike and organise some of this for himself. Moreover, this is a suggestion which also rings bells with the autonomous self-reliant values of the inner directed groups. The empowering of the working class to take this kind of self-responsibility is now being strongly resisted by the left-wing politician who wields political power as the potential provider of public sector jobs, and by many working people themselves who squirm at the terrifying prospect of self-reliance, releasing though it would be if they accepted it.

Inner directed values also call into question the entire welfare structure, the definition of the circumstances under which one might be entitled to benefit, and the manner in which benefit is to be provided. This reflects a growing recognition that many perfectly well qualified people are milking the welfare system at the tax-payers' expense. Ever more citizens are beginning to question the right of those able to work to be supported at public cost. Inner directed proposals are likely to be substantially more liberal than outer directed ones here – there is no lack of compassion for those who deserve it – but they will certainly be both different and controversial, and may well set the cat among both sets of political pigeons.

* Information Rich v. Information Poor

Here again, we have two aspects to the question. The first is the ability to hold, analyse and access large volumes of data, which will confer on those who have it in the 21st Century an advantage comparable to that held by the 18th century upper classes who held the land, and the 19th century middle classes who held the money. Secondly, and just as far-reaching in implication, is that inner directed values are liable to call into question the whole concept of secrecy and the holding of personal information by business and government.

Information is an energy that is useful only when it is widely dispersed and not allowed to stagnate in the possession of a few. The way for the information rich to become really rich is for them to spread around their store of it with relentless enthusiasm. Professor Tom Stonier,[3] who heads the University of Bradford's Science and Society Department, has shown categorically in 'The Wealth of Information' that where this happens it automatically expands so that everybody has more of it. That is an inner directed viewpoint.

This axiom may be said to be true of money also, but unlike money, information is inherently leaky, and has already been shown in this electronic age to be almost anarchic in its leakiness. Phone-phreaks who tap into the system and make long distance calls free are breaking the law and defrauding British Telecom of its revenue, but there is also a devil-may-care attitude about their activity that is insidiously attractive. The computer fraudster somehow does not seem to be doing anything as serious as the thieving employee who dips into the till, and the hacker is seen as cocking a well-earned snook at the establishment.

Similarly, though industrial secrecy has aspects to it that one might find possible to accept, now there is another and more seductive game in town. Because those who are accustomed to handling electronic information completely recognise the enormous value of sharing it, swapping it and spreading it around, they are beginning to do so with their opposite numbers in competitive organisations – on the assumption that what they get back in exchange is more valuable than what they give. This drives their non-inner directed superiors wild, locked in as they are to the traditional concept that a secret is a secret and that by letting it become common knowledge it loses its power.

Together with the global movement towards glasnost in government, in business and in all dealings where the big institution impacts upon the small individual, this concept of spreading information is very much at the heart of the inner directed ideal. The proliferation of personal computers will enhance it, as more and more people are able to conceptualise the new philosophical implications of electronics. The fact that inner directeds at the leading edge of society and computerised information at the leading edge of technology are both moving in this same direction means that the combination is programmed to become an immensely strong characteristic of millennial thought and culture.

Age, Sex, Class and Politics – The Easterhouse Effect

As already indicated, the division between our three main categories cuts more or less equally across the traditional boundaries of class, age, sex and region. Nevertheless there is a definite tendency for more young people to show inner directed tendencies, and for more of the DE social group to be found in the 'survivor' sub-category of the sustenance driven – this being the only section where class is anything of a feature.

One might guess that the politics of the three groups might be simply apportioned – sustenance driven equals Labour: outer directed equals Conservative: inner directed equals Democrat or SDP. In fact, things are subtler than this, their very subtlety providing an air of authenticity in this new world where there are no simple answers any more. We will see that political divisions are more distinctly defined when these three major categories are further broken down into the country's seven Social Value Groups, in the manner described in the following sections. Moreover, it should not be thought that there is some kind of inevitable elitist progression from concern for sustenance through outer directedness to inner directedness, which inevitably trundles forward under the influence of higher income and better education. This is important. The essential nature of inner directedness is interdependence, not division.

A case in point is what is happening as a result of the desperate unemployment levels in some of Britain's inner city areas. Take as an example the Easterhouse suburb of Glasgow. Correction, it is not even a suburb, it is a scheme, a product of the tiny minds of post-war bureaucrats who plumped down 50,000 people from the Gorbals in a no-man's land of ticky-tacky box houses and low rise flats. 50,000 people, with only five pubs, two supermarkets and virtually no bus service.

Its male unemployment rate is almost 40%, its main characteristic is total poverty of expectation – and yet there is cause to celebrate. Forty years after its birth, Easterhouse in early middle age came to terms with its mid-life crisis and has suddenly taken a grip on itself. Though together with Naples it is categorised within the EEC social spectrum as the nearest thing in Europe to a third world economic environment, nevertheless a few dedicated people within the community have begun pulling the place up by its boot-straps, based on the totally accurate assumption that nobody else was going to help anyway.

In this social Dunkirk, the core of the action is the Easterhouse Festival Society, a cultural organisation set up some ten years ago. It began quite literally with a festival. Shaking off their economic and psychological depression, a small group of people determined that if Edinburgh had a Festival, Easterhouse would too. So out they went talent scouting for musicians, actors, jugglers, stand-up comics, anybody – the one proviso being that the people involved had to come from within the community itself. To their delight they found a rich harvest of talent, which they then trundled round the community on floats – broken down old lorries decorated with coloured loo-paper.

Not only did the locals applaud the show, they also began to recognise that if they had artistic talent like this around, they surely had other kinds of talent as well. From then on, the essence of the Society's work was to help people find active ways of rejuvenating their community through their own creative flair. Thus it has –

* kitted out a flexible and approachable community building with all manner of artistic, dramatic and musical facilities; and run a continuous programme of sports, community events and celebrations in the area itself, besides sending out touring groups to the Highlands and Islands and to the Edinburgh Festival Fringe.

* formed a company that has created 200 jobs at an average cost of £900 each (compared to the average government expenditure of £5,500), and has provided support for other local employers as well.

* produced Europe's largest mural mosaic, triggering off the local authority to commit £½m to landscaping and leisure facilities in

association. When the mural was completed the Scottish press disdainfully conjectured how long it would remain unvandalised. They were to be disappointed. Stemming as it does from within the community rather than being imposed on it by some outside paternalist, it has attracted no vandalism and instead stands pristine as a focus for local pride.

* developed a network with community organisations in other areas. This covers not only Belfast, Liverpool, Birmingham, Edinburgh, and the East End of London, but Caracas, Calcutta and Beirut too, so that suddenly there is a small communicating group of people who share world ideas and experiences, co-operating towards a new interdependent vision of the future within the context of continuing structural unemployment, deprivation and conflict.

* attracted the interest of both the Prince of Wales and Anita Roddick, two inner directed leaders who have pitched in with their support.

The Anatomy of Inner Directedness

The above represents a remarkable germination of the new approach in what might be thought to be an unprepossessing seedbed, and is a clear example of inner directed values in action. How, then, to summarise these values, and how to gauge their impact on the way that the country conducts itself from day to day? We can fairly easily imagine the requirements of the sustenance driven group – the maintenance of the status quo and either an eternal truce or a favourable outcome to the age-old battle between rich and poor, whether in a castle or at a gate, according to the social position of the individual involved. And, apart from that, the cosy feeling of involvement and equivalence with an immediate circle of one's own kind.

The outer directed alternative is based at an individual level on personal esteem and show, but in a broader context on the floating off of all our inbuilt political and social differences by means of successful economic and commercial growth. This package its enthusiasts expect to be delivered through the medium of high technology, science, money management and a stiff dose of more-of-the-same industrialist Protestant work ethic. Economic cycles there may be, but the outer directeds' aim is to mitigate them by dependence on contra-cyclical remedies and the ever more craftily competitive manipulation of economic and fiscal laws.

In contrast, the inner directed philosophy suggests a sense of flowing with natural forces like the laws of economics, rather than attempting to overcome them by a Canute-style confrontation. As we have seen, the revolution it is now bringing about has a number of strands to it which relate to the various imperatives that inner directeds feel as members of this social entity.

The inner directed group does not fit easily into conventional modes of social classification. The conventional labour/capitalist confrontation was developed in the context of a struggle between sustenance driven and outer directed values. Inner directedness did not exist at the time to any significant extent except for a few 'social resisters' – political activists who sided with the sustenance driven at the time that the original confrontation took place. Now, however, with new attitudes creating a new model of society, everything is different. It is no longer appropriate to define social phenomena in bi-polar terms – north/south; rich/poor; have/have not; or even able/disabled. We are not in the realm of either left or right any more, but up.

The first element of this is that unlike the group-minded sustenance driven and the competitive outer directeds, the most advanced of the inner directeds are strongly autonomous, freedom-loving and individualistic – and that they wish the same corresponding freedom for others. They resent and avoid situations where they feel boxed in by outside events, and particularly by outside people. They have a burning wish to be accorded dignity by society and by those in it with whom they come into close contact – to be accepted as individuals whose values and opinions are important and should be given due weight. They abhor bureaucracies and hierarchies. They resent being pushed around and treated impersonally by big organisations in any capacity; in their turn they have no wish to push or bulldozer anyone else.

Smallness, informality and flexibility are their watchwords. Small is beautiful for them and any experience – whether it be work, leisure or personal maintenance – has ideally to be relaxed, laid-back and fun. They do not conform to rigid patterns in their daily lives, preferring instead to react as the mood takes them. They are difficult to fathom, but all those who wish to influence this increasingly important group must learn to dive that deep.

Inner directeds are more concerned with their own individual self-development than with working towards the benefit of an amorphous organisation. They are concerned with the quality of life rather than the quantity of livelihood, this applying not only personally, but also across the board as it relates to society and the planet as a whole. This is one of the chief derivatives of the growing concern about ecology and the environment, not only locally but on a global basis, and of the increased awareness of humanity's collective responsibility for the planet earth, Gaia, and all the other living travellers upon it. The principle of their self-development concerns them not only in the sense of regarding education as a life requirement for the purposes of intellectual growth, but also in the arousal and fulfilment of the psyche – and of the body, intellect and spirit. Given a future inner directed scenario, emotional development and intuitive development are thus likely to be as socially important in the future as conventional schooling, training and fitness are now.

The New Consumer

What we have seen so far indicates that the inner directeds already are and will continue to be the most important and hard to please consumers in the marketplace. In effectively relating to them, manufacturers, retailers and the providers of services have perhaps the greatest incentive to understand this Something Else that is going on. This is one answer to why the inner directed bandwagon will continue to roll – because it is good for business. But business must try harder – the people who make up this new market are maddeningly individualistic; they turn Henry Ford upside down and shake him – for them it has to be every colour so long as it isn't black.

Inner directed consumers are first of all more hungry for information than their predecessors; tackling the problems of their lives more specifically and intelligently, they want to know more from a position of already understanding much. They are more prepared to take time to weigh up alternatives and then pinpoint their choice so that it is closest to what they are really looking for. As such they are more discriminating and more prepared to complain and make demands – particularly more prepared to make demands about honesty and openness from the suppliers of their goods and services. Incompetence is not popular with these people but it is certainly preferred to manipulation. The one unforgivable thing by their book is when business tries to pull the wool over their eyes or acts in a morally slipshod manner.

As described already, inner directed consumers are concerned about autonomy, freedom and self-expression; about personal creativity and the enhancement of personal wealth; about health, fitness and education; and about caring for other people and for the ecological environment. Their attitudes to the products they consume are very much coloured by the content of these attributes or the lack of them, as they see it. They are able to understand complex messages and avid to acquire detailed information about their potential or actual purchases. They are strongly antagonistic to an authoritarian approach or to being patronised, under-rated or misread in any way. From the advertiser's point of view they are tricky customers. Endorsement advertising by some well known personality lyricising about the product generally gets the thumbs down – 'why should I take any notice of *him*?'

They enjoy advertising as an art form but take less notice of it than other groups. Thus though delighted by the zany surrealism of the Benson & Hedges advertisements, few of them actually smoke. Good television advertising amuses them, but they watch television less than the average – and then mostly for news and commentary or in selective forays into BBC2 and Channel 4, being more attracted to print and radio as communications media. Under their influence many future markets are therefore likely to be deeply concerned with quality and value for money first, and with durability next – the latter closely related to the inner directeds' strong conservationist leanings. Conservation of materials certainly, but conservation of the environment too, hand-in-hand with which goes a desire for naturalness in products, especially vegetable-based since exploitation of animals is at a thumping discount as far as they are concerned.

This group will buy things that are tailor-made, customised, and one of a kind – to them the joys of mass production are strictly for the history books. This gives rise to a distinct emphasis on modular production so that consumers can 'pick and mix' from a related or interlocking range of products, to create something specifically personal to them and for their own unique satisfaction. Happily the technology of batch production is at hand to provide just that, and once more technological and social change are therefore travelling in the same direction. This insistence on flexibility is closely related to the demand for informality and comfort that also characterises the inner directed personality. Comfort in all forms rates high on their list of priorities. Such people will no longer put up with being put out solely for the producer's convenience.

Outside the organisation, then, a better-informed public will show increasing discrimination and require that businesses conform to individual tastes and opinions. This entails a fragmentation of the consumer market and a great emphasis on niche marketing – which will continue to make inroads into both mass marketing and national brand marketing, as it has already gradually been doing for the past decade. But the demand for business to identify with the consumer means that there will also be more public pressure for it to conform to external mores. Thus we can expect to see added concern about business ethics and the burgeoning influence of single-issue groups. Furthermore, legitimacy will inevitably be withdrawn from bureaucracies by the growing number of people who reject them in every capacity. Business is in for a more difficult time than it is accustomed to.

The Growing Influence of the Inner Directeds

The writer once had the experience of making a presentation of these rather daring concepts to a group of senior managers from the Central Electricity Generating Board. Once the motivation of inner directed people and their growing influence on such delicate matters as nuclear power and acid rain had been described, one of the audience, an authoritative personnel man, was unable to contain himself any longer and shouted, 'what I want to know is: how can we identify these inner directed people in our organisations – and stamp them out?' He was not to be persuaded that in a world where inner directed values are becoming increasingly important, every organisation must contain employees at senior level who understand them, even if they cannot accept them. In future there will have to be people to help the dinosaurs at least vaguely conceptualise tomorrow's world, and then act as the organisation's emissaries in it.

However, whatever the tunnel vision of those just below the top, it is crucial that the real pioneers and decision-makers at every level in our society perceive this inner directed groundswell and act accordingly, for four salient reasons. First, as has been mentioned, the numbers of inner directeds are growing inexorably and in every developed country in the world. The pace may vary, but this is the major philosophical movement of our time, even though in some instances, such as here in Britain over the last two or three years, the movement from sustenance driven to outer directedness has been temporarily even more apparent and has thus somewhat disguised it. One reason for this gradual increase in inner directeds stems from the fact that there are disproportionately fewer in the oldest sections of the population and disproportionately more in the younger, so that with the passing of time more and more of the population is instilled with these values.

There is a second factor involved however. In times of such rapid change as we are now going through, individuals collide with what is known psychologically as the mid-life crisis. At any age between 30 and 50 they are likely to be suddenly beset by a dramatic turn of events, whether it be the death of a parent, the alienation of a child, divorce, a heart attack, cancer, or a financial upheaval – nowadays increasingly due to redundancy. In any event, for the crisis-ridden, the old days of inevitability are over – personal change and external change smash up against each other like anchored boats in a safe harbour when once in a blue moon a hurricane finally hits it.

In the shock of change these crises frequently throw up a whole series of fundamental challenges to people's basic concepts, as previous mind-sets and values are called into question and found inadequate to cope with the new experience. The Chinese pictogram for crisis is a combination of two others, those of danger and of opportunity. So when fate grabs someone by the scruff of the neck in this way, the whiplash jerk it gives them often opens up a whole new world of self-discovery and results in an exploratory shift towards personal inner directedness.

The third reason for the increasing influence of inner directed values is that they are less swayed by outside economic events than the rest. Sustenance driven and outer directed personalities tend to trade up and down according to the current fatness or thinness of their wallets, some of them temporarily invading each others' philosophical territory. So when times are good, naturally cautious survival-orientated people will tend to spend what they see as surplus money on a greater display of material show – instead of holidaying in Morecambe Bay they may progress to Marbella, or even Mauritius.

Conversely, when times get hard and the economic cycle begins to pitch downward, the first reaction of the outer directeds is to grit their teeth and continue as if nothing had happened; but once reality has penetrated, there suddenly comes a moment when this is clearly not possible any longer. They then all collectively knuckle down and slash consumer spending to the bone, in the realisation that the battle for competitive status is unwinnable by anybody for the time being. This is the rationale behind the observed phenomenon of the economic lag indicator of consumer expenditure, which hangs well behind the actuality of the economic cycle, as these more conspicuous consumers still vie in a desperate effort to maintain face until they all wordlessly agree to surrender at once in combined collapse.

In contrast, the inner directeds seem to hang on to their value systems much more tenaciously than do the other groups. They may gradually spend somewhat more or somewhat less because that is the way things are, but in an undramatic manner. Their interests, activities and general behaviour remain much the same, simply because they have subtler and more resourceful ways of maintaining them, and also because so much of the wide range of their behaviour pattern is capable of being maintained at very little cost.

There is thus a ratchet effect. Although the behaviour of outer directeds and the sustenance driven vaccillates according to the economic climate, once an individual has tuned into a measure of inner directedness, she is far less likely to stray from this fundamentally temperate motivation, however hot or cold it happens to be outside at the time. Inner directeds care little for external appearances; what matters to them is staying true to their convictions and preferences, and to the precise note of their own special tuning-fork. The final reason that theirs is generally more resilient than the competing philosophies is that inner directeds so often represent the vanguard of thought and ideas. What they pioneer is frequently then taken up – though maybe in a somewhat different form – by others down the line. The next chapter will start by showing how this happens.

4

NEW TRENDS IN HEALTH AND WORK

Fitness and Food

Jogging[1] exemplifies the leadership of inner directed thought. When it first surfaced as a weird and novel habit, here suddenly were these rather way-out people circumventing the park in their scruffy jeans and dirty tee-shirts, much to the amused disdain of everybody else. However, as they relentlessly pounded away the early morning dew, they also sowed the seeds of interest in the problems of late 20th century health.

Soon, a great many more people were also talking about getting themselves into shape and doing it. Not only inner directeds, but outer directeds joined the jogging circus – admittedly often so as to look good rather than to stay healthy – as a result of which the world of *haute couture* found it worthwhile to explore the market potential of this phenomenon. All of a sudden exquisitely tailored track suits burst on to the market, and £120 jogging shoes with specially adaptable springs in the heels according to the user's weight and running surface. Suddenly jogging was big business and everyone was in on it. What had happened was that an inner directed activity had become an outer directed fashion, so that the market as such was less casual but less loyal, more general but more fickle.

Similarly with health foods,[2] the writer's own city of Bath providing an excellent example. In 1984 there was one purveyor of organic food situated in an out-of-the-way warehouse. The assistants were covered in political badges, and merchandising and display were haphazard, the organic vegetables were earth-clodded, and much of the available space was taken up by a huge creche from which vantage point badly behaved children hurled hand-hewn wooden toys at all and sundry. The produce was delicious, relatively inexpensive and much resorted to by the youth and beauty of what might be termed the alternative movement.

A year later, however, in a prime shopping area of the city, another organic and health food shop set itself up, in parallel rather than in series. Everything was squeaky clean, the vegetables were wrapped in clingfilm, a lot of rather expensive and exquisite oriental produce appeared, with dinky wire baskets, Vivaldi in the background, and not a child in sight because of course the little darlings were all at home with the *au pair*. Wholefood had bust the fashion barrier. It didn't matter in the slightest from the point of view of the first establishment, in fact it was an advantage, like having an antique shop when another one opens up next door – more people come to the street. What had happened was that a new group of people had been introduced to the original concept, and had then taken it up and run with it in a totally different way.

The general situation has now simmered down to where it hovers between way-out and way-in, with an overall increase in interest in food labelling, lean cuisine and balanced diet in general, vegetarian restaurants, new-style organic takeaways, Belgian chocolates for a weekend treat rather than 'a-Mars-a-day', general fitness and complementary medicine.

In contrast with 1968, which saw the beginning of the health food movement, 'wholefood', 'natural' and 'organic' are now the labels the established food industry is most eager to adopt. Lentils are in and when eating them you need no longer wear sandals or burn a joss-stick. Initially, traditional business did everything it could to discredit the health-food trendies but, unable to beat them, it has not only now joined them but is trying to take them over by red hot marketing and promotional methods.

The wholefood industry is making record profits in Britain and its products are sold in more than 5,000 shops nationwide. Its consumption stretches from the House of Commons, which has recently introduced an alternative wholefood menu, to the High Street, where Wimpy now markets a BeanBurger and McDonald's is in keen pursuit with a range of wholefood salads. Frozen vegeburgers are available and so is packaged Veggie-Wiener-Schnizel made from textured soya protein, just two examples of the convenience wholefood products now flooding the market in plastic wrappers and aluminium foil containers.

These miss the point, however, running against the grain of the inner directed view of wasteful packaging; but the good news is that an entire library of wholefood and vegetarian cookery books is now available, including even those specialising in the ultimate in self-sufficiency, hedgerow cookery with wild ingredients, of which Rosamund Richardson[3] is the doyenne.

Yet again we see the same sequence of events. The inner directeds start the ball rolling and the rest of the population suddenly takes it and runs with it; though in a more fashion-conscious and shallower-rooted form, as big business cuts corners to cash in on the trend once a critical mass of support is reached. However the trend's leaders merely pass on to the next thing on the list so that everybody else has to keep panting behind to catch up. Gradually however, more of the meaning behind the behaviour rubs off and an increasing number of people pause by the wayside to listen to the whole story. This pattern is being repeated in any number of other spheres, every day across the country, and will continue to be so from now onwards.

The process signals more support for the contention that, for reasons of demographic change, of individual crisis, of stability in the face of economic variance and because of their being at the leading edge of opinion – in the long run, whatever the ups and downs of the curve, the values of the inner directed will grow in influence. Woe betide any business, any political party or indeed any individual that does not attempt to come to grips with them. This is the spirit of the new era, even if its substance is not made flesh quite yet.

All in the Mind

This new emphasis on bodily wellness is being matched by a new emphasis on psychological and mental development. The media have latched onto the growing interest in personality assessment, answering the call with an explosion of articles from women's magazines and *The Sun* with its 'Key to Life'[4] to *The Sunday Times* 'Life-Plan'[4] series. Each of these has been aimed at different markets but each market is clearly hooked. Meanwhile the growth of activity clubs, adult education networks of all sorts, group activities, marathons, war and adventure games, and the psychological approach to participative sport – all these represent leisure activities which have begun as part of the original inner directed personal growth trend, but have now rippled out to wash up against the other social value groups.

For example, while the inner directed may be interested in meditation or transpersonal therapy, the outer directed will be switched on to power-napping, an American concept where relaxation is also combined with self-knowledge, but focused to increase competitive ability in business. The recorded rise of interest in the martial arts likewise originated with the inner directeds, their object being to achieve an oriental balance between mind and body. However the outer directeds, having latched on to the growing fashion, got their kicks from its body-building and muscularity connotations. For the lower sustenance driven groups however, martial arts are seen as a short cut to streetwise physical power.

Bodily and mental activities frequently overlap, as in this case, and it is beginning to be recognised that the *mens sana* is a prerequisite for the *corpore sano*. Inner directeds fully realise the significance of listening to the whole self. A March 1988 *Observer*[5] colour supplement carried an item which mapped out the booming trend in psychotherapy. As psychotherapist John Rowan put it 'the demand for private therapy comes mainly from the middle middles . . . it's the halfway successes who have this feeling. The total successes haven't the time; the total failures haven't the money.' Designating 'success' in a materialistic sense one can equally categorise the three as inner directed, outer directed and sustenance driven.

The largely inner directed interviewees in the article evinced feelings of struggle, pain and excitement. Above all they recognised that they could be living fuller lives were it not for their own attitudes and responses which were preventing them from moving forward. Of course, some of the less rooted workshops now cashing in on this popular demand can leave people with a sense of temporary rebirth which is then followed by a psychological letdown. There are a number of charlatans around feeding off the new fashion for personal catharsis.

However, there are now over sixty established organisations representing different schools of thought in the psychotherapy movement, and they are proliferating both in numbers and in approach. Apart from those that signpost the more orthodox routes to psychological development, two interesting new techniques are music therapy and art therapy, both of which have the power to lift depression and even help quite serious psychiatric and mental handicap conditions, by enabling people to explore themselves and their problems in the safety of non-verbal media.

Surveying Health

This understanding of the constant interplay between the bodily and the psychological state is at the root of the emergence of a more holistic or rounded approach to medicine. It is reinforced by the inner directed insistence on being treated as a fully human patient rather than as a mere case with a reference number. Together these trends have combined to provide a powerful impetus for the complementary medical movement.

The Consumers' Association magazine *Which?*[6] published a piece on alternative medicine in its issue of October 1986. This was based on a survey of its 600,000-strong membership during May that year, the very month which saw the publication of a highly negative report on alternative medicine by the British Medical Association. In contrast, the sample of *Which?* readers who had used complementary therapies during the previous year produced statistics that were overwhelmingly in support of such treatment. 82% reported a cure or substantial improvement; 74% would accept such treatment again if the need arose; and 69% said they would recommend it to friends. Against this, 14% reported that their treatment was ineffective while a mere 1% claimed that their condition had worsened as a result of it.

The *Which?* report concluded with a list of recommendations headed by the need for more research and followed by better communication between complementary and conventional practitioners. The magazine also argued for acceptable national standards of training in these therapies and a single registration system for their practitioners, both being controlled by a council set up along the lines of the General Medical Council. In combination it was hoped that such changes would foster an acceptance of the therapies, establish a programme to explore their further potential, and ensure that patients were being cared for by fully trained therapists. A very reasonable list of suggestions.

According to a May 1988 Mintel[7] survey, most people are already treating minor ailments themselves rather than going to a doctor; one of the results of which is that over-the-counter drug sales have increased by 50% since 1982. Nearly £600m was spent on unprescribed medicines in 1987 compared with £400m on prescribed. Two thirds of women surveyed said that they went to their GP only if symptoms persisted. Nearly three quarters of the women surveyed thought that pharmacists were as effective as doctors in giving advice on minor illnesses. Hence, sales of painkillers such as aspirin and paracetamol have risen by 60% since 1982, while the total market for the top 25 home health care products has risen by 50%.

The message behind these reports was substantiated by another from the Taylor Nelson Group in 1986. The survey showed that 44% of the population believed in complementary medicine and that 26% had experienced it, the data also indicating that both belief and use are distinctly inner directed characteristics. The outer directed group tended to be more indifferent to complementary therapy, and the sustenance driven knew nothing about it. In their attitudes towards traditional medication the inner directeds as a whole are more responsible, more questioning of authority and more cautious about the use of medicine; while the sustenance driven blindly accept the authoritarian orthodox.

Inner directeds were far more liable to participate in health-related sporting activities of all kinds; and to control their diets, reduce tobacco and alcohol, cut down on salt and refined sugar and flour. In preventive health measures the survey's sustenance driven group scored consistently low; however this cannot merely be due to limited income because the cost-free advantages of walking as an exercise and of the reduced use of tobacco and salt are also less evident in the sustenance driven lifestyle.

At one extreme are the members of this social value category who tend to hold passive, fatalistic, dependent attitudes towards life in general as well as towards health in particular. Placing responsibility on other people or on institutions, they ignore the behaviour which is recommended to promote good health – and they also have the highest incidence of illness. Those at the other extreme, the inner directeds, have positive and independent attitudes to health and life as a whole. They assume responsibility for their own beings, they pursue activities and adopt practices which are known to be healthy. They are moreover more dissatisfied than most with the existing state of medicine today.

In the Taylor Nelson survey they showed a lesser tendency to have faith in their doctors than they used to, and more than averagely did they want to see an increase in private health care. In combination this exemplified the fact that they wanted to take responsibility for their own situations. About 60% of all respondents said that they would prefer to fight their symptoms rather than take medicine – almost exactly as many as those who agreed that 'doctors in this country tend to overprescribe'. Those who held both these views tended to embrace inner directed attitudes and reject sustenance driven ones.

There is thus now a far greater interest in the holistic treatment of disease and disability, where the patient or client is accepted as possessing a full range of sensibilities to be considered. There is also a continued rise in self care and self help, stimulated by improvements in electronic communication and other new technologies that provide better access both to the professionals themselves and to dependable information based on the best expertise. This coincides with rising consumer competence and the growing preference of patients for making their own judgements themselves given basic information, rather than having to endure the effects of the drug companies' high pressure salesmanship on the medical profession.

There is also increasing awareness of the toxification of our environment, resulting from years of industrial and technological development with too little attention being paid to its effects on health. At the same time we have greater understanding of biochemical individuality and the discovery of identifiable allergies of many more types than hitherto. There is thus an overall movement away from average prescribing to individualised treatment, all underlined and explained by the growth of informative media both in print and audiovisual form. In connection with all of this, it is intriguing to note that Health Secretary Kenneth Clarke's[8] radical proposals for GPs will link their pay not only to productivity but to patient appeal and preventive health abilities.

The Marylebone Health Centre in central London, run by two GPs from the crypt of a restored church, may hold the fourth key to cutting down the nation's £2 billion drugs bill – in that it supplements conventional medicine with a range of complementary therapies. In this way, the Centre saves over 70% on its drug costs compared to the average NHS practice. One of its prime movers, Dr Patrick Pietroni, argues that the government's plans for making GPs run their own treatment budgets thus provide a magnificent chance for reducing the drug bill and also the 14% of hospital admissions caused by drug side effects. Prince Charles is the Centre's patron, and according to Pietroni, 'he sees in it a lot of what he wants; the use of old buildings, regeneration of the community and a different approach to health care.'

The Empire Strikes Back

Meanwhile, it is the professional belongers who are, as on so many other battlefields too, engaged in a determined rearguard action to preserve the medical status quo against inner directed incursion. In May 1986 the British Medical Association published the Report of the Board of Science Working Party on Alternative Therapy. They had taken three reluctant years to compile it and had only done so under pressure from Prince Charles in his address to the BMA on its 150th anniversary. The Report dismissed all but a very few of the complementary healing disciplines as having no scientific basis and positioned these few as merely supporting orthodox medical practice in a minor role. A typical belonger response: 'we are the experts; if there are any good ideas around we've had them already'.

The Working Party saw any dissatisfaction with orthodox medicine as some aspect of 'a general criticism of governance' and blamed a 'hardly rational demand for instant cures'. It suggested that an uninformed public was 'turning back to primitive beliefs and outmoded practices, almost all purposeless and without sound base.' Revealingly, it always uses the aggressive and competitive qualification 'alternative' to describe these therapies, rather than the more cooperative 'complementary' with which their own practitioners describe them. Sharp rebuttals were published in response by those members of the BMA who had formed their own British Holistic Medical Association, and by the Research Council for Complementary Medicine. These claimed that the Report was thoroughly biased, by no means reflected the view of the entire BMA membership and had sadly failed to take the opportunity for joint action.

The surveys outlined above established a strong case against the BMA, which had not thought to ask any actual patients for their views. The very different and definite opinions that society in fact holds hotly challenge the BMA view of a naive and uninformed public turning to witch doctors out of a feeling of neglect. The Taylor Nelson report in particular showed quite clearly that the patrons of complementary practitioners tended to be among the best educated, best informed, most thoughtful, most open-minded and least irrational people you could meet in a day's march.

And yet, and yet. Galileo's great recantation 'but it *does* move' holds good today. The good news is that the rapidly growing British Holistic Medical Association has been set up within the BMA and that some doctors are beginning to refer patients to professional colleagues who also possess complementary therapy skills. Unfortunately this is also leading to a rush for instant expertise, such as weekend courses on acupuncture for doctors which in theory would allow them to practise on their patients a technique that actually takes years to perfect, permitted simply because those involved are qualified as general medical practitioners already.

On the other hand, there have been many beneficial results of this new awareness among traditional doctors, chief of which is that they are beginning to recognise that their patients are no longer prepared to be treated as mere case numbers and stuffed with addictive tranquillisers for want of any better idea. Neville Hodgkinson[9] revealed in *The Sunday Times* that Glasgow University had announced that medical students were to be examined in their ability to communicate with patients as part of their degree course, and that other medical schools such as Leicester and Manchester had also pioneered schemes to improve the teaching of this human skill.

To date doctors have often thought that bedside manner was largely irrelevant to the serious business of curing disease, but now at Cambridge University there is a full-time teacher of doctor/patient communication skills, Penny Morris. She is undertaking a 5-year project in which half of one year's intake of students are receiving additional communication training. Videos, recording and self-assessments made at the beginning of the project will be compared by independent investigators to see if the study group has done better than its control equivalent.

According to Morris, many doctors shy away from human contact because they want to avoid its inherent uncertainties. 'They feel more secure with facts, but medicine is a rapidly changing science and the facts they are taught now will get out of date. Doctors need to know how to cope with uncertainty; then they will be better able to share what is not known with patients, instead of trying to pretend there is always a magic wand they can wave to make illness go away'.

As one course student put it, 'in the past the doctor has always been on a pedestal, the one with the knowledge, the superior being. (But now) you are thinking much more about how the patients are feeling and what their problems are. We are taught all this science, yet we don't see the conditions people live in, the stresses they are under, which have a big relevance to whether they have diseases.' Here, as in so many other ways, the inner directed philosophy is winkling itself into all the nooks and crannies of the everyday lives of an ever-widening number of people. The more caring approach has already given rise to the natural birth movement on the one hand and the development of hospices for the terminally ill on the other, and is now starting to illuminate a great many life cycle points in between.

Self Responsibility and the Future of Health

In summary, then, there is this desire among many individuals to be allowed to take responsibility for their own health on the basis of the prevention of disease rather than its cure. The traditional 'parent/child' relationship between physician and patient is becoming increasingly strained as these new attitudes to health become more widespread. What exactly happens, however, when a patient wishes to assume this responsibility? The old professional association has perhaps to give way to one where there is another and more personal contract between the parties. In the United States some health maintenance organisations have offered reduced rates for people who behave in ways known to promote good health. This reflects a practical market orientation but falls short of a relationship which will ultimately have to become a personal as well as a commercial one.

There are bound to be regulatory problems in its development. Dr Wendy Savage, an obstetrician at the London Hospital who recognised the benefits of natural childbirth, encouraged a substantial degree of personal responsibility among the expectant mothers under her care, which was clearly a great help and release to a large number of her patients. However, she was strongly criticised by some of her professional colleagues and supervisors when other patients claimed that she had been negligent in their treatment.

What seems to have happened in at least some of these cases was that, having accepted the substantial personal responsibility associated with natural childbirth, they tried to opt out when things began to go wrong. The question is, in this very different doctor/patient relationship, who carries the can in such an instance? There was no doubt in the minds of Dr Savage's critics, but their belonger-based attitudes may well become increasingly inappropriate in future.

En route there will be many difficulties, not only the legal implications but the conflicting opinions of different philosophical approaches and, it must be admitted, a strong dose of downright professional jealousy. All these will stand in the way but ultimately, and not without a good deal of controversy, all will be resolved. There are already a number of successful experiments – for example the Bristol Cancer Centre and Dr Patrick Pietroni's Marylebone Health Centre that has already been mentioned here – where complementary and conventional medical assistance are combined to the great benefit and satisfaction of the patients.

Here then is yet another symptom of the fact that the secret changes that are occurring in our society are in the direction of care and concern, of individual freedom and autonomy and, most important, of personal responsibility. The inner directeds who hold these new values and the others who tentatively begin to take aspects of them on board, will continue to appreciate the brilliant successes of high-tech medicine but will increasingly regard them as having the secondary, though vital, function of organic damage limitation and control. In contrast they will place their initial emphasis on healthy living, the prevention of disease, complementary medical techniques, and personal involvement in and responsibility for the maintenance of their own health.

The crisis in the National Health Service – driven by a constant ratchet of expectations based on miracle drugs, wonder solutions and white-coated geniuses – is tragically self-induced. The medical profession, in ostensibly curing what used to be the incurable, is hoist by its own petard – first in the appalling cost of so doing and secondly because of the all too frequent neglect of possible side-effects, given the commercial pressures under which the drug companies operate. Thalidomide, Opren and now Valium – all were welcomed as breakthroughs in their time and all have brought a legacy of misery in their train.

Today's misery, however, is compounded by the expectations of the sustenance driven who imagine that the system is going to take care of everything. The Conservative government has shown very clearly that the system is a bottomless pit in which it is not prepared to pour unlimited resources. The Health Service cuts are largely the result of too much money being spent on the high-profile, dramatic and incredibly expensive cures and not enough on the undramatic but effective methods of prevention and education at grassroots level.

The future will involve a greater emphasis on wellness, rather than disease. Wellness is not simply the absence of troublesome symptoms; it is a physical state in which one experiences the proper functioning of the body, derives pleasure from the experience, and works consciously to maintain it by pursuing a lifestyle to match. As the emerging paradigm is now breaking clear, with the social and philosophical changes that herald the birth of a trans-industrial society as opposed to an industrial one, it also brings with it the recognition that this holistic view will prevail in the end.

Hence also the demonstrated popularity of complementary medicine among the inner directeds, children of the trans-industrial age, treating them as it does in a whole sense. The term complementary is important here because it acknowledges both the success of the new and the forgotten good of the older, grafted together in an entirely different manner. In a whole sense again, both will be needed in the years to come if we are to ensure the rightful prevalence of general good health.

Work – A Spectrum Of Attitudes

Moving from health to work, it is clear that in this world too, the inner directed influence is growing. Professor Ralf Dahrendorf[10] has rightly stated that real changes are not political. They occur where people live and work – in industry and commerce, and in the home. It is here that adjustment is needed, however painful it may be. His thesis is that instead of our trying to fit people round a rigid system, the system must in future be applied to fit round people's evolving circumstances and commitments. This is happening – mothers with children can now work from home as computer programmers for ICL and for FI Group; the British Steel in Ebbw Vale has helped to retrain redundant workers and set up new job possibilities for them – more varied and interesting than their old ones, and with the sense of the belonging, trust and participation that is derived from more humane practices.

As a further example, in the Notting Dale urban technology unit, young people with no academic qualifications at all are given hands-on experience in electronics. Those who seem inspired and talented are then also provided with research and development and teaching skills to help them form their own small companies. These are now, but need not be, isolated cases. The future of work as an activity looks as if it is either going to be non-existent or meaningful and enjoyable. The choice is up to people themselves and the unorthodox methods they can dream up when fun, ambition, participation, small-scale local activity and networking are at a premium.

This is a wholly inner directed view. It is nothing like the worlds of either the outer directeds or the sustenance driven, indeed the attitudes to work of the three major groupings are not only distinct, but almost mutually exclusive. The inner directed works for accomplishment and fulfilment. She requires that work is demanding and exciting and utilises her personal talents to the ultimate. Inner directeds have such varied demands on their capabilities that if their work is not fulfilling enough they may opt for shorter hours in order to develop themselves outside it in other ways.

These views are catching on. As long ago as December 1981, *The Guardian*[11] published the results of a survey that listed employees' prerequisites for work satisfaction in order of importance. At the top were fulfilment, working towards a common aim, comradeship and doing a good job. Status and financial reward were respectively twelfth and sixteenth in order of priority.

Inner directeds and their ideas are frequently found in the new trans-industrial businesses and the service industries – the world of computers, consultancy, personnel, training, research and development. In contrast the conspicuous achievers, the outer directeds, are most likely to be orientated towards sales and marketing. This is the explanation for the frequent problems that arise between marketing people on the one hand and research and development people on the other. Psychologically, they come from quite different places. The former are always pressing to get the new product out where it can fill some yawning gap in the marketplace; the latter constantly need another six months to perfect it before they let it loose on an unsuspecting world.

Outer directed workers aim for advancement and high income and are willing to grind themselves into the dust to get them. But inner directed people are hard workers too – as long as they are motivated by what they are doing. However, the competitive achiever is going to put up with a lot more as long as his ultimate rewards are clearly visible. He plans his career with a fine degree of accuracy – 'if I'm not assistant manager within 18 months, I'm off'. In contrast, the inner directed tends to adopt a less rigid attitude, to have a shrewd idea where she wants to end up, but to go with the flow of events as they develop.

Outer directed workers are dedicated indeed, but dedicated to their own ambitions, and will let the boss down at the drop of a hat. 'Look after number one' is the cry. They can be excellent to work under because their charisma and flair often brings success to those who are hanging on to their coat tails. In contrast however, when consumed by power lust they can behave ruthlessly towards colleagues and subordinates. The cut and thrust among a whole group of outer directeds working together can make an organisation as attractive a place to work in as a piranha tank.

The sustenance driven are basically all for a quiet life as far as work is concerned. Survivors will work well and cheerfully as long as they are effectively led, either by a belonger father figure or a power-driven conspicuous achiever or experimentalist. They feel uncomfortable with inner directed leadership – it is too unstructured and they prefer someone who will tell them exactly what to do and let them get on with it. They are as dependent on the employer as they are on the doctor for health, the state for welfare and their company commander for survival at war. They do not want to be responsible for making any decisions themselves. Theirs not to reason why. What they require above all is bread and butter security, and high income for the jam on top.

Of course, it must always be remembered that the sustenance driven are by no means all working class, and that there are a large number of belonger ABs who fall into this general category. These are yesterday's managers, and unfortunately too many of them are still often in today's top positions. If so, either they or their organisations are going to be clobbered in the current swing towards assertively outer directed management. The middle ranking company, the dozy medium-sized stockbroker or solicitor, the Wolverhampton widget manufacturer with archaic plant and equipment – these are on the way out with their sleepy paternalism towards both employees and customers.

Their places will be taken either by large aggressive organisations which acquire the opposition or break its back in single combat in the marketplace; or by a series of small flexible specialist 'boutiques', likely to be organised and run by inner directeds. As for the former category, there will for long enough to come be sustenance driven minions around to do the bidding of their outer directed masters. Habit dies hard and they would feel uncomfortable if they were not in this dependent kind of relationship.

New Organisational Structures and Patterns of Work

One aspect of work which shows very clearly the different attitudes of the social value groups is the possibility of telecommuting[12] – working from home or from a remote place using electronic networking techniques, and communicating with rather than commuting to the central office. Already in Britain there are a number of advanced examples of this mode of working, and although it is beginning to happen all over the world it is here in this country that the management of it is at its most sophisticated. Though all work cannot be undertaken in this manner, there are strong indications that an increasing proportion of it will be in future.

Working from home rather than from an office appeals particularly to the inner directeds, who enjoy the flexibility and independence it brings. However the sustenance driven suspect it, having as they do such a strong aversion to change, while the survivors among them fear that it will weaken union ties and threaten jobs as a means of increasing productivity. Meanwhile, the outer directed are also unenthusiastic. They want to be in the thick of things where the competitive action is, fearing that at home they will be less able to display their successes and their status. With the accelerating influence of the inner directeds and the technical and cost factors in its favour, it is nonetheless liable to become an increasingly significant mode of work in future.

Outer directeds prefer to operate in rigid hierarchies and play snakes and ladders at work. In contrast, the inner directed detests the bureaucratic or military pattern of business organisation. These people prefer new and complex structures and inter-relationships, such as the heterarchy, a loosely defined group of equivalent colleagues who have different expertise but a strong element of mutual respect for each other. Team leadership and responsibility may shift from person to person as circumstances change, demanding a different calibre of response from the organisation. Here, A need not inevitably be over B who is in turn inevitably over C. The favoured circular working pattern is where A, B and C are in loose association and whoever has the experience required for a given project will lead it. Thus at one time A may well be managing B and C, but for the next project C could direct A, B and X.

Another new inner directed method of working is the network, typical of consultants, an association of individuals who have little organisational relationship, until one of its members identifies an opportunity or a requirement for action. Then he will contact appropriate associates and form a heterarchical node within the network. This nodal organisation operates until it has fulfilled its function, when it dissolves again and the members disperse back into the network pool. An alternative structure is that of overlapping cells, similar to a network except that the cells themselves have a permanent shape and mode of operation; their interrelationship derives from people who have a common membership in several of them.

The old-style organisation has always been hierarchical with an expert who makes the decisions sitting at the top of the heap while the others below do what they are told. But the hierarchical structure has great problems for the inner directeds, particularly the self-explorers, who need a looser framework in which they are allowed to take their own responsible autonomous decisions. Harking back to a medical equivalent, these people will not accept bureaucratic procedures whereby patients are woken up to take their sleeping pills.

Waning are the days of the organisational tree with the chairman at the top and ten thousand worker ants struggling away at the bottom layer. That was a characteristic of the industrial era, built as it was on comparative status. Now we are beginning to see variants of the organisational sponge, a trans-industrial form in which individual units work semi-autonomously together, almost like consultancies or enterprises within the whole. These polyps are linked by a central matrix of information, financial and technical services which supports them structurally, and which they in turn nourish by their individual profits in the marketplace as they work within electronically defined financial and operational parameters. The sponge with its softer and more feminine outline is more appropriate to the trans-industrial age, just as the shape of the organisational Christmas tree was appropriate to the thrusting masculine industrial one, now past its maturity and into its decline.

Nonetheless, for decades to come there will still exist traditional organisations led by abrasively outer directed conspicuous achievers, who attract round them a mass of belonger acolytes to do their bidding till they drop. The problem with such an organisation is that there is only room for one leader, actual or potential. Crown princes are elbowed out and when the massive beech tree is finally cut down by retirement, takeover or cardiac arrest, the forest beneath is bare of talent except for a few aetiolated saplings that have lived too long in the dark. Anyone with any nous has already left the organisation and put it down as an interesting experience in the cv. But although the old conspicuous achiever/belonger relationship, the gaffer/worker or lord of the isles/salt of the earth connection is outmoded in principle, for some time it may persist in practice.

As a group within society, inner directeds are always aiming for autonomy and freedom. For this reason they prefer institutions, particularly the organisations for which they work, to be small, informal and flexible. If the institution happens to be a multinational company then they will create for themselves a small, informal and flexible unit within it. For them work and leisure are somewhat blurred; they take their leisure seriously as a means of fulfilment, but they demand that work should be fun, exciting and fulfilling too. It must be nourishing not only to the wallet and the intellect, but also to the emotions and the spirit.

People of this cast of mind are now moving into the position of enjoying a portfolio of occupations, some of which can hardly be defined as either work or leisure in the purest sense. The story is told by Professor Charles Handy, chairman of the Royal Society of Arts, of his meeting a young woman at a cocktail party and asking her what she did. 'I'm a freelance television script-writer' she said, thus gaining his immediate admiration and respect. But she went on to admit that only one of her scripts had actually been accepted so far and that she had only been paid a pittance for it anyway. 'What do you do for money, then?' asked Handy. 'Oh, for *money* I pack eggs on Sundays', she replied.

Note that she did not consider herself as a Sunday egg-packer which allowed her to eat, but as a freelance television script-writer, which allowed her to fulfil herself. With the increasing strains on traditional employment due to international competition and hi-tech alternatives – and both robotics on the shop floor and information technology in the office are relevant here – there is also a melting of the historical barrier between work and leisure. So often what have in the past been mere part-time occupations or hobbies have perforce become major sources of income to people as redundancies have sliced into the heartland of traditional work.

Early retirements, sabbaticals, part-time working, out-working, job-sharing – all the other fashionable variants of the general drive towards cutting down the time worked in a traditional nine-to-five framework – have combined in this process. As Handy puts it, the old 'law of 48' (48 hours a week × 48 weeks a year × 48 years in a working life) has been diminished to a formula whose factors are more like $36 \times 44 \times 38$. 110,000 hours in a working life have almost halved to 60,000 and are still under pressure. The inner directeds will adapt to this better than anyone else.

A clue as to how this might all come about is revealed in the previously quoted remark made by Sir John Harvey-Jones, when he anticipated the full-time UK workforce of ICI as falling from 66,000 to 3,000 by the year 2015. This conforms very closely to the scenario that Handy[13] unfolds in 'The Future of Work', and elaborates in 'The Age of Unreason'. His view is that business will ultimately consist of far more small organisations than now, but that even large ones will be considerably reduced in bureaucratic scale. He envisages them as comprising a central core of professionals and managers who work their guts out all day, all week and all year for a limited period of time and either blow up or retire ostentatiously to the Caribbean as millionaires. These will be the outer directeds of the future – without whom, it must be admitted, the powerful transnational organisation could find it hard to function.

Outside this core however, will be a middle ring which Handy calls the contractual fringe. In other words, it will become increasingly fashionable for organisations to shed their peripheral activities and concentrate on what is for them the mainstream. This represents a sort of further privatisation of the private sector, and is already visible. Catering, printing, pensions administration, market research, publicity, chauffering – all such activities outside the core of producing and selling Bonzo Crisps – will increasingly be subcontracted to a great raft of outsiders, who may well include the organisation's ex-employees themselves. This will be the area in which the inner directeds flourish.

[63]

Handy's third level is the outer ring (or third leaflet of the shamrock) of either temporary or part-time workers who will still have to get their fingernails dirty or monitor the robots that do so – probably on a 24-hour basis and therefore involving shift work during unsocial hours, given the new international thrust of business and the necessity to operate across timescales. These of course will mainly be the sustenance driven, primarily survivors who are after security plus good pay and are prepared to work in the middle of the night to get it. However, they may well include a number of self-explorers who are only there for the money, which will release the time for them to do other more meaningful things, like Handy's eggpacker/television scriptwriter. The seeds of this economic future are already germinating in the present, although the harvest may be some way off.

The Inner Directed Employee and the Future of Management

It is self-responsible working patterns and freely autonomous organisational structures that enable inner directeds to function best. Under these conditions they develop like the branch of a tree that grows in such a way as to acquire the greatest advantage of light, within the limits set by the overall shape of the tree itself – and by doing so also provides the greatest advantage to the organisation of which it is a part, whether tree or business. It is this natural fluidity of individual and collective growth that will enable the inner directed organisation to adapt to changing circumstances as they occur. Survival, in other words, not only of the fittest but of the most flexible.

However, on the downside for the busy boss, the inner directed employee will also be more and more concerned with the objectives and behaviour of the firm for which he works. The nature of the product, the relationship with employees, the source of funds and the identity of customers and suppliers are all areas in which he may take an interest, in addition to the need for a sense of personal growth and incentive. Companies will have to be good open corporate citizens if they are to excite and maintain their employees' loyalty in future. They will thus need to develop a holistic and integrated corporate personality and behave responsibly in all aspects of their business. This is a substantial undertaking and will require firm leadership and expert communication.

Tom Peters,[14] author of 'In Search of Excellence', described American business as overmanned, overlayered and underled. Its current leadership is not leadership in the round but based on the outer directed principle – 'we pay you: we kick you'. Temporarily one hopes, this is also beginning to be mirrored here in this country, and explains the growing preference of so many people to abandon multi-layered and autocratic employers in order to start their own inner directed businesses.

In 'The Art of Japanese Management', Richard Pascale[15] and Anthony Athos listed seven factors that needed to be considered by the management of any organisation. The first four they called the hard Ss – strategy, systems, structure and skills. These are essentially outer directed values. The second three they termed the soft Ss – style, staff and shared values, which are more inner directed in nature. It is interesting that even in a society like Japan where inner directedness is at a discount, these factors are accepted as just as important as the other more obvious and traditional business imperatives.

Should this whole thesis be accurate, so that the world in general begins to follow a more inner directed path, many other aspects of business activity will also be influenced. Organisations will have to develop certain abilities if they are to function effectively. First and foremost, they must understand the motivations of inner directed people and respond specifically to them, not only in their markets and with their work-forces but also as far as the rest of society is concerned. Secondly, they will have to learn to act flexibly and not necessarily in accordance with rigid predetermined plans. Lateral thinking will be at a premium here.

Thirdly, organisations must accept, validify and utilise the intuitive powers of their people. Quantitative methods of business analysis and decision-making may now be in the ascendent, but in the process a lot of quasi-scientific gobbledegook is given the houseroom it does not deserve. What is gradually becoming apparent is that major decisions must also contain a substantial component of hunch, flair or intuition, which we will learn to harness more precisely in future. Imagine trying to construct a computerised model to forecast trends in women's fashion, or the uptake of some new information service – these are the kinds of problems that are increasingly going to underlie the trans-industrial scene in which intellect alone will not suffice.

Fourthly, business people must be willing to learn from their own and their teams' mistakes and use them as a resource from which they can improve future performance. I am indebted to my consultant colleague John Frank[16] for the term 'error harvesting' here. Outer directed managers are generally unwilling to admit mistakes and analyse them dispassionately, and in today's business the tendency is to bury them six foot deep. The ability to admit errors and to learn from them must be developed as an aspect of corporate flexibility and responsiveness.

Finally, it will be necessary to communicate with and motivate a variety of people. The organisation must recognise the need for the different social value groups it contains to work harmoniously together, by stressing the essential nature of the team concept and underlining the necessity for all to cooperate interdependently. This principle also has a more general application. In its specialist world of work the business is a microcosm of society as a whole. All these considerations will characterise the successful organisations, the successful societies, and indeed the successful individuals of the next century and the new millennium.

5

FROM THREE TO SEVEN

Analysis and Synthesis

In theory, then, it may sound as if we are split into three groups of totally different people, three rival clubs, each with absolute qualifications for membership. Naturally, however, the truth is a lot subtler. Everybody is different from everybody else and the way life works is that we are all distinct individuals, wildly resistant to being categorised as either Clone A, Clone B or Clone C. In reality, we have all been supplied with a very specific cocktail, containing the various isotopes of A, B, and C in different proportions, with which to construct a psychological armoury to face the world.

We each have the elements, the aspects of all three parts. There are moments when we all need to struggle to exist, need to be recognised as winners, or need to become freer and deeper within ourselves. There are moments when we do appreciate each of each other's common humanity. However, what seems to happen with the great majority of people is that one or other of these imperatives is felt more urgently to the exclusion of the others. Our general motivation and behaviour are influenced towards one particular set of values and beliefs.

As already stressed, the Maslow Theory is by no means an elitist or exclusivist one. This 'nested hierarchy' comprises a psychological series of demands that we all share at some level or other, whether or not we are actively conscious of them or prepared to acknowledge them. Every inner directed knows what it is like to feel outer directed or sustenance driven sometimes; every outer directed knows what it is like to feel sustenance driven too.

But the reverse does not hold so well, of course. Having not yet discovered the part of themselves that exists further up Maslow's ladder, the golden goose at the top of their own beanstalks, the sustenance driven tend to be bewildered and threatened by its manifestation in others. Tragically, those who are not in touch with their own potential, so much more wonderful and extraordinary than they have ever realised, will often do their best to smash the full realisation of its equivalent possibility in others.

In order for us all to reach this millennium of interdependence, therefore, this dream of adulthood for the human species, it is first necessary to conduct a careful analysis of the points that now divide us. To be effective it must be blunt and may be painful. Danaan Parry,[1] an American professor of the study of conflict, has complained that the process 'divides the world into blockheads, assholes and wiseguys.' This is perhaps fair comment about the breaking down part, but not once it is used in combination with the building up. It is only when we can see the facts about ourselves and each other with utter clarity that we can embark on the positive process of synthesis – of recognising all our human strengths and building on them open-handedly together.

The Map Is Not The Country

More of that later, however, and back to basics for the time being. Over 80% of the population is ruled by one of these three major archetypes, which predominates in their motivation and behaviour. Some 15% are governed by two of them which more or less overlap in influence, while a tiny proportion are at the beck and call of all three at once, and presumably find it difficult to make their minds up about anything very much. Meanwhile, society as a whole acts as if it is divided into these three major sections battling it out together in the marketplace, in the electoral process and in the arena of public opinion to decide whose voice is the loudest. The subtleties of individuals are lost in the tumult of the crowd.

Mention has been made of Arnold Mitchell's[2] 'The Nine American Lifestyles', in which the author split the three fundamental categories that are common to all developed countries into nine identifiable American subgroups. The principle can be extended to any country, though the numbers vary in each case. Canada for example has twelve, since though the population is far smaller, its social structure is more complex because of the existence of both the Francophone and the Saxophone cultures side by side.

In the case of the UK the three major categories are broken into seven minor ones, termed social value groups. Once again, this does not imply that the British can all be slotted into a mere seven pigeonholes. Of all nations, they would be perhaps the most unlikely candidates for that. What we have here is simply a map, and like any other map it is effective but limited. Without going to the place itself you cannot imagine all the richness of its detail. The map is not the country. But, given an Ordnance Survey you can see where there are railway cuttings, churches, swamps and electricity pylons. It is a useful representation once you know its rules, but nothing more. The description that follows is also merely a useful representation; but it can help travellers find a route through the highways and byways of society and see at a glance where they are going and where they have been.

Nevertheless, there are certain clusters of people who conform very distinctly to common ideals and philosophies. These sit right in the middle of their social value groups and anchor the quintessence of their collective concerns. They are surrounded by a vaguer cloud of others who more or less agree with them, but who also spread out and overlap into different areas. Most people, as we know, have conflicting motivations and are therefore in this equivocal position of straddling more than one group. However, they can almost always be categorised for statistical purposes in order to obtain a valid cross-section of the population as a whole. As explained, the British nation does behave statistically according to the social research polling system that has been used as if it were subject to this sevenfold division; and Taylor Nelson/Applied Futures' sixteen years of experience in surveying it shows that as an analytical tool and an aid to forecasting, the credability of the method cannot be sneezed at.

The publication that provides most details of the British equivalent and the whole Taylor Nelson rationale is a 1985 article in *Futures* magazine, 'UK Social Change Through a Wide-Angle Lens', by W Kirk MacNulty.[3] At the time he wrote it, MacNulty was a consultant to Taylor Nelson Monitor Ltd,[4] the forecasting arm of the Taylor Nelson Group headed by his wife Christine, who had previously worked with Arnold Mitchell at SRI. In mid-1988 the subsidiary was the subject of a management buy-out from the Taylor Nelson Group, and set up as Applied Futures Ltd, now owning the right to market the consultancy applications of social value group analysis. It is on the work of these two organisations that the following analysis is based.

Remembering all necessary caveats, let us now look at the seven archetypes representing the seven social value groups into which the population of the UK is more or less divided. The British groups are designated in Table 1 with their characteristics, their 1989 proportions, and their aggregation into the three major social categories. Taking the UK population as a whole, this analysis is highly relevant to anyone interested in the sociology of the country – whether academically, from a business angle or from a personal desire to understand one's fellow human beings and work better with them.

The plan now is for us to take a quick comparative trawl round their slightly more detailed features, before examining them individually under a high-resolution lens in the following chapters. Note first, though, that the groups on the move are the self-explorers and the conspicuous consumers. The former consolidated their gradual progress in 1987, notching up an additional 1% compared to the previous year, while the latter, spurred on by Thatcherite radicalism, increased by a massive 4% in the same period and at 22% are now the country's largest social group.

The Seven Groups Displayed

*   *Self-explorers* (15%) are the hard core inner directeds, primarily motivated by self expression and self actualisation. The self-explorer shares the societal concerns of the more bigoted social resister, but is more likely to reject doctrinaire solutions in favour of the holistic view that change is an organic process, occurring naturally as awareness unfolds. He matches the experimentalist's passion for autonomy and individuality, but without an undue emphasis on materialism. However he is financially sophisticated and more liable than most to hold a range of savings and investment media.

Of all the social value groups, self-explorers have the broadest horizons, the highest tolerances and the greatest propensity to tackle problems on a global scale. They also have a strong tendency towards spiritual values, but shun organised, conventional religion. They are particularly involved with matters of health and self-development and with freedom and care for others. They are at the leading edge of the inner directed movement – what they think today much of the rest of the world tends to think tomorrow.

As a consistently strengthening group, self explorers form a turbulent but often very effective coalition with the shrinking band of social

TABLE 1. THE SOCIAL VALUE GROUPS[5]

Social Value Group	Characteristics	% 1987	Aggregation into major categories
Self-explorers	Ethical, tolerant, open, understanding, introspective, non-materialistic and individualistic	15	Inner directed – 36%
Social resisters	Altruistic, concerned with social views and supporters of standards but also doctrinaire, intolerant and moralistic	14	
Experimentalists	Unconventional, technological, creative, self-confident, physically fit, risk-orientated, self-indulgent	11	
Conspicuous Consumers	Acquisitive, competitive, assertive, conscious of appearances, authoritarian and materialistic	22	Outer directed – 35%
Belongers	Conservative, pragmatic, traditionalist, conventional, self-sacrificing, tribal and pedantic	17	
Survivors	Sustenance-driven, class-conscious, community-minded, traditionalist, cheerful, awkward if treated badly but quietly hardworking if treated well	15	Sustenance driven – 29%
Aimless	Either old, lonely, purposeless and disinterested; or young, hostile, anti-authoritarian and frequently violent	6	

resisters. They are forecast to grow regularly, but maybe slowly for the time being, as long as the political and economic emphasis remains on the conspicuous consumer ethos. They are somewhat stronger than average in London, among the ABs and the young.

* *Social Resisters* (14%), in contrast to the self-explorers, are the old-fashioned political carers who see involvement more as a social duty than as anything that touches them personally. Their motivations are fairness, and the realisation of a quality of life that corresponds with their own principles, whatever these may be.

Social resisters are essentially of two main types – ageing idealists of both left and right, and single-issue junkies of a slightly younger generation, who in spite of their egalitarian principles have pretensions to a *vita* which although not predominantly *dolce* is nonetheless relatively so. Terribly unusual salad dressings and all that. They are altruistic and concerned with social issues such as peace, nuclear disarmament, ecology, morals, law and order, and individual rights.

They are, furthermore, likely to be concerned with spiritual values, but in a somewhat orthodox way. Social resisters generally have a fixed, doctrinaire attitude about how issues are to be resolved, and thus their stance often appears intolerant and moralistic. The group is forecast to decrease in size and statistical significance, but will continue to exert an influence greater than its numerical strength might imply. After all, they are so strident.

* *Experimentalists* (11%) are the first of the two transitional groups that straddle our three major categories, in this instance the inner directed and outer directed. In past years experimentalists were young and predominantly male; they were the tigers in their twenties and early thirties who wanted to try everything before they settled down. They were also transitional in the sense that the phase related very specifically to a certain period of life. However, it is now clear that though they are younger than average there are increasing numbers of experimentalists of all ages and both sexes.

The more orthodox and typical of them tend to shift at the prime of their lives either to a more distinct inner directed or an outer directed mode. Many of them experiment with hang-gliding and potholing, but there are also an equal number who experiment with yoga and meditation – whatever is new to them turns them on. They are also highly credit-orientated; they have expensive tastes and want to fulfil them immediateliy. Up-market and big spenders, the outer directed among them have joined with the young conspicuous consumers to create the yuppie phenomenon.

Their motivation is fast-moving enjoyment. While they are materialistic, and technological gadget-fiends, they are also highly individualistic; it is from this quality that their inner directedness derives. They reject traditional authority and established procedures, and are a powerful force for individual autonomy and the development of new organisational structures and relationships. Many of them embrace higher values and have this tendency to flip over eventually into a more non-materialistic behaviour pattern.

* *Conspicuous Consumers* (22%) have no time for high-faluting inner directed nonsense. They are materialists par excellence, and many experimentalists eventually end up in their camp. They are now the largest social value group in this country, but are even more numerous in other countries such as West Germany, Japan and 'middle America'. Here in Britain the AB London yuppie is the obvious example of the breed; but they are also concentrated in the C2 socio-economic group, especially in the north, where small-time show-offs flourish wonderfully.

They are driven by the need to get on and get ahead, and to be recognised as successful. Their aims are to increase their wealth and material well-being; to improve their social or working status; and to strengthen their power and influence over other people. They are motivated by acquisition, competition and esteem. They are traditionalists and they are also materialistic, pushy and concerned about appearance and position. Conspicuous consumers are mainly women; 60% are female, as opposed to the 40% of 'conspicuous achievers', the male equivalent.

Their thrust and drive has until recently been diminished in Britain by the belongers who consider that the impulse to claw one's way to the top is ungentlemanly, and by the self-explorers who feel that it is unrealistic. Nevertheless, at present conspicuous consumers are, as mentioned, attracting large numbers of both experimentalists and belongers themselves into their ranks in the wake of the Thatcherite revolution, of which more later. They represent the mainstream of the outer directeds and there are still plenty more where that came from.

* *Belongers* (17%) are the second transitional group, overlapping both the outer directeds and the sustenance driven. The former represent a

particularly high proportion of the upper echelons of the British establishment. Upper crust belongers are not so much smart, as *there*, because they either have been or pretend to have been so for generations. It is their abiding hope and belief that as long as there are enough of them around, everything will stay the way it always has. However, for this they need to rely on the large number of belongers in the lower orders of society, who support their betters and the dear old system to the death.

They are by and large older and drawn to a quiet, undisturbed life. Belongers are conservative, traditional, conventional, pragmatic and devoted to their families, whom they place above all else and on behalf of whom they often make substantial self-sacrifice. Since their horizons are so constrained by this orientation, they also tend to be worried, pedantic and governed by rules.

They are wholly against change, and their only interest in the future is to ensure their own and their family's security in it. The ten-year trend shows that this group is slowly declining and indeed dropped by two percentage points in 1986/87. Belongers used to be the largest group in every country – the backbone of England, they were called at the time of the First World War. Their commanding philosophy is, 'there's no place like home'. Home is where the heart is for the belonger, and outside it and the family nothing else matters much – witness the fact that they carry significantly more life assurance and more household insurance than the average.

Belongers are excellent cannon fodder. There are an inordinate number of brigadier belongers, sergeant-major belongers, police belongers and civil servant belongers. Sir Humphrey Appleby in 'Yes, Minister', with his successful resistance to any kind of change, is the perfect belonger. When it comes to their commercial behaviour, because many of them are in the upper reaches of society they feel an urgent need to maintain the style of life to which they and their families have become, or would like to become, accustomed.

This is why, as suggested, a successful British businessman so often opts for early retirement and a Georgian manor house on the Test, in contrast to his go-getting American equivalent who is thinking about how to make the next $50m. Apart from the landed lot, however, many other belongers have but modest social and economic requirements, and fit more naturally into the sustenance driven category, with its essentially peasant ethos.

* *Survivors* (15%) the central sustenance driven group, want above all

to 'get along', but reckon that the world is conspiring against them to prevent it. They have no concern about either the emotional and spiritual values of the inner directeds or the materialism of the outer. Their overall attitude assumes that the system is going to bale them out, but if it fails to do so they will bend it. Their profile is almost the exact opposite of the self-explorer's, whom they misunderstand and despise.

As long as no one takes advantage of them, survivors are a hardworking, quiet, traditional and cheerful lot with a strong community spirit. They have a powerful class-consciousness and represent the backbone of Labour party support. They tend to be concentrated more highly in the north, amongst the young and in the DE socio-economic group. The ten-year trend shows them to be declining slowly, although their numbers have recently been swollen by many of the young unemployed.

* *Aimless* (6%), the other sustenance driven group, is split into two divisions, the very old are who purposeless and apathetic, and those of the very young unemployed whose only motivation is short-term pleasure for kicks. They share the common characteristic of letting life slip by without caring much what happens to them, or feeling that they are able to control it.

The old aimless are ineffective because they are not able to be anything else, the young aimless are ineffective because they see no reason to be anything else – that is, except that their inadequacy can frequently erupt into resentful or mindless violence. A combination of demography and social pressures will ensure that this group maintains its strength of numbers, or maybe even increases in future.

Some Group Inter-comparisons

To demonstrate the contrasts between the groups and the distinctive differences in their behaviour, let us take holidays as an example, for which the requirements of each particular type are, in a nutshell –

* *Self-explorers* seek discovery, independence, flexibility and some kind of internal dimension, too. Their holidays may range from a spiritual retreat or an educational tour on a go-as-you-please ticket, to involvement in an environmental or community project or the exploration of some remote region.

* *Social resisters* need above all else to be in control. They feel they have a duty to go on holiday because that is what one does in order to keep sane. They may not look forward to it with any great enjoyment and they particularly dread placing themselves at the mercy of cultures or circumstances alien to their own way of thinking. The holiday has to be 'just right', or there will be complaints galore.

* *Experimentalists* want something at full throttle which sparks off as many sensations as possible and stokes up the fire of their adrenalin with its novelty and/or risk: say, some particularly attractive sport that relates to the environment they choose to go to, such as scuba-diving off the Great Barrier Reef or off-piste skiing in Aspen, Colorado. However it is not all sport that they are after. Any kind of new experience fascinates them, any kind of new place, new food or the novel titillation of any of the appetites and senses.

* *Conspicuous consumers* go for exclusivity, point-scoring and glamour. This may mean the Orient Express, a five-star hotel in Bangkok, or maybe Calais if nobody else in Station Road, Grimethorpe has actually ever been there yet.

* *Belongers,* in contrast, are all for a planned family holiday which is safe and private – that is if they want to have a holiday away at all, since they are really perfectly happy at home looking after the garden. ('I hate abroad', said King George V.)

* *Survivors* are after entertainment and letting their hair down, demanding the stereotyped ritual of a holiday but combined with a cultural anchor in the shape of bangers, chips and tea, ideally an oo-la-la home-from-home, in other words. Joining in the fun is all important, as is the anecdotal element, which involves collecting a wealth of ribald stories to tell the neighbours when they get back.

* *Aimless* as usual divide into two sub-groups. The older ones need something cheap where they can have a bit of peace and quiet; all the young ones want is to get blotto and indulge in blotto sex and violence.

To summarise, each of these social value groups inhabits a different world. Or rather, their members think they do, because to each of them the same world is a different place. We can dream up some indicative slogans as illustration:–

[76]

Self-Explorer	If you want a better world, you need better people
Social Resister	If you want a better world, you need a better system
Experimentalist	The world is my oyster – and there's a pearl in it!
Conspicuous Consumer	Look at me up here, world!
Belonger	The world isn't how it used to be . . .
Survivor	The world owes me a living – haven't I given it enough already?
Young Aimless	Sod the world!
Old Aimless	Eh? What World . . . ?

Semi-Permeable Membranes

It should not however be felt that these definitions are rigid throughout life – by no means so. They are separated by semi-permeable membranes and interact with each other as if in a constant state of variable osmosis during an individual's life cycle. Table 2 shows the ways in which movements can occur between the social value groups, as people pass through the various stages of their development. They reach adolescence carrying with them the attitudes they received from their parents and peers, and there is thus a primary route made up of solid arrows which indicates that they are fairly liable to remain in that same social value group throughout their lives.

However more than a few children of the self-explorers, social resisters, conspicuous consumers and belongers leave these groups early on, and embark in their teenage years on an experimentalist trip. In addition there are two exceptions to the rule that people, more often than not, remain in the same group. First, most experimentalists are unable to sustain the physical demands of their risky and dramatic style into mid-life, and tend to become either self-explorers or conspicuous consumers. Then there are also powerful political, educational and economic forces that cause some

TABLE 2. DEVELOPMENTAL MOVEMENTS BETWEEN THE SOCIAL VALUE GROUPS[6]

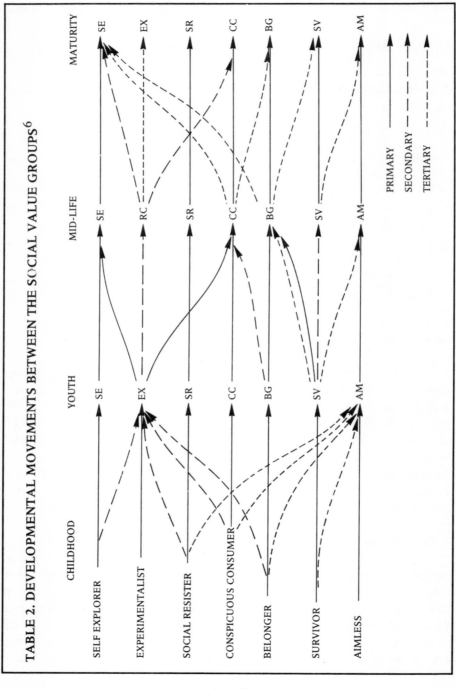

survivors to leave their social value group and drift up into the belonger group in their early adulthood – 'we're all middle class now', and so forth.

In addition to the early move into experimentalism, there are two other developmental movements of secondary importance that are designated in the Table by dashed arrows. To begin with a few experimentalists do stick it out and adhere to their demanding lifestyle in contrast to the majority who either become self-explorers or conspicuous consumers as above. Secondly, many young and middle-age belongers tend to become conspicuous consumers, some of the latter having been one time survivors who pass rapidly through the belonger phase. The belongers are thus being fed from below but float off into our other groups above.

Movements of tertiary importance are shown by dotted arrows. A few belongers, driven by economic necessity or loneliness, become survivors in later life. A few conspicuous consumers eventually become self-explorers; others however turn into belongers at this stage as age and failure dull their competitive edge. In contrast, quite a few survivors pull themselves up into a wholly new self-explorer mode, entirely missing the outer directed stage. But others understandably become aimless, dropping out of the conventional lifestyle. This also happens to some younger members of a number of other social value groups if they become unemployed.

Distinction should be made between these fundamental movements and individuals' short-term reactions to boom and slump, which result in an oscillation between the outer directed and sustenance driven modes. Cyclical factors apart, we should therefore expect a slow but steady increase among the self-explorers and a varied growth, sometimes as now extremely rapid but at other times non-existent or even slightly negative, among the conspicuous consumers.

The Ultimate Possibility

So where do we go from here? Taking Maslow's hypothesis a little further, what of the empty rung at the top of the ladder? Could this next social value group be the self-realiser, known in the Zen philosophy as the True Man of No Rank, whose purpose in life is to be the best of himself; the Swordmaster, who can take on ten opponents at a time and whose only weapon is his smile. There are few of these around at present – most of them are probably members of contemplative monastic orders in the Pyrenees or the remoter parts of Tibet. No matter, though, the emergence of the self-explorers has been so rapid during this century that maybe the next will see the dawn of this new self-realisation phase.

But to focus down to the shorter-term, the new millennium will also mark the recognition of the fact that, like the two sexes, the three major groupings of inner directed, outer directed and sustenance driven actually need each other. For the time being it is this that must be our major concern. We all have our faults and our magnificent virtues; it is only when we work deeply together that we can truly fulfil our human purposes.

More cooperation is needed, and less competition, even though we should recognise that we live in a competitive world which has nothing wrong with it apart from ourselves. What we have to do now is first to redefine, and then to recombine again, having rediscovered our own and each others' natures in the process. It is therefore this process of redefinition and rediscovery that will exercise us in these next few chapters.

6

THE SELF-EXPLORERS

It Must Be True – I Read It in the Papers

There are some for whom all this is going to be too theoretical. To them it must be said that the best way of testing the theory is to try it out in the everyday. Armed with the concept of these seven social value groups and some clues to how the members of each think and behave, the doubters should then look around them for confirmation. It must be confessed, though, that there is a problem here. As has been stressed, this analysis is not a personality test, but a statistical mechanism that year on year provides a dynamic model of society. Social researchers are adamant that it cannot be used for pigeon-holing individuals under one category or the next.

They remind us that with the regression analysis method by which these seven clusters are outlined, some people will typify a group very closely while others will be on the fringe of their designation or may even overlap into more than one. Real people are complex but in literature and the performing arts they are depicted more straightforwardly. It would probably be easier to pick examples from literature as stereotypes. For example, Alex and his drooges in 'A Clockwork Orange'[1] are aimless, almost all the characters in 'Dallas' are conspicuous consumers, Soames Forsyte is a belonger as is Phil Archer, and the Webber family in Posy Simmons' *Guardian* strip are social resisters to the life.

There is another solution and it lies with the press. Public figures are regarded as fair game in the media, and their activities are reported and dissected in ruthless detail. However, even though some of them make a fair shot at it journalists can never get behind into the absolute reality. It is a less than three-dimensional picture that emerges, halfway between the whole truth and a literary invention, but it is this incompleteness that makes press comment suitable for examining the theory. By using it we are not assessing the individuals themselves but the media's idea of them.

So now coming up is confirmatory evidence in the form of comment and rapportage from the responsible heavy press, covering the two years, from mid-1987, as annotated and acknowledged in detail in the Appendix of Notes and References. These paraphrased and quoted items, inter-woven with indicative reports on parallel current issues, will provide strong corroborative evidence of the existence of the groupings already described and examined in theoretical terms.

To satisfy the pedantic, the writer freely admits that none of the indi-viduals described has been surveyed as such, but nor have any of them been labelled here as members of a particular social value group. It is the *perceptions* of their attitudes and behaviour by the media in these various references that are suggested as examples of how that group ticks – a profoundly different assertion.

God Bless the Prince of Wales!

Back to the real world, however, and our first social value group, whose specimen representative is the Prince of Wales,[2] the quintessence of Millennial Man. Immediately this same paradox of identification asserts itself. The Prince, with a thousand years of tradition behind him, has the most solid belonger background of anyone in the entire country. He is also very much an experimentalist. The image of royal action-man is one that he has sustained since his teens with his passion for active and potentially dangerous sports – steeplechasing, hunting, windsurfing, diving, para-chuting and polo, not to mention off-piste skiing.

At one stage it is said that he had a private dream of riding in the Grand National. The Queen failed to talk him out of it, apparently, but eventually the Princess of Wales succeeded. This energetic physical activity may all be driven by an inner need to prove himself to his father in particular and everyone else in general, as offering a counterweight to the introspective, caring and spiritual side of his personality. Nevertheless the vast majority of what he clearly stands for is straight down the middle of the self-explorer road.

Like that of all members of the Royal Family, the Prince's position has to be one of political detachment. However, within this framework he has staked his personal commitment to a number of high profile and often controversial causes. Prince Charles represents the future, and he clearly sees it as his responsibility to encourage what he feels the future should be about. He keeps constantly urging us forward, all the time walking the fearsome tightrope of public opinion with extraordinary skill and determination.

As Alan Hamilton points out in 'The Real Charles', it is extraordinary how its founder Kurt Hahn's ethos, summed up in the Gordonstoun school motto, 'Plus est en vous', has been applied undiluted to so much of the Prince's approach to life. And Anthony Holden amplifies the same point in 'Charles, A Biography', listing his influences and interests as Kurt Hahn, Carl Jung, the United World Colleges, organic farming, alternative medicine, architecture with a human scale, urban regeneration and concern for wildlife in both the animal and plant kingdoms.

Holden views these as all 'pieces of a giant jigsaw which fits together as a cohesive world view. Between them they amount to a Princely Bill of Human Rights based on Charles' belief of the innate qualities of the individual, his right to live in conditions in which he can take pride as part of a caring, prejudice-free community which functions smoothly and effectively . . .' In other words, a totally holistic and self-explorer philosophy.

He has openly embraced the cause of complementary medicine, as became abundantly clear when he was President of the British Medical Association. His views on architecture appeal to the importance of community life and the need for buildings to relate to the human scale. The architectural profession has been sent packing with his unapologetic description of a proposed extension of the National Gallery as a monstrous carbuncle, his comment on a plan for Mansion House Square as a glass stump and his labelling of a new Plessey factory in Plymouth as a Victorian prison.

In October 1988 he roasted the profession on television, taking viewers on an aesthetic tour of British architecture, praising the good, criticising the bad and blasting the ugly in a highly professional 75 minute documentary. A MORI poll commissioned by the Daily Mirror found the public overwhelmingly in his support, with 67% strongly agreeing with him, 13% mildly agreeing, 17% mildly disagreeing and only 3% strongly disagreeing. His book, 'The Vision Of Britain', a statement of his views on architecture and the future of humankind, should be a sellout.

As an extension of this thought-process he has particularly expressed the cause of the inner cities which he has tackled in a non-political but highly personal and energetic manner. His interest combines the practical and the humane. His anxiety to meet people in centres of urban deprivation stems partly from his compassion, but partly also from his desire to encourage everyone to demand a say in what happens to them, by stressing the importance of a sense of community and the effectiveness of self-help. This overall emphasis on the rights of the individual, and on the need to empower people to lead their own lives in the way they consider best for themselves is fundamental to his own belief system, and wholly characteristic of the self-explorer ethos.

A great deal of this derives from the spiritual path which he has trodden largely under the direction of his friend and mentor Sir Laurens van der Post, author, philosopher, adventurer and godfather to Prince William, who has in a sense become personal guru, by appointment. Now in his eighties, he has taught Prince Charles the ability to observe life through the eyes of a mystic. His philosophy combines the work of psychologist Carl Jung, his personal experience of suffering as a wartime prisoner of the Japanese, and a deep respect and reverence for the bushmen of Southern Africa who live in total harmony with nature, the nomadic hunter-gatherers who represent the last dim memory of our earliest human ancestors.

The bushmen's spiritual beliefs are based on the tripartite communion of each individual with nature, with village and with tribe; a unit of body, spirit and the natural order within the community and a true celebration of wholeness and interdependence. Jung teaches us about the collective unconscious, and this relates to van der Post's conviction that modern man is a schizophrene with a light, rational 'European' side and a dark instinctive 'African' side. These two poles must be united if destruction is not to overtake us as a species, he argues. 'Something like the bushman, the first man, remains alive in all of us in some basement of the European spirit.'

This recognition of everybody's need for a holistic existence in which the conflicting elements are reconciled – within each one of us as well as within society as such – is central to much of his writing, and has deeply penetrated Prince Charles' psyche as a result. Van der Post invited him to commune together with his bushmen friends in the Kalahari desert in early 1987. This must have given the Prince a taste for wilderness and remote landscapes, as later that year he also spent time on a small Hebridean island working with its little population of crofters.

His emphasis on closeness to the earth and a communion with the plant kingdom has given him what one might describe as a hard row to hoe with the popular press – 'A-loon again!' sneered one tabloid headline when the Hebridean story broke, and many a self-explorer must have felt a painful stab of sympathy for him. He is very much in the vanguard of the organic farming[3] movement, and though in this respect his opponents speak of him as being 'in cloud-cuckoo land' and complain that his ideas are 'about as relevant to ordinary farmers as caviare', the reality is that the public is beginning to listen to this and the other marching songs of his secret revolution. But still there is that hard core of mindless resistance. There is nothing more reviled by the sustenance driven than what they consider to be pretentious wetness. It is ironic that this kind of behaviour is not only a symptom of advanced self-development but actually reveals a deep empathy with their own situation. The fact that they react so disproportionately is an indication that they feel profoundly threatened, but know at the same time in their hearts that he is right. A similar reaction was evinced when he addressed an audience of lumberjacks in a remote part of central Canada about the beauties of nature as a source of spiritual enlightenment.

During the March 1989 London conference on chlorofluorocarbons (CFCs) he insisted to delegates that there was an overwhelming case for their complete elimination, and charged governments with an obligation to intervene, accelerating or enforcing environmental measures. He then turned to other significant problems such as our polluted seas and the desertification of our rainforests, commenting 'if we can stop the sky turning into a microwave oven we will still face the prospect of living in a garbage dump.' He praised those who warned of these dangers and sympathised when they were initially 'dismissed at best as cranks, and at worst as extremists', adding in parenthesis, 'I know how they feel.'

But you can't keep a good man down. Speaking in Sydney in January 1988 during the Australian bicentennial celebrations, the Prince added his support to the cause of the aborigines campaigning for land rights. During the ceremony an actor, Jack Thompson, commented that 'after 200 years, Australians are finding out what the aborigines have known for 40,000.' The Prince jumped straight in with his reply – 'those are my sentiments entirely'.

Not that his concerns lack a practical edge. His presidency of Business in the Community is witness to that. Under its banner and with the spur of his encouragement, many companies are now following the lead of the few large ones which started this initiative, notably Pilkingtons, IBM and NatWest, to restore life and employment to the inner cities. The movement gained impetus from the whirlwind tour of Toxteth given by

Michael Heseltine to assorted captains of industry in 1981 which left them shaken and determined to help. But it is the leadership of the Prince of Wales that has been such a key feature of this development.

He is quite prepared to acknowledge the contradictions between his immense personal wealth and his philosophy that happiness lies within the inner life. 'I may have everything I need materially in a sense, but there are other difficulties. One worries a great deal about the responsibilities and everything else, trying to do the right thing, to have as balanced an approach as possible.' He has remarked that he would actually enjoy working on a building site,' because it is a marvellous way of getting to know people. You live a much more normal existence with people. They lose their anxiety and merge.'

There is a poignant dichotomy here, as many of his necessary activities reflect the highly traditionalist belonger background from which he comes. An appropriate quotation is one from Machiavelli's 'The Prince': 'there is nothing more difficult to take in hand, more perilous to conduct or more uncertain in its success than to take the lead in the introduction of a new order of things'. We are incredibly lucky to have him, and he deserves all the support and love that we can muster.

The Royal Lead

The Prince of Wales is beset by hazards, not the least of which being the fact that he will no doubt continue to be misleadingly reported. He has however won tremendous popular affection, and is going about his business with nobility, sensitivity and dedication. It may indeed be that his siblings are hearing the same drumbeat. It is remarkable how the Princess Royal's intensely personal involvement with the Save the Children Fund has captured the imagination of the public and totally altered its perception of her.

Prince Edward,[4] too, has managed to create a role for himself which satisfies the expectations of his public position, his family and himself. His decision to leave The Royal Marines in the face of intense pressure from the regiment and from his father was a mark of his individuality, and his determination to work in the theatre, resisting other traditionalist suggestions such as the diplomatic corps, also exhibits an attractive streak of personal determination. How interesting it is that three of the four royal children show so many indications of possessing inner directed tendencies.

This is not always popular with the present government – note Norman Tebbit on *Panorama*[5] rubbishing Prince Charles and his influence, on the grounds that he was debarred from having 'a proper job'. What he may well have been voicing was concern that some kind of unofficial opposition seems to be building up among certain sections of the establishment, notably the Church but also including members of the Royal Family. Apart from Prince Charles, Prince Philip is not averse to making caustic remarks about acid rain; and the Queen's distaste for Mrs Thatcher's materialist philosophy is well known, even if officially denied by all.

There does seem to be some evidence of integrated timing among the Royals.[6] For example, coincident with Prince Charles' call against CFCs at the Saving The Ozone Layer conference in March 1989, the Duke of Edinburgh in his BBC 1 Dimbleby lecture entitled 'Living Off The Land' spoke of the strain put upon the earth's resources by the need of farmers to produce extra food for growing nations. Intensive agriculture, he argued, though having made possible an unprecedented increase in population, was also creating desperate problems for future generations and had become a victim of its own success.

Further support for the Prince came from the Queen a few weeks later, when she marked the conversion of the royal fleet of cars to leadless petrol by having children release 10,000 balloons from the forecourt of Buckingham Palace and, in her annual message to the Commonwealth, called for a common partnership to conserve the world 'not only across the oceans but also between generations.' It was also interesting when less than 24 hours after the Prince of Wales, speaking as patron of the European Year of the Environment, had expressed grave concern over global environmental issues (warning that one third of all forms of life on earth could be extinct within six years), the Duke of Edinburgh attacked 'the arrogance of the human race in claiming to have conquered nature'. In this address to the Royal Society of Arts he said, 'the use of the word conquest seems to imply that Man has somehow managed to put something under subjugation'. This echoes Bacon's remark that mankind must 'torture nature's secrets from her'. In the light of events in the space of time between the two quotations, the Duke's contention is not difficult to substantiate.

The Prince's Euro-speech called on political leaders with a sense of vision to save the environment before it was too late. 'The trouble is that there is not enough evidence so far that those in politics or in industry believe that the British public is indeed ready to dip into its pocket to support environmental measures.' In contrast, he then detailed a whole change in public attitude that he saw taking place, a growing realisation that we were not separate from nature. 'Because so many more people are beginning to think like this, they are not prepared to tolerate the avoidable abuse of our environment – such as pollution for example, whether of rivers or the sea, by nitrate run-off and sewage effluent, or of the air in the form of emissions of sulphur dioxide and nitrogen oxides from power stations or cars.' Classic self-explorer doctrine.

Bernard Shaw's *The Apple Cart* postulates a socialist Britain of the future, where the King is on the verge of being forced to abdicate, but saves himself by reminding the Prime Minister that if he were to do so he would be released to form a political party that would sweep the government out of office. In a way, the Prince of Wales now exercises the same kind of appeal, though circumstances are admittedly dissimilar at the moment. Nevertheless, he is one of tomorrow's world leaders, around whose philosophy a growing number of the thinking people of this country are going to congregate.

1968 And All That

Born in 1948, Prince Charles shares the characteristic of age with the young people of the 1960s generation all over the developed world. Much of the current momentum of the self-explorer movement is the result of a practical consolidation of the swinging sixties and early seventies when we never had it so good. The sweet scent of flower power and cannabis was in the air, the Beatles gave the beat, and the signs of deep social change began to appear on the streets. These young people were said to be undisciplined because their fathers had been away at the war, and they gave many an old fogey a heart attack at the time.

Much of their movement petered out, however, as having acted out their dreams in their late teens and early twenties they knuckled down to the serious business of starting work, getting married and raising a family. Responsibilities temporarily eradicated the desire to crystallise all those beautiful thoughts, and though subsequent cohorts of students still carried the torch, it was glimmering but faintly after the dousing it got from the OPEC I and II recessions of 1974 and 1980.

Nonetheless, the values of the beat generation, immature though they may have seemed at the time, remained in the back of these people's minds as they progressed into their mid-lives. Here, as always, a period of reflection ensued, as they suddenly realised that it would not be long before they were in the driving seat once their elders and betters had given way to them. At the same time, though, they have been confronted by the pressures, frustrations and traumas of personal life, combined with those of ever-increasing social and economic change. It is therefore hardly surprising that some of these old values are now beginning to bubble up to the surface again in the minds and actions of opinion leaders, who have now acquired the maturity to re-state some of their original tenets in more thoughtful and sophisticated tones.

Of course, some of the erstwhile hippies, with their sixties idealism, their 'new left' counter-culture against the Vietnam war, their campus riots and Watergate protests of the 1970s, have become upwardly mobile socialites and corporate strivers. For them, the Age of Aquarius has become the Age of Aries, ramming home the message of consumer power and forgetting their earlier rejection of it.

But after twenty years or more, the late 1960s are now big nostalgia business. The 1960s revolution is seen as a pivotal recognition of multiple perspectives. Apart from social revolution, the era generated intense interest in the validity of individual beliefs and attitudes, marking the acceptable realisation that each of us is a unique lens interpreting our own reality through our own glassware. The rediscovery of this old spiritual truth means that society has begun to see itself as being governed by a collection of such lenses rather than by a cut and dried set of superimposed values.

There had been a remarkably international feel to 1968, with a sense of absolute global integration about it. The whole planet seemed to be on the move with the Vietnam War, the May Evènements in France and the Prague Spring. Everyone was a citizen of the world, and there was an evolving consciousness of optimism, energy, imagination and self-confidence. Some of this energy was admittedly channelled into unproductive and dotty activities at the time. On the other hand 1968 led on to the birth of the Feminist and the Green movements which, though they have gone up a few blind alleys since then, are nevertheless a vast improvement on what was there before, and have contributed to the foundation of something even better to come.

1968 was a response to the long boom of the 1950s and 1960s. It was the recession of 1974 following OPEC I that undermined its spirit, which assumed everlasting material wellbeing and had little to say about priorities during times when resources were limited. It had no interest in modernisation, it was anti-science and held technological change at a discount. The subsequent counter-counter-culture of the microchip seemed a reversal to many of these faded flower people, but in fact this antithesis to the hippy thesis could well combine with it to produce a remarkable and wonderful synthesis as a legacy for us in our new millennium.

Thus many of the issues raised in the sixties and since buried have now returned to re-engage us. The media are looking at the second coming of the sixties generation and dividing it into two moral and economic categories: the poor-but-virtuous and the rich-but-compromised. In the US there are quite a few carpenters with university degrees and tax lawyers homesick for the Himalayas. However the generation's real energies have begun to move positively again. Ideals, tempered by years of exile, now seem practical, and can actually be shown to be profitable.

A new and transformed leadership is preparing itself for display like a crocus under the snow. This is the suggestion of Annie Gottlieb[7] in 'Do You Believe in Magic?', subtitled 'The Second Coming of the Sixties Generation', Gottlieb concludes her book with a description of a 1994 event called World War IV, a war on war itself in which 'we are engaged in an urgent and joyous fight for our survival. The enemy is not out there; it is that war-making thing in the human spirit, fathered by fear.'

In the United States the 1960s phenomenon was closely linked not only to cannabis but to the psychedelic drugs such as LSD, described by Jay Stevens in 'Storming Heaven' as the hippy sacrament, a mind detergent capable of washing away years of social programming. The mind detergent of the 1980s has been not LSD or pot, however, but cocaine, the release of Wall Street bankers and Philadelphia lawyers rather than of dropout draft dodgers and airhead idealists. The boom that followed the two OPEC-induced recessions spawned a new phenomenon, the yuppie, whose rise and fall we will be considering shortly.

The New Age Philosophy

The American yuppie has taken up rather faster than his British counterpart many of the trends set in motion by his compatriot self-explorers, but has done so in a more opulent and self-conscious style. Just as in the past they hijacked the jogging movement initiated by inner directeds for health reasons and elaborated it as a vehicle for *haute couture*, outer directeds there are invading what is coming to be known as the New Age of spiritual consciousness.

Admirable though this may be in its pure form, in the heat and glitz of California it deteriorates. Here the rip-off brigade are making a pile of money charging people 200 bucks a throw to watch them fall into an unconscious trance, permitting the Crown Prince of Mars or some 30,000 year old Mongolian warrior to take over their bodies and 'channel' psychobabble to the ecstatic audience. This is the tacky underside of the largely positive trend towards spiritual inner directedness.

Such a powerful spontaneous upsurge of interest in the supernatural has some of its roots in the beliefs of the early Christian Gnostics. They considered that within each person as part of themselves was a tiny spark of God, elusive but accessible with effort and practice. It is by striving to resonate to that part of a greater whole, that we reach the ultimate goal of linking this spark – what Jung terms the transpersonal self – to the greater God through experiencing our own holism. Out of this flows the idea that everything is both a creation and an interpretation of this God-consciousness and indeed that the Universe itself is a dimension of God.

To take a parallel from modern physics, a holographic photograph, besides being three-dimensional, also has another unusual characteristic. If the holograph is contained on a glass plate which is then broken into pieces, each piece retains an image of the whole original, rather than just a small part of it like in a jigsaw puzzle. The New Age argument is that we are all spiritual holograms, all holons – single entities both comprised of and comprising other wholes.

This wholeness leads to a sense of oneness with all created things and is a reason, even if sometimes an unconscious one, for the inner directed's strong attraction for conservation, ecology, the natural order and the development of the self in body, mind, emotions and spirit. The mystical aspect which is fundamental to the New Age also has philosophical links with such Christian sages as St John of the Cross, Dame Julian of Norwich, St Teresa of Avila, Meister Ekhart and Pierre Teilhard de Chardin. It connects too with the Sufi Muslims, the Kabbala discipline of Judaism and concepts borrowed from Buddhism, Hinduism and Taoism. Carl Jung and his followers, among whom were Abraham Maslow and Roberto Assagioli, have provided the philosophy with an up-to-date psychological interpretation.

In its pure form this is to many an increasingly attractive concept – it gives meaning to the world; it points to a single reality behind all myths and religions; it regards death as but one temporary step along the way; and posits truth as not merely a matter of blind faith superimposed by an autocratic religious structure, but as something to be found and grasped by everybody within themselves. It's great weakness is the weakness of the inner directed movement as a whole. It is so individualistic a credo that effectively there are no rules to it, so that everybody can play the game in any way they want.

In the rarified atmosphere of California, like in first century Athens, they are constantly seeking an opportunity either to tell or to hear some new thing. No trouble for an ambitious salesman on the make to cling like a leech onto this search for identity among the rich and ridiculous, just as the television fundamentalist preachers feed off their foolish sustenance driven compatriots. These two groups, however, are fired with antipathy towards each other, in this as in so many other respects. The war between mystics and fundamentalists is now just beginning and has a long way to go. Ultimately it may well engulf every religious movement in the world if we fail to defuse it. Alas, increasing media attention is going to make this more and more difficult.

Meanwhile, though, let us take a look at some of the other issues close to the hearts and minds of self-explorers and see where current events are taking them. It will become evident that, forgetting the blatant excesses of these Californian manipulators, some important and interesting moves are going on nearer home.

Do-It-Yourself Education

For example, in the field of education it may just be that Secretary of State Kenneth Baker's radical proposals for placing more decision-making power in parents' hands could have some unexpected results. Thoughtful parents are already taking a self-explorer route, voicing deep concern at the bureaucratic decisions of some Education Authorities. In the Suffolk seaside town of Southwold, for example, the education committee of the County Council and the Local Education Authority have cosily agreed between themselves that three schools should be shut down, depriving the area of public education for all children over nine.

The new alternative plan is for them to be bussed up to twelve miles away to huge centralised comprehensives. Investigating the story for *The*

Observer, Michael Davie[8] interviewed three officers of the Suffolk Education Authority, who control the organisation of Suffolk schools in strict accordance with the procedures laid down by Whitehall. Davie found that they spoke a language incomprehensible to ordinary people, talking about education as if it were some obscure intellectual speciality.

The principle bone of contention was the closure of Ruidon High School, an 11-16 comprehensive with 265 pupils. There seemed no clear reason why anybody might have thought that Ruidon was too small, so Davie asked whether there was a particular number of pupils that made a school the right size. The County Education Officer smiled patiently: 'Wouldn't life be easy if everything was as cut and dried as that?' When asked whether a larger school would be able to offer the children certain subjects such as Russian or Computer Sciences, he explained that to talk about particular subjects was 'simplistic', it was a question of a smaller school being 'more restricted' and his aim was 'to improve the provision'.

Opposite, in the green corner, a totally united community faced the faceless ones. Davie tried conscientiously but unsuccessfully for three days to find one person in Southwold or Ruidon who approved of the proposals. Local businesses, local papers, parents, all the local parish, town and district councils, and all the political associations, were implacably opposed to what they saw as the potential deterioration of their town into an old people's twilight retreat. The managing director of the local brewery wrote: 'It is our considered view that without the focal point of our local school whose contribution to the community is immense, it would not be very long before most young families and young people left the area altogether'. As another long-standing resident commented, it was as if a plumber had come along and performed a heart-transplant on a perfectly healthy patient.

Kenneth Baker has said: 'We want to extend choice to everyone', citing small schools as 'the cement of society in the community'. Ruidon High School has produced educational results in line with the rest of the country, and it would cost more to shut it down than to keep it open. The school grounds and buildings were also being used for all sorts of activities, from the Youth Club to old people's bingo, that would suffer if the school was closed just for bureaucratic convenience or whim.

It is beginning to be felt that in principle bureaucratic convenience and whim are not good enough any more. So, many parents who find themselves in this kind of predicament are going to slip out from under the system and break the chains of their dependence upon a remote centre.

[93]

The classic self-exploratory alternative is simply to take over the responsibility and do it themselves. For example, the school at Ticknall, Derbyshire is a former primary school which closed because of shrinking numbers. Derbyshire County Council refused to help fund it because officials believed that its mixed age classes and small size could not provide adequate education for children from 4–14.

However, headmaster Philip Toogood came up with a radical answer – to allow parents to educate their children partly at home and partly at school, negotiating with it to teach them for whatever proportion of the week they each agreed upon. The school charges no fees and is now owned by a 200-year old educational trust. At present there are only 15 pupils but numbers could rise to 60, though this would be the maximum, in line with the Human Scale Education Movement's belief that children's social and educational development is best undertaken in small units.

Some pupils attend full time, but parents retain a substantial role in the educational process, both as regards their own children and often in the collective sense as occasional teachers and minders. Eventually it is intended that they will even bake their own bread and make their own lunches, as they do at another and earlier flexi-school, The Small School at Hartland, Devon, which has been a manifest success.

As Philip Toogood puts it, 'the pupils will not be taught how to be taught but will learn how to learn.' By using the open-learning techniques that are becoming ever more available, they can cover any subject and are not pinned down to a restrictive conventional curriculum. Eventually it hoped that the school will become an adult education centre as well, but even before this it will be more closely connected to the community than normal, as parents with skills teach there and pupils do much of their learning outside it.

This may seem all too adventurous for some, but it could well offer an attractive alternative to the residents of Southwold if they were prepared to take the plunge. Certainly not all the parents involved in this kind of experiment are likely to be self-explorers and indeed they may well cover almost all the social value groups. However, it is probable that the blue touch-paper will first be lit by someone with self-explorer tendencies.

But the interesting thing is that once people start shedding their dependence on the system, although some may take it as a licence to trample on everyone else's fingers in the name of independence, they nevertheless generally end up, as here, with a strong sense of interdependence and community. Furthermore, once people start branching out autonomously in one area of their lives, be it education or yoga or whatever, the seeds of this behaviour seem to take deeper root and it is not long before they are transplanting the principle into other aspects of their behaviour.

Conservation and Consumption[9]

The movement for the conservation of resources and the durability of products provides another example of spread of the self-explorer philosophy. How interesting it is that when apparently cornered by the League Against Cruel Sports, the shooting community leaps on to the fashionable conservation bandwagon. Its new public relations emphasis is that well-keepered estates encourage the growth of the songbird population, as the predators that kill both them and the game birds are kept down. At the same time, 'game strips' round the edges of fields are left untouched by sprays, not only to shelter game birds such as partridges and pheasants, but to encourage the development of the wildflower and insect populations (alias weeds and pests) because here also the protection of game demands it'.

Meanwhile there is a somewhat different story from the National Farmers Union, which accuses the Department of the Environment and local councils of trying to preserve a 'chocolate box' image of the countryside. It cites, for example, the case of farmer Brian Moore of Weeton, North Yorkshire, who built up an ice-cream operation to absorb surplus milk production but was given 6 months to end it by the DOE after public complaints about the litter and traffic congestion being caused. On the other hand, the NFU has grudgingly had to admit that many British farmers now under siege from EEC regulations – designed to protect inefficient continental smallholders but which have resulted in supply build-ups and cuts in price support – are turning to nature conservation as a crop, based on the increasing interest of a public prepared to pay for the privilege of witnessing at first hand the protection of diminishing species in the world.

On New Year's Eve 1987 the World Wildlife Fund warned that 1,000 animal species faced extinction within the year, most of them the victims of man's relentless expansion programme. While publicity tends to centre on the giant panda, the mountain gorilla or the white rhinoceros, it is the less dramatic insects and plants that are frequently of vital but little-known use. The properties of numerous obscure plants and animals have

[95]

been found to be of crucial importance to medical research. The Madagascar rosy periwinkle is a source of vicriblastine, highly effective in the treatment of leukaemia and Hodgkin's disease. Having been used for generations by tribal healers, the plant is now responsible for the fact that whereas in 1960 four children out of five who contracted leukaemia in the developed world died, today four out of five survive.

The contraceptive pill is largely derived from the Mexican yam and quinine comes from the bark of a Peruvian tree. The chemical didemonin, isolated from a Caribbean squid, is being tested for important clinical applications. Dr Julian Caldicott wrote in the British Medical Journal that already one pharmaceutical product in four is derived from wild plants, 'yet only one species in one hundred has been screened for potential value. Much remains to be done and since four-fifths of all plant species live only within tropical forests it will be done only if these forests can be conserved.' In the face of this, who can deny that we are truly interdependent with the Amazonian Indian who has known the properties of these plants for the past 25,000 years?

Meanwhile Professor William Jarrett of Glasgow University is poised to carry out human trials on a vaccine that gives new hope in the fight against Aids and is derived from the bark of the Brazilian oak, used by the same Indians in the Amazonian rainforests as a blood-clotting treatment for wounds from poison darts, but which is now seriously diminished in numbers. The similarly threatened black bean tree from North Queensland is also under the scrutiny of Aids researchers.

As Prof. Jarrett says, 'the more the diversity of the rainforests is lost, the less we can look to them as a source of salvation in future. When we cut down rain forests, we simply don't know what we are destroying.' The forests of the equatorial belt are being ripped out at the rate of 100 acres a minute, half of them having disappeared since the beginning of the century. The timber is harvested and the land planted with crops which exhaust it in just a few years, forcing farmers to move on and burn new areas of forest, driving out the tribes who live there.

Until the very recent past, short-term economic and political pressures have meant that the warnings of environmentalists like Sir David Attenborough and Dr David Bellamy have passed unheeded. Estimates of the number of undiscovered species of life are now in the region of 30 million or more, three quarters of which are seething and swarming together in the unparalleled richness of the jungle canopy and floor. As the most magnanimous eco-system on earth, covering only 7% of its surface but containing more than half its known species, the tropical rain forest is the main subject for anxiety. In South America and elsewhere the World Bank is still financing dam and hydro-electric schemes despite its alleged attention to environmental factors. 'Governments then have to encourage the clearance of forests to make way for cash crops in order to pay back the debt incurred in building the dams', complains tele-biologist David Bellamy.

A *Sunday Times* February 1989 colour supplement, 'The World Is Dying – What Are You Going To Do About It' described our planet as 'despoiled, rotten, over-crowded and barren', and held us all to blame and all to suffer. It revealed that every hamburger represents the cutting down of 55 square feet of tropical rain forest. Mrs Thatcher has criticised Brazil over its programme of rain forest destruction and indicated that the government was looking very hard at lending schemes for Brazil in the light of this, provoking an angry backlash from President Sarnay, who categorised her attitude as 'green imperialism – part of a campaign to impede Brazil from becoming a world power'.

The very keystone of tropical forestry is economic nonsense, however. Brazil burns entire provinces, exports a fraction of the timber it salvages to Japan and then buys it back again as finished furniture. But the rain forests are quite capable of paying for their own survival in a host of ways. In Zaire the natural products of bulb fibre and bark are torched as a waste product, whereas in Europe they command huge prices. Consultants Euro-Gulf, working in 345,000 hectares of Zairian rain forest, have proved they can obtain the same financial return by cropping 8,600 hectares of it as they could by razing the entire area.

A watershed in planetary appreciation of the rain forests occurred in March 1989 in Altimira, Brazil, where representatives of 38 tribes of Amazonian Indians met to protest against the construction of a huge hydro-electric dam on the site. The Shamans (medicine men) of the tribes had all independently concluded that it was time for them to teach their white brothers and sisters their secrets, because the earth as a whole was in need of them. Environmental groups, scientists, and government and bank officials from all over the world were invited to the gathering and the white brothers and sisters were courteously welcomed, but only allowed to speak for five minutes each because 'when a white person speaks for more than five minutes he tells lies'.

Suddenly coming up against this kind of truth is uncomfortable. But what is happening in the deepest sense is that people, led by the self-explorers, are beginning to recognise themselves as being unremittingly and irrevocably bound up in the whole. Saving the rain forests might in the past have been thought of as altruistic. But now the realisation that the lives of all our grandchildren are going to be wrecked by our own stupid behaviour is coming home to us.

The word 'altriusm' has as its root the Latin for 'other'. But 'otherness', is dead – we are all so personally affected; 'sacrifice' is dead – we are all too intimately involved. What is happening now is that 'virtue' is no longer required, and the interdependent pain of our planet is shrieking out to every one of us as its individual cells to help rescue it. The planet is the extension, the body of every one of us – and as more and more people begin to realise this, no longer does one need to waste time imploring someone else, 'please don't cut off your leg, it would be a bad idea'.

Conservation, then is not simply a question of maintaining an artificially pretty image of the English countryside, but is increasingly recognised as necessary for our survival – not least because of the appalling climatic changes that the destruction of our biosphere is already beginning to produce. This is not referring to sodden Wimbledon fortnights. It is about millions dying in Northern Africa, worldwide flooding of low lying territories and the acceleration of the 'greenhouse effect', where because there are fewer trees to absorb the increasing levels of CO_2 we produce for our utilisation of fossil fuels, there is a danger that the polar ice caps will melt substantially and engulf us. The meteorological office estimate that inevitably the rise in mean temperature in the UK will be something like 5 degrees Celsius by the year 2050. Furthermore, many wild plants under threat are now realised to be vital sources for the improvement of food crops through cross breeding. In particular, both yields and disease resistance of rice have increased enormously through the introduction of new genetic material from wild strains. Seemingly insignificant insects are also of crucial economic importance. The African oil palm, introduced into South East Asia, had until recently to be laboriously pollinated by hand. Research in the Cameroons identified a tiny weevil as the natural pollinating agent, which since being sent east has produced such an increase in fertility that there is now a temporary palm oil glut.

There has also been considerable publicity surrounding the hole in the ozone shield[10] over Antarctica. The ozone layer of the upper atmosphere filters out the harmful ultra-violet rays of the sun and thus protects us from skin cancer, eye cataracts and other diseases. Ultra-violet rays also suppress immune systems in humans, animals and plants and upset the delicate balance of global life support.

The most probable cause of the damage is the use of the chlorofluorocarbons that are to be found in most of the world's aerosol cans, and in polystyrene products like packaging materials, egg-boxes and hamburger cartons. CFCs are odourless, non-toxic, safe in storage and have no effect on their contents. Unfortunately, since the mid 1970s, they have also been under the deepest possible suspicion of damaging the ozone layer, even though many of their manufacturers continue to mumble that the case is not proven.

The London conference on saving the ozone layer agreed to ban the manufacture of CFCs by the millennium, but this will do no more than decelerate the danger. Being unusually inert, CFCs last for a century or so in the atmosphere, and just to keep the pollution level constant their use would have to be cut immediately by 85%. However, in an age when self-explorer awareness and action are both growing so markedly, some people have stopped using these aerosols anyway. There are now plenty of non-polluting sprays on the market and only 60% of the 800 million aerosols made in Britain every year contain no CFCs at all any more, with Johnson's Wax and Wellcome significantly reducing their use. Fast food concerns like McDonald's and Wimpy are phasing out polystyrene containers too, and manufacturers of all shapes and sizes are looking round for substitute materials.

Large companies are not going to take steps like this without a huge public surge in demand that they should act in a responsible manner. The same applied to the withdrawal of tartrazine (E.102) as a food additive when it was linked to hyperactivity in young children. Typically, at the vanguard of the movement once again we find The Prince of Wales, who in a speech in February 1988 strongly criticised Britain's record on environmental legislation.

First he singled out the Central Electricity Generating Board for its reluctance to take action to reduce acid rain. Then on the subject of the ozone layer, he said, 'I personally, as I become older and more autocratic, have banned aerosols in my household', adding that as many husbands have discovered, the problem was finding alternatives to hairsprays. However, returning to the attack he stressed that many industrialists were out of step with the considerations of ordinary people when it came to attitudes to the environment, a criticism he has already applied to architects, of course.

His speech to the delegates of London's Saving The Ozone Layer conference in March 1989 was wholly appropriate to the occasion and wholly consistent with his personal list of imperatives. He is indeed the President of this invisible club of the awake.

Expect, then, a seeping down of concern for the environment to occur throughout the whole of society, initiated by these inner directeds, and particularly the self-explorers. 20,000 people a month, and rising, are now joining green groups like Friends of the Earth, Greenpeace, and Ark. 87% of these likely to vote said that a party's environment policy would be an important factor in deciding where to put the cross in the European Parliamentary elections in June 1988 – in which the UK Green Party boosted its share of the vote from virtually nothing to 15%. Assume, then, that it will become increasingly fashionable for individuals to –

* use unleaded petrol

* use household products that are not harmful to nature

* save energy in the home

* recycle household rubbish

* eat less meat and animal fats

* insist on organic fruit and vegetables

Furthermore, expect electoral pressure on both central and local government to intervene, regulate and spend in order to –

* promote energy conservation in all fields – in particular, by firming up on fuel efficiency requirements for cars and by raising petrol taxes, if taxes are to be raised, thus also raising drivers' personal interest in saving fuel

* stop subsidising private transport – the major source of offending pollutants – at the expense of rail

* reform Britain's toxic waste shambles

* clean up our drinking water and rivers, our air and our soil

* encourage waste recycling

* promote natural gas usage – the cleanest hydrocarbon fuel available – and promote research into alternative sources of energy (and this does *not* mean nuclear)

* encourage 'debt for nature' swops with Third World countries, subsidising debt relief in exchange for steps taken by debtor nations to protect natural resources

* support worldwide family planning campaigns

* ratify the Antarctic Agreement and the 1982 convention on the Law of the Sea, which seek to regulate indiscriminate mining and other commercial development

* make the environment a summit issue

From environmental considerations to consumer durables – regarded in economic circles as the yardstick for measuring an individual's or a society's standard of living – but how realistically, when it comes to the point? That sharp-pencilled, sharp-minded scourge of the absurd, *The Observer*'s Katharine Whitehorn[11], has complained that nobody knows what the phrase 'consumer durables' really means.

'An increase in the production of such goodies is always seen as a deliciously significant step, but it is only when you have heard the phrase about a hundred times that you start realising that it does not mean what it says'. She goes on to argue that though some purists may see all consumer durables as pointless status symbols, there is an important difference between a pure piece of nonsense luxury and a vital working tool which if broken or repossessed can mean desolation.

She therefore sensibly suggests dividing the category into three subheadings. First are 'consumer aspirationals', which almost everyone nowadays demands whether they are of any use or not, such as cars, TV and hi-fi; then genuine consumer durables, which are practical objects like irons, stoves and washing machines, where 'durable' should be a description monitored by the Office of Fair Trading lke 'flameproof' or 'pre-shrunk'; and finally 'consumer ephemerals' that catch the public's fancy, burst into fashion and slip out again, like the ten-speed personalised gizmos for taking silicon chips out of horses hooves. Self-explorers would entirely endorse this redefinition, so who knows, it might actually catch on.

More About Work

Meanwhile in the world of work[12] things are also moving the self-explorer's way, as has already been indicated. The growing emphasis on bonuses and share options means that the relationship between employer and employee is becoming less one of master and servant and more one of partners in an enterprise. However, the relationship is also sometimes more a matter of commitment to the job than loyalty to the firm, and teambuilding can thus be adversely affected.

What is emerging is a new breed of executives that London management consultants Inbucon call 'journeyman professionals' – people who want a share of the action with the implication that if it is not big enough or exciting enough they will move on or maybe go freelance, à la mode de Charles Handy. Although such people have till now always been part of the organisation's innermost core, their demand for intellectual and emotional fulfilment as well as for financial reward is turning many of them into up-market contract workers.

On the continent there is already a trend for top managers to hire themselves out on a highly paid contract of 3 or 4 years' duration, and a number of British headhunters are also latching on to this concept of 'interim management'. However under these conditions, the employer tends to feel less responsible for staff welfare, at any rate where reward levels are such that people should be financially able to look after themselves.

This is bad news for your average sustenance driven plodder. The relationship between employer and employee is transformed here into a benevolent mutual exploitation, putting the burden on employees to take a self-interested grip on their own careers. Few executives are equipped to do this at the moment, particularly scientists, engineers, accountants and others who are solidly in the left-brain professional mode and tend not to create career plans for themselves. Once again, though, the trend is towards a gradual shedding of dependence, on the employer just as on the State, and a gaining of independence; and through that to the eventual creation of an interdependent network.

An indication of the new independence of bright executives is the growing rebellion against job relocation. The Institute of Manpower Studies, surveying the problem in 1987, found that though companies were increasingly anxious to relocate people, people were increasingly reluctant to move. Inadequate pay increases, disrupted home and social lives, interrupted education, differences in house prices between north and south and the unattractiveness of certain relocation areas were pinpointed as just some of the reasons.

As John Atkinson, Research Fellow at the Institute of Manpower Studies and author of the report 'Relocating Managers and Professional Staff' stated, managers and other professional staff are certainly getting more resistant to mobility; but not because these people are stick-in-the-muds, they are simply becoming more choosy about where they will move and when they will move. Clearly, executives want more control over their working lives and over the way work fits into their domestic circumstances, fully recognising that relocation packages are not primarily designed as a service for the employee, but to suit the organisation's administrative convenience.

The self-explorer's need for flexibility and independence is here again being picked up by many in other social value groups, especially those at their fringes. People are not going to be pushed around; however, they do want to contribute to their organisations and will do massively when properly motivated, but on their own terms. Having nowadays an altogether more rounded attitude to life, their home, their neighbourhood, their children's education and their own development are just as important to them as the exigences of their work. These people are also more confident that they will be attractive enough to a new employer if their free approach brings them into disfavour where they are.

A recession would of course curb this trend but many of these individuals will still feel capable of drumming up something new and positive for themselves in a self-employed capacity. Meanwhile managers who do refuse to be relocated are rarely penalised directly these days, though they may well lose seniority and be dropped from promotion lists. One solution that can be acceptable to both sides is that of remote working, a highly inner directed concept for the future that has already been touched upon.

As architect/philosopher Buckminster Fuller said 'I can either make money or I can make sense'; and many are now echoing this thought. The most determined of them argue that by choosing to make sense the means to do so will automatically flow, but possibly only with relatively little time or money to spare. For that game you need a lot of sense, but a lot of faith on top of it, too. Not an activity for the shallow-rooted. Even so, a great many self-explorers are deliberately cutting back on their material ambitions or opting for a life of voluntary simplicity. The well-known West End theatrical producer Cameron McIntosh was asked in an interview what was his ultimate ambition after such enormous success before the age of 40. Did he want to end up incredibly rich and powerful? His answer was 'No, I want less power and more holidays – especially in Scotland'.

One of the best bond saleswomen in the City, Vashti van Smit, turned her back on £150,000 a year salary as a vice-president of the American investment conglomerate Kidder Peabody to join Mother Teresa's hospice for the poor in Calcutta, wandering on foot through the Indian countryside, tending the sick and caring for the needy. When asked why, she said simply, 'I have been thinking of doing something totally different for some time'. Caroline Phillips in *The Times* also highlighted some of the young and upwardly mobile who were already spurning the time-is-money get-rich-quick ethic of the 80s.

She cited Fiona Stuart, senior business analyst at the Henley Centre for Forecasting, which monitors social and economic trends, who has demonstrated how more and more of the privileged are deciding to become *downwardly* mobile, being prepared to forego a rise or even take a pay cut if faced with longer working hours or less job satisfaction. 'Having sold their souls' she says, 'they now want to retain their integrity. New aspects of life are assuming a greater importance to them: time and interest become increasingly valuable commodities.'

The trend seems to be gathering strength among women. In general, men accept a salary cut only to get into a smaller business where they will have more say, which is understandable perhaps, given their usual mortgage commitments. Phillips featured three women who had idealistically left the top decile of the rat race and taken reduced salaries in jobs which gave them more fulfilment. One had moved from a holiday company to a charity; one from an advertising agency to being advertising editor of a magazine; and the third was a solicitor who moved from a highly aggressive City practice to a much smaller and more human one. All of them had experienced a financial shortfall, all of them believed they had done the best thing.

She concluded, 'Given the considerable earth tremors at the leading edge of the salaries market, who can possibly say that they are not right to opt for satisfaction plus greater security, in exchange for mindless struggling in the face of uncontrollable circumstances'. Once again the self-explorer message is asserting itself.

Three Grains of Sand

In the hourglass that measures human destiny three other grains of sand have passed through the narrow gap that leads from past to future. There are many more, but these caught the eye as they fell.

A flip through *The Sunday Times*[13] magazines during the month of October 1987, at the moment the annual Taylor Nelson survey was being conducted, shows that in this very conspicuous consumer medium, where outer directed values predominate, a large number of items were absolutely inner directed in content. The October 4th issue contained a highly favourable report on The Small School at Hartland in Devon, already mentioned in this chapter, and a survey of exercise videotapes. October 11th had 'Pictures from a Silent World' about the drawings of Stephen Wiltshire, a 13-year-old autistic child with a genius for architectural drawing, black and born into an underprivileged home. The cookery column carried an item on suitable wines for vegetarian meals.

October 18th featured an article, 'Spain's Other Tourists', chronicling the disappearing way of life of Spanish nomadic herdsmen and their ancient customs; plus 'On Their Own Two Feet', a report of an alternative method of helping handicapped children developed at Budapest's Peto Institute. Then the October 25th issue included 'The Battle of the Bogs' about a bitter land feud in the remote Scottish highlands where environmentalists and conservationists were fighting off invasion by conifers, planted as an investment by absentee landlords. It also featured Professor Chris Baines, the environmentalist and botanist in the regular feature 'A Life in the Day Of'. Finally the issue of November 1st contained a 'Tried and Tested' survey of sugarless jams, and a piece entitled 'Three Score and Then' about some extremely inner directed, interested and lively old age pensioners.

The second grain of sand dropped when the city of Coventry, nominated as a demonstration recycling city in the recently concluded European Year of the Environment, extended this brief to embrace a very much wider environmental commitment. It plans to set up a council team to knock on about 80,000 doors in order to coax out public attitudes and raise awareness on issues such as water pollution and acid rain; as well as local concerns like litter, traffic noise, air pollution and recycling. The aim here is to end up with a population which is much more aware of environmental issues, which knows how to raise the pressure to get major concerns resolved, but which also knows how to handle waste materials produced by individual activities like domestic cleaning or car maintenance, and how to start projects such as improving a polluted canal, cleaning up a piece of land, or taking part in energy conservation schemes.

The final grain fell in the form of a letter to *The Times* from Neil McIntosh, director of Voluntary Service Overseas, stating that VSO receives 30,000 enquiries a year from people who would like to work for them, but that of those they could only afford to recruit and send abroad 700. The mirror image of this potential goodwill was demonstrated by the case of Peter

Coleridge,[14] Oxfam's Middle East coordinator, who was kidnapped with a Lebanese colleague and held hostage by the Abu Nidal. He wrote at about the same time in *The Observer* of the psychological hell of his imprisonment and interrogation, and the heaven of his release less than a week later. Part of this heaven was the realisation of the vast network of support that had been active on his behalf inside and outside Lebanon.

'People had come from all over Lebanon during our captivity to express solidarity and see what they could do. Nearly 30 organisations had drawn up an escalating series of measures they were prepared to put into effect had we not been released – starting with a march on Abu Nidal's offices in Sidon and going on to sit-ins and a hunger strike. All this was not just an expression of solidarity for us as individuals but for the work of this network itself, of which we and Oxfam are a part. It was a spontaneous expression of people power and it was intoxicating . . .

'The last hope in Lebanon today lies in what these people are doing for themselves; their work is their hope and their life. An agricultural cooperative in a remote village of the Beka'a Valley; a vocational training school in a refugee camp near Tripoli; Friends of the Handicapped which organised a peace march of disabled people through the coastal towns of Lebanon last October; a carpentry workshop making educational toys for kindergartens; a physiotherapy centre in Sidon . . . the people running these projects are a dynamic network of individuals, groups and organisations committed to a process of finding an alternative to the violence and fragmentation as seen on TV.'

So, even in shattered Lebanon the millennium of interdependence is making its presence felt.

The Bad News

The reader may be excused a little tetchiness if he or she feels that all this is somewhat too good to be true. How is it possible for there to be so many paragon self-explorers – 15% of the population after all – without their having an even more marked effect on the entire country? Two answers to that, then. First, they show signs of being not entirely homogenous; of splitting into two sub-groups with rather different priorities – the 'caring' and the 'autonomous' tendencies – for whom respectively life's main emphasis is on cooperation and on freedom. This division into the group-minded and the individualists somewhat weakens their thrust.

Secondly, at present the self-explorers feel a touch vulnerable in their new philosophy, in the sense that they are still in the exploratory phase both of themselves and of it. They are therefore sensitive to the mocking laughter of the rest of the world, which sometimes makes them defensive and critical of others who have not reached their sublime state of development. Put another way, the self-explorers are often not only holier than thou but wholer than thou. Not to mince words, they can be the most thundering prigs and, in racing parlance, they too frequently talk their own book.

Many of them are dismissive of what they call 'the tyrant intellect', over-emphasising arguments that have been outlined in this chapter already. But in some cases one can be tempted to react to this with a certain irritation, conjecturing that for those who may be utterly soulful but not over-endowed with intellect themselves, it is tempting and psychologically easy to scoff. Everything in the end is a question of balance. The gifts of science and technology have been enormous. It is only in their slavish disregard for everything else that humanity has rendered many of them dangerous and inappropriate.

Self-explorers, often having the rare and balanced quality which enables them to understand the position of other groups, need to use that quality to the utmost if they are to avoid offensive exclusivity. This group must encourage, cajole and endorse the positive aspects of the others, since it is apparent that none of them are going to fulfil this function alone and by themselves. Self-explorers must in fact become the facilitators and *animateurs* of society, bringing a new dimension to the way that it looks at the future and at itself. In a nutshell, they have to shed the vulnerability that their position involves – that of being misunderstood and ridiculed by other groups. It is only through their selfless leadership that the mind, the heart and the will can at last be generally accepted as being of equal value.

7

THE SOCIAL RESISTERS AND THE EXPERIMENTALISTS

The Social Resister's Recipe

Illuminating remark by self-explorer to social resister – 'I'm terribly sorry, I'm afraid my karma has run over your dogma . . .'

Yes, though conjoined by concern about a great number of issues, in reality they are very different. The social resister's recipe for a better world, it will be remembered, demands a better system, as opposed to the self-explorer who hopes for better people. Note that though sharing the inner directed desire for a better world with the self-explorers, social resisters have a narrow and more rigorous view of it. They are followers of the single issue rather than generalists, and the holistic vision is really not for them. They can be of any political persuasion or none at all.

Mary Whitehouse with her fierce demands for improved moral tone in the nation's broadcasting demonstrates this tendency. Victoria Gillick with her campaign against doctors prescribing contraceptives to teenagers without their parents' consent, could well be another. The more strident members of the pro-abortion lobby and the more strident members of the anti-abortion lobby also fall into this category. But in almost all respects the most fascinating candidate for the social resisters' rose-bowl and signed testimonial is the undisputed political phenomenon of our time, Margaret Thatcher.[1]

Margaret Thatcher – Another Archetype

Here, however, one must add an immediate caveat. Just as Prince Charles exhibits a number of strong belonger characteristics, so does she. Her trumpeting of the virtues of a traditionally structured family is a strong clue here. For this reason and with her constant theme that the country should return to Victorian values, she appeals to many back-street belongers, 'our people', as she calls them. Note, though, her almost total alienation from the old-money high-and-mighty AB belongers of the Establishment. She has no time for them at all.

Her unswerving belief in free-market economics as a state religion has fuelled the industrial and commercial boom, the beginning of the end of which may have been signalled in the autumn of 1987, but which together with reductions in personal taxation has meanwhile given the conspicuous consumers a field day. Moreover, her insistence on self-determination and standing on one's own two feet – the get-on-your-bike syndrome – has attracted the sub-group of the self-explorers who particularly value the virtues of independence and autonomy; even though to those who are of a more caring disposition and comprise the other self-explorer sub-group, she is anathema.

Thus there are those who resonate to her as a belonger or as a conspicuous consumer, while yet others see her as an independent self-explorer. These, and there are many of them, will argue that what she actually does and how she actually feels imply a more caring disposition than the way she is generally reported in the media. A consummate politician, she has built a whole raft of personal constituencies to support her. But at bottom, what she says and particularly the way she says it, seems to reflect a social resister attitude.

Margaret Thatcher has created a public policy forum that covers the entire question of right and wrong in our society. The Government's anti-crime policy has provided a strong emphasis on crime prevention by parents, teachers and the Church. There is a national debate on how to include the education of moral values in the new school curriculum. She has courted controversy with her flagellation of the Church for what she sees as its reluctance to assume moral leadership, and with her forthright declaration of personal belief, based on the commandment, 'thou shalt not whimper'. She offers a relatively glad hand to glasnost, but still evinces a pretty steely cynicism towards what she sees as the continuing evils of Communist imperialism.

As far as the Prime Minister is concerned, the Victorian ethos entails a restoration of the accepted value of qualities like thrift, patriotism, integrity, charity, hard work, wealth creation and most of the other virtues she would claim to be her own. By nagging the nation to smarten up, she sees herself in shining contrast to the permissive dilettantes of the sixties who now dare to mock her brand of moral rectitude.

In this she is supported here by Professor Gertrude Himmelfarb, who avers that we are largely mistaken about the ethical principles for which the Victorians are supposed to have stood. Some claim that our generation imagines that these principles were invented by a triumphant middle class for the purpose of crushing the poor into submission, by attributing all social evils to their fecklessness, drunkenness and sexual incontinence. From the effects of these vices, the poor could only be saved by the providence, restraint, sobriety and compassion of the rich; by diligent attempts to emulate such virtues themselves; and meantime by accepting with patience and humility the consequences of their condition.

Himmelfarb takes a contrary view. Her point is that 'To the degree to which Victorians succeeded in bourgeoisifying the ethos, they also democratised it. That ethos was not, to be sure, an exalted or heroic one. Hard work, sobriety, frugality, foresight – these were modest mundane virtues, even lowly ones, but they were virtues within the capacity of everyone; they did not assume any special breeding or status or talent or valour or grace – or even money. They were common virtues within the reach of common people. They were, so to speak, democratic virtues'.

This argument positions Victorian morality not as an enslavement of the poor but as their liberation. Mrs Thatcher fits herself beautifully into this picture because she desires above all else to universalise the middle classes. She wants people to own their own houses, to own their own shares in a booming private sector, to enjoy far more choice in the education of their children, and to do what they like with their own earnings. She abhors the belief that people are generally incapable of manifesting these Victorian virtues and indifferent to attaining their rewards, thus necessarily remaining for ever the objects of their rulers' compassion and patronage.

For many, her version of the social resister's 'better system' has worked and their world is indeed better for it. According to a recent poll, 76% of British people believe themselves to be middle class, and it is crystal clear that the majority of the population is now enjoying what were formerly middle class standards. The spread of private ownership, and with it the greater width of choice and freedom, has dramatically altered both the perceptions and the aspirations of ordinary people. But there are gaps in this story.

Where the National Health Service is concerned, for example, the Prime Minister was brought up on the idea that the practice of medicine and nursing was inspired by 19th century notions of personal vocation and public service. However, in those days the action was played against the backcloth of a prosperous economy founded on a flourishing industry and burgeoning empire trade. Then, nurses were recruited from an ever-growing middle class and neither expected nor received adequate pay. Their rewards were not so much financial as emotional, including a better social life than was available for most of their contemporaries. In contrast, today a nurse's outside social life is now worse than that of her contemporaries, restricted by the need to work inconvenient hours, while at the same time the social aspect of hospital morale is diminished by the realities of cuts, shortages and stress.

Opponents of the Himmelfarb view remind us that the 19th century was as well known for its child labour, prostitution, disease, street rioting and hypocrisy as for its virtues. If these are necessary concomitants to the Victorian values she has in mind, the sooner Thatcher and they are banished the better, they protest. Furthermore, the universalisation of the middle classes implies the elimination of the working classes. Those who cannot or will not make this transformation will suffer direly in a competitive game whose rules are alien or incomprehensible to them. Those who have aspirations which remain unfulfilled while they watch others scoop the pool will suffer too.

So a lot of people are likely to become very angry indeed. Like in a children's game of sardines, the fewer there gradually are, the angrier they will get, the last few tearfully seeking that hidden treasure-house of giggling companionship. Ironically, they will fall slap into the arms of a bunch of alternative social resisters, the lunatic hard left whose self-imposed duty it is to drag everything down to their own level of hatred, the Labour Party's 'Ragged-Trousered Misanthropists'. So often, as with Margaret Thatcher herself, these leftist single-issue, system-orientated social resisters have a brilliant penchant for motivating members of other social value groups to do their bidding. Their dedicated and relentless drive is a source either of inspiration or disgust and they are archetypal in the strength of their message.

Possibly one of the reasons that Margaret Thatcher is so powerful is that she characterises the British archetype of Britannia herself. Britannia first emerged in Romano-British times as an emblem of the subjugated country, but with the spread of Christianity she was overtaken by the cult of the Virgin Mary of Walsingham. She was revived at the time of the

Restoration of the Monarchy by Charles II, and epitomising money, sea-power and the Amazon virtues has since pierced deeply into the nation's collective unconscious. Sitting there in full armour, her lion by her side, she is confident and relaxed but ever-ready to leap up and into the action.

With echoes of Boadicea and Elizabeth I she is psychologically, as Dr Rupert Sheldrake[2] puts it, 'a tutelary leader, a goddess giving protection'. In the Falklands war Mrs Thatcher played this role to the hilt and Sheldrake points out the ironic symbolism of her most important future weapon being called Trident. 'If the Americans had thought for a thousand years they could not have come up with a name for this weapon that was more appropriate or better guaranteed to have the most positive impact on a large section of the British people – and of course on Mrs Thatcher herself'. For her, Britain is symbolically in the thick of confrontation – St George and the Dragon; rather than in the breadth of cooperation – the Lion and the Unicorn.

Whenever she is considered, other Royal analogies keep popping up. Lord Hailsham, the former Lord Chancellor, puts her in the same category as Elizabeth I. 'Her handling of men is not altogether dissimilar. If you had been a courtier of Elizabeth I you would never know whether you were going to get the treatment of an admired male friend or a poke in the eye with an umbrella.' Doubtless the same was true of Boadicea and of Britannia herself. However, though the public had become accustomed to Margaret Thatcher's royal 'we' when she was talking collectively on behalf of the Government, her statement 'we have become a grandmother' projected her into a wholly new dimension of triumphalism.

Julian Critchley describes Margaret Thatcher as 'imperious, infuriating, indestructible and the *prima donna inter pares*'. She also inspires uncontainable hatred. 'That woman!' seethed Edward Heath, belonger extraodinaire. Dr Jonathan Miller, impresario, medico and experimentalist, sees her as 'loathsome, repulsive in almost every way – her odious suburban gentility . . . catering to the worst elements of commuter idiocy'. Apparently she once confided to Brian Walden 'they don't like me – but they respect me'. A total zealot, she ignores the signs of a changing world, scorning U-turns and denouncing compromise.

She has an absolutist vision and pursues it relentlessly. Not for her the delicately arcane mechanisms of government but the cold discipline of political certainty. When first in office she announced her intention of running what she termed a conviction Government, which would not waste time on internal arguments. 'I go for agreement', she has said, 'agreement for the things I want to do'. Ten years later, according to

Michael Jones of *The Sunday Times,* there are not three ministers in her Cabinet who would tell her she is wrong on anything.

Furthermore, she is determined to change the lot of us, not merely in the way we live but also in the way we think. 'Economics are the method', she has openly admitted, 'the object is to change the soul'. The kind of soul she has in mind for us is modelled on that of her father, Alderman Alfred Roberts, who formulated his cramped and disciplined philosophy in the grocer's shop on the corner of North Parade, Grantham. The regime – church four times a day on Sunday, no drinks in the house, only the rarest visits to the cinema, no boys, no dancing – bred not rebellion in his daughter Margaret but an inextinguishable determination to saddle the entire country with it, making us verily a nation of shopkeepers.

For good or ill, though, she has made a lasting impact on this country. The unions, yesterday our rulers, have been deposed. 1979, which included the winter of discontent, saw 30 million days lost through strikes, whereas in 1986 there were only 2 million. Those in work are on average 22% richer in real terms since she took control. There are three times the number of shareholders, while many more of us than before are now home owners, private patients and the parents of children at private schools. But though we may be all right, how about Jack?

The Jacks in this pack of cards now also include many violently protesting belonger institutions[3] at the top of the social scale – the City, the law, the medical profession, the opticians, the universities and schools, the media, the museums and the arts. All vested interest and restrictive practices are for the chop. She has turned their cosy worlds upside down both by opening them up to competition, and by making politically motivated appointments so that inevitably 'one of us' gets any job with establishment leverage. Note, though, that this is not to promulgate Conservatism directly, but because she wants to make them save money or to spend it 'more efficiently', regardless of any other consideration. She does not want anybody in any position of influence who might criticise or get in the way of her vision. Perestroika indeed! No wonder she gets on so well with President Gorbachev.

And how about Third World Jack?[4] Coincident with the two great Thatcher morality speeches to the Church of Scotland and to the Conservative Women's Conference in May 1988, extolling generosity to others as a Conservative virtue, figures were quietly released showing that Britain's overseas aid had fallen from 0.52% of gross national product to a measly 0.28% during her premiership – four times as great a cut as for public spending in general. Get on their bikes? They haven't any bikes.

[113]

But in spite of the Bishop of Durham's Easter 1988 attack on her, describing her government's policies as 'verging on the wicked', and voicing the view that it was morally wrong for her to deny that she was making life harder for the impoverished, she stifled Church of England criticism of her heartlessness by accusing them of failing to give a lead on crime and personal immorality.[5]

However, at home in her independent Samuel Smiles society, there are some who are now in far more pain than they have been used to, and it is not necessarily their fault. She must be thanked for having begun to unhook us from the dependent habits we had slid into since the Second World War, but at the same time we must recognise that her Valhalla is only a stage on the long journey towards interdependence. Her determination to sweep away the last vestiges of dependence should be supported, but what cannot be is her apparent lack of understanding of others. 'The lady's not for turning', she insists, but there are many who consider she is not for learning either.

So much a product of her time, it could be that her time is almost up. A necessary part of the ecology of things, like a vulture which feeds upon the dead flesh of the status quo and thereby fulfils the useful purpose of ridding the environment of a decaying corpse, she does not represent an ultimately advanced form of life. Eventually she will be superseded, but how? She will certainly not go gracefully; her downfall is likely to be turbulent, and arise from the turbulence of the angry and disappointed.

Some of the denizens of her independent world express their independence in selfish, nasty ways. They are therefore beginning to be met with a form of counter-independence, a cultural revolt, equally selfish and nasty, but envious instead of avaricious, violent instead of greedy. The first rumblings are audible, and getting louder; soon we will be unable to ignore them. But if the whole British or even the world economy should lurch out of control, bringing down with it all our previous card houses, that will be when the tumbrels really roll. It will be she whom we will all blame, however powerless she may or may not have been to contain the situation. Once this happens we will not, in the words of Hilaire Belloc,[6] 'take care and keep a hold on nurse for fear of meeting something worse'. We will turn on her and rend her in pieces as a sacrifice to appease the gods of destruction.

Abortion And Animals

The social resister, equipped only with tunnel vision, finds it almost impossible to appreciate that destruction lies so frequently within the self – this being the root cause of his difference from the self-explorer. The inner conflict may be so unbearably painful that the only recourse is to project it outwards on to some hated object. This object may indeed be an objectional one, like sin, or war, or environmental despolation. Social resisters share these concerns with self-explorers but for different reasons. You have only to listen to the violence of the language – 'fighting for peace', 'exterminating sin' – these are sure-fire social resister catch-phrases.

These are the fundamentalists of society, while as we have seen, the self-explorers are the mystics. The Ayatollah Khomeni was a pan-galactic social resister; so from what one hears are the Rev Ian Paisley and doubtless many Jesuits. The downfall of the American televangelists Jim Bakker and Jimmy Swaggart in the wake of separate sex scandals demonstrates the Achilles heel of the breed – they cannot recognise or redeem the shadow within, and their failure to attain wholeness colours their life in a single un-remitting hue. They harbour anger and fear, and are basically resistant to change as such, accepting the idea of it only to induce their own rigid model.

As mentioned, social resisters are *par excellence* single-issue supporters, and extremely effective ones. The near-success of David Alton's 1988 bill to change Britain's abortion laws[7] was a triumph for social resister lobbyists who momentarily outflanked the opposition in a brilliant campaign. The photograph of an 18-week-old foetus sucking its thumb was a devastating weapon of persuasion.

Life, the anti-abortion group and the Society for the Protection of the Unborn Chld combined forces with the Roman Catholic community and then also mustered support from other religious groups. Together they organised a mass lobby of handicapped people to ask MPs if they thought they should have been killed before they were born. In the face of this pressure, many MPs changed their minds and voted for the Bill's second reading because of the weight of letters from constituents. As one put it, 'there are only two lobbies that matter, the animal lobby and the Catholics'.

However, unlike the pro-life lobby, the animal rights movement[8] reveals a sinister characteristic which is shared by a number of other social resister causes. Its members add on an extra dimension to their impact by persuading a contingent of aimless to do their heavy work. Hence the bomb scares in scientific establishments, the harassing of scientists them-selves, the planting of incendiary devices in department stores which are selling furs. However, it is particularly visible in the Hunt Saboteur movement. Known among themselves as 'Sabs' and by the hunting fraternity as 'Antis' these social resisters are recruiting young aimless and training them to pull riders off horses, blow divertive hunting horns and spray hounds to put them off the scent.

The dedicated of the fraternity spend their entire spare time disrupting hunts, seal culls and grouse shoots. The most dedicated of all even push unsuspecting float anglers off their little folding chairs into the canal. Spokesmen for the British Field Sports Society are pessimistic about the future, claiming that saboteurs are becoming more violent. 'We are get-ting a hard core of fanatics, and the more violence and abuse there is, the greater the chance of hunt supporters losing their tempers too'. This of course is exactly what the social resisters would like. They love the smell of blood.

Explosions in Bristol University where the veterinary school has a record for experimentation on animals, threats to academics' lives and those of their families, fire bombs planted in stores selling animal furs (four House of Fraser shops alone suffered damage estimated at £25 million), and butchers being sent letters with razor blades along the edges of envelopes – these are the characteristics of the Animal Rights Militia, which has claimed responsibility for them.

Take, also, the Welsh Nationalist[9] group, Meibion Glndwr, whose cam-paign of arson started in December 1979, since when it has caused over £1 million of damage to holiday homes and estate agents' offices in 150 attacks. It is now apparently being infiltrated by the so-called Tripoli faction of the National Front. Social resister organisations either fight each other to the death, or collaborate warmly, as in this case. These two have in common a brand of politics known as Third Position, which purports to back neither capitalism nor communism, but admires such stalwarts as the Ayatollah Khomeini and Colonel Gaddafi of Libya – both, of course, fundamentalist social resisters themselves.

The Experimentalist's Recipe

The experimentalists are the darlings of Mercury, god of risk and gain. An exciting life is what they are after, and to them the world is a magic oyster with a pearl inside it. They are enthusiastic and attractive, always in search of a new sensation whether it be bodily, mental, emotional or spiritual, explorers of their whole environment rather than merely of the self. They do have in common with the self-explorers the fact that many of them experiment with new forms of self development, but they tend to go at these challenges like a bull at a gate. Strangely innocent, they are nature's sensualists, tricksters, fools, entertainers, eccentrics and innovators.

The home of the future is about to become the wonderland of the experimentalist. In this respect she performs an important function. Once she has breached the technology barrier and provided a market for the manufacturers and retailers, the other side of that barrier becomes more commonplace and accessible for many other social value groups.

As long ago as 1979, the chief executive of an American electronics firm informed the writer that he was able to telephone his Los Angeles home from London and ask it to turn the sprinklers on, to set the lawn mower off on a programmed path avoiding the flower beds, to close the curtains and ensure that the porch light was put on at eight o'clock and off at eleven, together with the lights in the hall, kitchen, dining room and sitting room; giving way to those in the bedroom and bathroom, which were for final extinction at various times between 11.30 and midnight so as to fool burglars who might notice a regular pattern.

This calling up of appliances, the refrigerator, the alarms, the oven, the lights, the security system, the music, the bath or whatever, is characteristic of the house of the not-too-distant future which the home-owner will be able to play like a fugue. The toccata is represented by the fact that a dozen or so companies worldwide are now preparing entire automation systems for both new and existing homes.

The new levels of convenience and security, and the time and energy saving they will provide, promise to inspire a vast market and create a whole new experimentalist industry. Home automation can be practical, frivolous, or anywhere in between. Its appeal is wide; it can do wonders for handicapped people, holiday-home owners, people who work at home, the elderly and the gadget-happy. It is destined to take off before the end of the century, and we will have the experimentalist consumers to thank for it.

They seem almost like an intermediate life form, suspended Peter Pans who never quite grow up. But for most of them this is merely a passing phase before they become fully fledged self-explorers (if their motivation is largely inward) or conspicuous consumers (if their motivation is largely outward). There was a time when they were predominantly male and under 35, but now they encompass both sexes and all ages. Here are two likely examples – one facing outward if the press is to believed and one inward – who will be familiar to most contemporary readers.

Archer and Branson

Jeffrey Archer[10] is one for whom nothing in life has gone unpublicised. His career has been a roller-coaster ride of dizzy heights and stomach-churning depths. In his Oxford days his most famous coup was getting The Beatles to perform at an Oxfam concert by arranging that they should also have dinner with Harold Macmillan. 'Get the right ingredients, sweetie, and you can raise money for your local traffic warden', as he advised at the time.

On that particular occasion Jonathan Aitken found himself standing next to Ringo Starr and they struck up a conversation about Archer. 'That guy', said Ringo, 'he'd bottle your pee and sell it for £5'. Journalists find irresistible his genuine and infectious enthusiasm and the fact that he is happy to play their silly games. 'When so many people around me are listless and cynical', says one, 'it's somehow uncomplicated and cheering to be in his company with his optimism and idealism, and he makes you feel you are important to him. I like being around him. I like people who make their own luck, whose lives conform to soap opera principles. Someone who takes a hammering and gets himself up off the floor'.

On Desert Island Discs he chose the record 'Oh Lord, it's hard to be humble when you're perfect in every way'. Describing his schooldays he commented, 'I was allowed to ring the bell for five minutes till everyone was in assembly – it was the beginning of power.' He deftly side-stepped the open grave of his libel action over newspaper allegations that he had picked up a prostitute. There is obviously no stopping the man. He cannot bear even to lose a game of squash. It is not enough for him to know that he is the fastest selling paperback writer in the land; he wants ever more readers still. It is this obsessive ambition that has often lured on those hoping to gloat at his disaster. The urge to bring him down proved irresistible, but for Archer, every backward step is another springboard – *'reculer pour mieux sauter'* determined.

Richard Branson,[11] founder of the Virgin Group, seems to typify the inner directed experimentalist in contrast with Archer's apparently outer directed stance, but there are plenty of similarities. Ever since his schooldays Branson has combined a keen business brain with an image of Boys' Own adventure. Twenty years ago he created a magazine called *Student* and cheekily wrote to everyone he wanted to interview. At that time the youth culture was in vogue and the responses from the famous rolled in.

As a friend of his said, 'While we were all wondering about the next fag behind the bike sheds, Richard was writing to Ted Heath or George Brown. He was a go-getter'. It was obvious to his contemporaries that he was going places, but he tried a customs fiddle when Virgin was facing bankruptcy and the court ordered him to cough up £60,000. In later years he bravely admitted this publicly on television as an explanation of why he was the only businessman to offer work to ex-cons in answer to an appeal by the New Bridge, a prisoners' charity. Inner directed experimentalists do learn, and humbly, as a part of that process, do teach.

Given a chance, or better still a dare, Branson would pull the flags of all nations out of his left ear. At the end of January 1988 he ended his first trip to the Soviet Union after signing and initiating deals ranging from the £2 million takeover of a Crimean holiday hotel to a scheme for alleviating the country's lack of condoms. He also used his 3-day visit to break the ground for his Virgin group to bring Soviet rock and classical musicians to Britain, and to export British talent to record for the state Melodiya label. He has resolutely got stuck in to the Gorbachev doctrine of opening up the Soviet economy to western influence, with a unique cooperative arrangement with the state tourist company *Intourist* to take over the 121-room Oreanda (an old Russian word for Virgin) Hotel in the Black Sea resort of Yalta.

Virgin has always had a reputation for being the unconventional David challenging the traditional Goliaths, whether in the recording or in the airline business. However, Branson resents being classified as a hippie capitalist, insisting that he spotted gaps in the leisure and pleasure markets and set out to make money from them. He has liberal views on issues like abortion, homosexuality, cannabis and race, but is very much on the right of the spectrum on unions, taxes and whingeing layabouts.

So Branson has a certain charm as far as the powers that be are concerned. In 1987 Margaret Thatcher announced his appointment as the first chairman of UK 2000, a vehicle for harnessing the young unemployed into the service of the environment. The media promptly labelled him 'Mr Clean' and 'Minister of Rubbish', but ignoring the flak he has continued to head-up the campaign. In its first year it undertook 250 projects to beautify the cities by cleaning up eyesores, planting trees, restoring parks and waterways, creating woodlands and nature reserves and preserving the industrial heritage. It has achieved its main objectives of bringing voluntary organisations together, attracting sponsorship, giving people worthwhile jobs and improving the environment – typifying Branson's own concerns. In spite of all the sniping from the sidelines, it is likely to survive, thought maybe in a transformed state.

His latest project is selling Mates condoms to the world in a joint venture with Anita Roddick of The Body Shop, of whom more later. These are being marketed at about half the price of the regular brands and in a far wider variety of outlets. This is not a case of Branson jumping on the Aids bandwagon however, he has been campaigning for proper advice on contraception since he ran a student advisory centre in Piccadilly in the late sixties. The profits from this enterprise will be channelled to a charitable foundation and the strategy is to use the launch of Mates as the first of a series of self-financing businesses which will plough profits into charities aimed at combating cancer, Aids, drugs and child abuse.

Their main target will be the inflated profits the drug companies make from cheaply produced medicines, essential children's items and basic medical equipment. 'Why should 90% of the money go to drug companies' shareholders when it could be used for charity?' he asks. 'We would say to people who have good ideas for a medical breakthrough to bring them to us and let us market them for charity instead of taking them to a commercial firm to make money out of'.

Like Archer, he is likeable and intelligent, and his self-promotion is relentless. As he describes himself, 'There are two Richards; one would like to be an adventurer, the other runs a public company and has a family'. An old friend commented, 'He is one of those people who get an adrenalin high at a very early age and never really get off it. He is always on to the next thing, always enthusiastic. I suppose in a way he is still a schoolboy.'

At his airline's inaugural press conference he arrived wearing a brown leather aviator's helmet which imbued the occasion with something of a Biggles flavour. As the first 747 took off, a voice announced to the passengers, mainly journalists, television crews and celebrities of a greater or lesser degree, that they would be shown a view of the take-off from the cockpit. The backs of the heads of the supposed first and second officer and engineer flashed onto the video screens, and all three turned round revealing themselves as Ian Botham, Viv Richards and Branson himself.

But Still The Paradox

That schoolboy joke fits the experimentalist to a T. On the face of it, both Branson and Archer seem to epitomise the type, just as do Naomi James and Anita Roddick the female version. But you never really know about people. Is it a fact that their behaviour genuinely reflects their motivations, or are they just brilliantly camouflaged? We have seen how complex the answer to this answer to this question can be when previously considering Prince Charles and especially Margaret Thatcher.

Take Arthur Scargill for example, who ostensibly parades himself as the showcase survivor but in fact does so to play on the emotions and values of his NUM survivor membership so as to ensure their support. What is not widely known is that he has a huge set of fabulously expensive albums hand-tooled in the finest leather, in which he keeps all his press cuttings, including every time he is mentioned, however disparagingly, in whatever medium. Do not be surprised if he moves on to the International Miners' Federation in Europe at the same time as the National Union of Mineworkers is being quietly assimilated into the Transport and General Workers' Union. Be prepared for him to disappear into the soft atmosphere of cigar smoke and good dinners, remote from the real world of full and frank discussions and flying pickets. He is a closet conspicuous achiever, for whom power is the ultimate kick. They and their like, the conspicuous consumers, are the next to come under the microscope.

8

THE CONSPICUOUS CONSUMERS
AND THE BELONGERS

For Love or Money

After the see-saw world of the experimentalists we now come down with a bump in real outer directed country. Though many experimentalists and much of their motivation closely correspond with conspicuous consumers and outer directed values, they are transitional in nature, and may well embrace inner values too. As we have seen, they could flip either way or indeed stay as they are for the rest of their lives. It is all somewhat conjectural.

With conspicuous consumers however, you know where you are. In the money. The core group of the outer directed, sandwiched between about half the experimentalists on the one side and about half the belongers on the other, they have at the very centre of their system the urge to succeed. 'Look at me up here!', they crow, or at least 'look at me getting up here!' Yes, these are doers not be-ers, but by no means necessarily thinkers.

Obsessed with the impact they are making, other people's acclaim and esteem is what they are after, to slake their burning thirst for inner confidence. They may not be loved, but by jimbo they desperately want to be admired – that is the prime motivation of their existence. Perhaps they do not feel themselves capable of either true love in its deepest sense or the ability to arouse such love. They are more than willing, however, to settle for a lesser grade of love, but in compensation they need it by the magnum.

Normally, it is wrong to think of the average conspicuous consumer as the historical product of the capitalist system. In this country the established capitalists are more likely to be belongers, who although many of them exhibit outer directed tendencies are not so paranoid about the need for visible success. It is also not true to say that most conspicuous consumers are rich. In fact the majority of the group belongs to the C1C2 socio-economic sector rather than to the ABs. Somewhat more of them are women, the true conspicuous consumers, than men — who are perhaps better termed conspicuous achievers.

Meanwhile, however the species also exists in an altogether higher and more successful waveband, which contains the role models for the rest of the shortlisted candidates for success. Here we can conveniently consider the way the press depicts the Saatchi brothers, Lord Hanson and Robert Maxwell.

The High-Flyers — Saatchi and Saatchi[1]

As chronicled by Philip Kleinmann in 'The Saatchi Story',[1] when the brothers started their business in 1970, nine of the ten top advertising agencies in London were American based. Sixteen years later, by majoring on solid and imaginative creative work and a brilliant acquisition policy, they had become the biggest in the world. In recent times no British company starting from scratch had ever before aimed at becoming world leader in its field and succeeded. What they demonstrated was recognition of the value of a high profile and a relentless absorption with acquisitions that would stick.

In 'The Brothers; The Rise And Fall Of Saatchi And Saatchi', Ivan Fallon described the frenetic driving atmosphere they created in the agency, where the motto was 'two ads a day keep the sack away'. There were many who found Charles arrogant and overbearing, hubris-ridden and unlikeable. 'He either did not mind the criticisms or ignored them. What he did care about was being noticed, and he was achieving that'. In March 1989 Saatchi and Saatchi were certainly noticed, as their profits crashed amid a welter of sell recommendations from brokers' analysts. Are we downhearted? No! The brothers announced they were building a company that would last a hundred, maybe two hundred years, and swore that they were going to tighten controls, concentrate on getting margins and efficiency right, and recover their reputation.

Charles and Maurice founded their business on a number of small companies, employing a formula that combined money-saving and motivation and has by now been widely copied; takeovers with something

up-front as part of the agreed purchase price, leaving the existing management in charge and making future tranches of payment contingent upon
its performance over the next few years. By 1975 the Saatchis were
number four in Britain, by 1979 number one, in 1983 number one in
Europe and by 1986, after their takeover of American agency Ted Bates,
number one in the world.

Not enough for them, however. They had to be the number one service
industry in the world, signalling this inflated aim with a somewhat alarming attempt to take over the prestigious merchant bank Hill Samuel and
also one of the most overripe and sleepiest pears in the financial sector, the
Midland Bank. The City in general and The Bank of England in particular
recoiled in horror and mounted an elaborate rearguard action to ensure
that both preys escaped the net. These were two bids which they
undoubtedly knew they had no chance of carrying off.

However, the Saatchis are players in a different and deadly serious game
– the game of tomorrow, as opposed to that of today. Their brazen opener
signalled that they would inevitably mount other and more successful
raids on the world's establishments in future, having catapulted themselves into the top league of international takeover bidders by spending
time, money and effort in their apprenticeship.

It is their fishing philosophy to spend good money on bait. When
Jennifer Laing, now returned as a deputy chairman of the company,
temporarily packed her bags in the late 70s to work for a rival agency, she
found a red Ferrari parked outside her door one morning, a present from
Saatchi and Saatchi who were determined to woo her back again. The
gesture was deliberately well publicised and its value in the status-
conscious agency world counted even more than the fact that she did
ultimately rejoin them. Similarly, the Conservative Party account, which
the company won in 1978 and held through three general election campaigns, provided a unique subliminal benefit. There was no profit in it
whatever, but it took the name of Saatchi into the political vocabulary.
Every comment, whether good or bad, was free publicity.

Charles, the elder of the two, collects contemporary paintings rather in
the same way that his company collects subsidiaries. He recently rang the
dealer of artist Lucian Freud with an order for six paintings. Freud, a
meticulous and painstaking worker, already has a long and patient
waiting list. The dealer said that possibly over the next twelve years he
could help him acquire a small but pleasant collection. Forget it, said
Charles, if it was going to take twelve years, he was no longer interested.

The High-Flyers – Hanson[2] and Maxwell[3]

The old-time belonger City establishment, defending its vested interests against such a brash approach, typifies the reaction of the sustenance driven when confronted by these highly outer directed motivations. Just after the Saatchis indicated that they were pushing the boat out towards the Midland Bank, the City experienced another frisson of repulsion with the confirmation that Hanson Trust had also acquired a significant stake in this historic but ailing clearing house. As Lord Hanson's running mate and blood brother, Sir Gordon White, declared of London's square mile, 'It is full of people just waiting for us to lift their wallets and rape their wives'.

Lord Hanson himself is one of Thatcherism's most enthusiastic exponents – always prepared to fire off a letter to the press or a loaded feature article defending the market economy. 'It is the central tenet of my faith that the shareholder is king', he said. Like the Saatchis an acquisition fanatic, he has made his company one of the top twenty in Britain, securing himself a Wilson knighthood and a Thatcher peerage in the process. He has delighted his shareholders and appalled the Square Mile. The outstanding management phenomenon of post-war Britain, he is still as keen and aggressive as ever; with his grasp of essentials and his direct-ness of purpose, he is a man who inspires belief and loyalty.

He may still be a rough-edged Yorkshireman, but he is taken extremely seriously. As one City expert puts it 'Such men have only one drive in life, getting bigger, richer and more powerful; and he can't lose. He only has to look at a company and its shares rocket'. But at the same time another City figure adds 'There is too much of the gold bracelet about him, even today – I find him arrogant even if charming'. His taste for the full life runs to a red and white personal helicopter, a custom-built Roller, houses in London, Berkshire, California and Florida, and a yacht moored permanently at Cannes.

'Not quite our sort' murmur the City belongers. They are too right. For them, his most famous faux pas was when, having taken over the Imperial Group, he arrived at the boardroom of its subsidiary Courage and announced 'Those two paintings. Nice. Very nice. Have them sent to my office.' After a long pause during which the temperature fell to absolute zero, the deposed managing director explained that they were family portraits of his ancestors. 'Right', said Lord Hanson, 'right. That table, send that instead.' The Saatchis would have been proud of him.

It is dangerous to pass comment on Robert Maxwell, publisher of the Mirror Group newspapers, or even to quote those who have commented upon him. Possibly, even to read those who quote those who have commented on him could merit a writ. However, here goes.

Three biographies of Robert Maxwell hit the streets in March 1988, two of which were unauthorised and whose publishers were immediately sued. As a result the first, 'Maxwell, a Portrait of Power' by Peter Thompson and Anthony Delano, had to be pulped and reprinted in emasculated paperback form, vast damages being simultaneously paid to the Great Ormond Street Children's Hospital. The second, 'Maxwell the Outsider' by Tom Bower, awaits the outcome of another writ at the time of writing. Only the authorised 'Maxwell' by Joe Haines which extols his war heroism and inordinate benefactions to mankind, serialised with great prominence in his own newspapers, was awarded the imprimatur.

Woodrow Wyatt, reviewing the field, described its subject as a 'ludicrously vain, comical and uncouth exhibitionist, longing hopelessly for affection and esteem, while trampling over his staff and his own newspapers'. Nay more, over other staff and other media too. Commenting at a press conference that 'Messrs Thompson and Delano . . . failed to carry out their elementary duties as journalists to check their facts before rushing into print', Maxwell was not amused when asked by a representative of *The Bookseller* magazine how many complaints of inaccuracy *The Daily Mirror* received in a week. 'You are an idiot', Maxwell responded, 'I don't want to talk to you', and then characteristically invited the questioner to sue him.

The bouncing Czech, as he is styled in the City, drinks tea out of a cup twice the size of everyone else's, the rim of which is embellished with the legend 'I am a very important person'. He tried to thank BBC executives for *The Radio Times* printing contract by giving them signed £50 notes. He is extravagant, exuberant, irrepressible and impossible to work for. It is said that during a policy disagreement with a colleague in his Rolls Royce on the motorway, Maxwell demanded that the chauffeur should stop. 'Get out' he said to the colleague, who obligingly did so. 'Now walk', he concluded, and drove off, leaving the wretched minion to get back to base as he could. This is known in the trade as management by laceration.

Born Jan Ludvik Hoch on the Czech-Romanian border and of Jewish parents, he seems from day one to have striven for influence through hard work, intelligence, flair and chuzpah. He hops, according to Piers Brendan, from one fiasco to another, from the 'I'm backing Britain' campaign to rescuing Aston Martin, from saving the Edinburgh Commonwealth Games to saving Ethiopia. Haines' extracts from his letters reveal his flamboyant language, his elephantine humour and his ruthless streak. At his first meeting with the print unions at *The Daily Mirror* in July 1984, after he had bought it the day before, the audience became restive as he continued to speak. 'Do you think that I am on an ego trip?' he asked. 'Yes' shouted the audience in unison. 'I have invested £90m in this business and don't belong to the Salvation Army. I am the proprietor, I am the boss, there can only be one boss and that is me'.

However, he recognises and acknowledges his equals. Geoffrey Goodman, the paper's long-serving industrial editor, was detailed to arrange a secret meeting between Maxwell and Arthur Scargill at a hotel near Sheffield during the miners' strike. Goodman observed, interestingly, that when they met the two men got on very well together. 'They were practically interchangeable', as he expressed it.

In October 1984 Maxwell saw the chance to help both the starving of Ethiopia and *The Mirror* in one fell swoop. He travelled out there accompanied by a substantial retinue and enormous coverage in The Mirror Group press, his place at the centre of attention contrasting weirdly with the images of ghastly famine. Meanwhile he was still sending messages back to *The Mirror*, dictating what action the newspaper should demand to solve the latest crisis in the miners' strike. This is par for the course. He is said on one occasion to have held three separate meetings and three telephone conversations at once.

The 1986 Commonwealth Games in Edinburgh were originally set up on a self-financing basis, but with eight weeks to go before the opening, the chairman of the organising committee was faced with a deficit of £5m. In the middle of June, Maxwell announced that The Mirror Group would assume responsibility for the Games' finances. However there was confusion as to exactly what this meant. Maxwell felt no commitment to contribute a penny himself though 'guaranteeing unconditionally that the Games would go ahead'; as far as he was concerned this was because somehow he would successfully acquire new sponsors. As it happened he did not do so and the Games went down the tubes in a welter of controversial arithmetic.

The deficit stood at £3.8m two years later, according to accountants Coopers & Lybrand, just £0.2m less than when he took over the financial reins, having stood next to the Queen and the Prime Minister on the dais with The Mirror Group's red and white colours dominating the stadium and its scoreboards. The Queen apparently named one of her rather more dominant corgi puppies Maxwell after he had gone just a little over the top even for him, by patting her on the back.

The Work Ethic

Work, and successful work, has been the flavour of the month for quite a lot more than a month by now. 'If work is so wonderful', complained the old fashioned Labour politician some years ago, 'why don't the rich have it all?' Aha, but nowadays the answer is that they do. In the supposed leisure age, work is the ultimate form of self-expression and to the still vast numbers of unemployed, it is what you have if you are lucky. With the awareness that a lot of people have no work, the concept of leisure as a way of expressing oneself is now slightly ironic when there is too much of it around.

The chief executive of Korn Ferry, the international headhunters, wrote in *The Times* in February 1987 to announce that today's business go-getters are 'aggressive, restless, greedy, urban technocrats . . . interested in money to the point of obsession. Let them make a million and they'll strive for ten. That's the way they are and that's the way we want them'. A year before that, Alan Sugar, founder of Amstrad, had publicly said 'If there was a market in mass-produced portable nuclear weapons, we'd market them too'.

In the recent past, moral interference with market mechanisms has been considered presumptuious. A determinedly secular society has demanded, and got for its pains, a non-judgmental economic system. This segregation of money from morals is felt by many of those who make the decisions to be at the very heart of modern commerce, underlining the absolute dominance of 'the bottom line' in commercial affairs.

The new involvement in work is valuable in many respects, however. It has transplanted itself into the development of a more agreeable, participative and almost domestic working space which has become extremely pleasant for those involved. New service industries have also created an extraordinarily exotic variety of new careers for the lucky ones who are well educated and well placed. For many of them, these new working lifestyles have crossed the traditional border between the domesticity and gainful occupation, now that technology allows people to work largely from home or on the hoof. What might formerly have been considered hobbies have developed into middle-class careers in the gentrification of crafts and small shops.

This relates to the fact that the major threat to young merchant bankers and corporate financiers is of burning out, a dread phenomenon that sometimes strikes and destroys them when they are in their late twenties and early thirties. Increasingly large numbers of them are playing the new system of breaking out before getting burnt out. Some turn into aggressive entrepreneurs – but many become actors, authors, nurserymen or purveyors of restored Victorian baths to their old, mates in the City at vast profit. Vivien Donald[4] in 'Offbeat Careers – 60 Ways to Avoid Becoming an Accountant' advised City yuppies to follow their hearts rather than their heads and think of becoming a chicken sexer, an embalmer, a clown, a piano tuner, a puppeteer or a Gentleman Usher of the Black Rod. Not a few are taking her advice, some perforce as we shall see. Whether voluntarily or not, they may be right.

This entails the evolution of the Protestant work ethic into what one might call the catholic work ethic, in the original sense of the word. The acceptance of being pushed from behind has given way to the acceptance that anything goes. What is now different is that the work ethic has almost become the work aesthetic.

Next we shall investigate a funnier and sexier manifestation of the conspicuous consumer, the yuppie, a species which may possibly, however, be endangered.

Anatomy Of The Yuppie

Yuppies[5] are smart, organised and demanding people. They symbolise change, privatisation and professionalism. They have, however, been sloppily categorised to date. They are not the same as the Sloane Rangers who are predominantly well-bred, but they are not wide boys or solo risk-takers either. They are the ones of all classes who know they have choices and plan their progress with an unremitting drive for instant gratification.

The more competitive, aggressive people, medically characterised as 'type A', have been known for some time to be more prone to heart disease than their less mettlesome 'type B' colleagues. However, 'type A' has now been split into two groups, the first having an abnormally high rate of heart disease and stress-induced symptoms, while the second group actually thrives on stress. The first may still be conspicuous consumers and achievers, but the cream of the yuppies falls into this second category.

The name 'yuppie' is derived from one of two possible acronyms – either Young Urban Professional People or Young Upwardly Mobile

Professional People. The provenance may be obscure, but six species have been delineated within the genus by Questel Qualitative Research, an affiliate of the AGB market research group. Two of them are not really conspicuous consumers as we would identify them. The first are the Hedonists, the accidental yuppies whose major motivation is to enjoy life, and who savour wealth, prestige and position as a matter of luck. This group would fit absolutely into our experimentalist category. Then there are the Embarrassed Capitalists, with a social conscience, who are anxious to be successful but without harming others. Slotting perfectly into the self-explorer pigeon-hole, they are aware of social issues and feel responsible about current affairs, and spend freely but for genuine value.

The other four classifications are straight conspicuous consumers and achievers. The first of these is the Blatant Competitor, driven by the desire for power and believing that lifestyle and possessions are the primary indicators of success. These people are obsessed by trends, wear the latest clothes, drive powerful cars and, although ostensibly wild and carefree, are secretly agonised by the fear of failure. Flash Harry, the second type, is a product of the working class who is keen to make it and show he has made it. This Harry or Harriet tries to emulate the middle classes and spends extravagantly to win acceptance. In contrast, the Armchair Materialist is usually working class, wealthy and successful, but with a narrow outlook. His social life is low key and extravagance is shunned in favour of investment.

Finally, the Traditional Strivers want to be successful and established. Their aspirations focus on an impressive home with classic comforts and modern equipment, while children are delayed to leave room for a hectic social life. The writer came across a beautiful specimen on the Friday evening commuter train from Paddington to Swindon – who got out his radio telephone and rang home, loudly: 'Darling' we're not doing anything at the weekend I'm afraid – couldn't get a flight anywhere. Train's about 15 minutes late. Can you do a couple of toasted smoked salmon sandwiches and I'll get a bottle of champagne from the off-licence on the way back.'

Crudely expressed, there are a great many people about nowadays who would echo Ivan Boesky, the disgraced New York arbitrageur, in saying 'Greed is all right, by the way, I want you to know that. You can feel greedy and still feel good about yourself'. Many people now in work know that their rising living standards have been derived from market economics and have understandably embraced the Thatcherite philosophy – that individual power is good and collective power is corrupting.

Not many of them recognise the corollary that a society that goes for winners must inevitably have losers, and that increasingly the devil takes the hindmost. Car telephones, swimming pools and moving to ever cost- lier homes are among the normal expectations of these conspicuous achievers and consumers, who have lost the taste for contented poverty if they ever had it. In defence, they claim that so-called greed simply means refusing to be satisfied with what you have got and is just another name for creative drive, laudable self-help as distinguished from supine apathy.

'Serious' is the current London in-word. *Serious Money* is Caryl Churchill's play which with perfect timing took the lid off the City for those who had never seen nor smelled inside it. Financial people who rarely go near a theatre at all have been queuing up for seats, too. The play portrays events since the deregulation of the City of London in October 1986, including the Guinness scandal and the Boesky insider trading affair. Aficionados admit it to be not far from reality except for one point. Here everybody survives, everybody is an insider, everybody is in the know, no-one is being deceived, no-one is repelled by the crassness and stupidity of the whole thing, everybody is both on the make and makes it. Alas, in the real world there are real and serious losers − witness the fact that the City of London police have recently set up a Serious Fraud Squad.

Peregrine Worsthorne[5] of the *Sunday Telegraph* writes of 'a sense of bourgeois triumphalism abroad', as the well-heeled celebrate that the class war is over and that they have won it. The Rev Harry Williams,[6] writing in *The Times* in June 1987, described how he found himself sitting next to a yuppie at a lunch party while dressed in his ordinary and somewhat shabby clothes. When he ventured that he was a monk, the reply was, 'Ah, that gives you a respectable reason for being poor.'

Another new and important word has emerged in the upwardly mobile vocabulary − 'covetables' − designer trinkets and gadgets that are faddish and overpriced. Matthew Parris, writing in the *Sunday Telegraph Magazine*, caressed the seriously brazen phase in which the nation was then finding itself, 'feasting its eyes', as he put it, 'once more on the outer, having had a mild flirtation with the inner self.' Extrapolating examples like David Bowie and George Michael, he described approvingly the show-off style that fashion people call 'expressing the personality', the physical boast of what you are. 'Showing off is a fundamental human drive and a key qualification for success. Ceasing to show off − like ceasing to eat or wash − is a sign of mental illness.' Totally wrong, of course, but irresistibly seductive to serious readers of the *Sunday Telegraph Magazine*.

How To Spend It

Seen in Bishopsgate, a red Porsche with a sticker in the back window announcing 'my other car's a Porsche'. For many, for enormously many, the car says it all. Tony Hill of Elite Registrations is comfortably the biggest in the field of what are known as cherished number-plates.[7] Jimmy Tarbuck drives around in COM 1C, conjurer Paul Daniels in MAG 1C. The Lord Mayor of London has LM O on his Daimler and the head of a Japanese multinational has FUJ 1 on his.

Naturally many of Hill's customers are rich – they would have to be if they were out to beat the top price ever paid for a plate – £22,000 in 1986. However, not all those who have the determination to show off in this way are necessarily loaded. Hill had one customer who saved up for five years to buy the plate of his dreams. And the public sector is poised to cash in, too. ELV 1S, D1 ANA and CHR 1S are still stored in the Swansea Driver and Vehicle Licensing Centre computer – but not for long. Transport Secretary Cecil Parkinson is planning to market a little treasure trove of plates numbered 1–20 that have been hoarded since 1983, plus a few others. VIP 1 has been nominally priced at £100,000.

Yuppitis is catching and addictive. Those who have no recourse to the real thing seek substitutes. For example, clay pigeon shooting[8] has enjoyed a remarkable vogue among City types; it is cheaper than Ascot, classier than golf and more competitive than a night at the opera, so they all say. Hailing it with unconscious irony as the 'new traditional' way to entertain foreign visitors and clients, the young City tiger from Fulham equips himself with a hired 12-bore, mudless green wellies and a pristine Barbour in the pockets of which he stuffs his Filofax and remote telephone. Everyone involved pretends it is real game shooting because the genuine article is totally out of their reach, both financially and culturally.

On Monday October 19th, Black Monday itself, *The Times* carried a Charles Bremner article 'Guide to the Good Life',[9] which homed relentlessly in on the latest and flashiest American magazine *Millionaire*, designed for a readership of nouveaux riches and proud of it. Subtitled 'Lifestyles of the Working Rich' both its advertisments and its editorial appealed to raw indulgence – 'Absolute Power Corrupts Absolutely', shrieked the full page Maserati ad.

Its publisher, Douglas Lambert, the Florida millionaire who started *Playgirl*, told his readers that 'the attitudes of the 1960s have gone; you deserve all the good things in life'. The first number carried a string of profiles of self-made millionaires and advised on the merits of rival private jets. Tips for millies on the move included the vibrating radio pagers which avoid disturbing the sleeping audience when bleeped by one's stockbroker in the middle of a smart New York concert.

Meanwhile, London is on the threshold of the upmarket brown bag revolution of gourmet takeaway, a service that some of its best known restaurants are now operating, following the lead of those in New York and Los Angeles. This is for the well-heeled busy-busy 25–40 year olds who are not ashamed either of their microwaves or their inability to cook. For around £17 per head you can have delivered to the door fillet of brill with mint and mustard seed sauce, or roast pheasant with creamed celery panache plus suitable starters and puds on either side.

The Times columnist Penny Perrick also featured a hire company whose slogan is 'when only the best will do'. This provides the dinky hostess with every element of temporarily gracious living down to the last damask napkin, with full instructions for eight different ways of folding it, including a rosebud, a birds nest and a cardinal's hat, the latter specially for when you are serving caviare and salmon on a Friday, no doubt. Other goodies include an EPNS champagne fountain with gilt decorations; an executive chafing dish for chafing executives with; and the Drake carving trolley which, 'enhancing any surroundings, has a huge domed lid which swings open to reveal the pièce de résistance'. On the subject of pièces de r, the same week, in the same paper, some enterprising continental was also featured as hiring out the odd Poussin for an evening – but in this instance, to hang opposite the odd hired Fantin-Latour.

Why is it that a four-slice toaster which has won design awards with its chic appearance but toasts no better than its competitors sells for about four times the price of rival brands? Welcome to the world of discriminating materialism, that's what they say. According to the Henley Centre for Forecasting,[10] people who buy the Dualit toaster are 'connoisseur consumers'. Keeping up with the Joneses has now reached a more sophisticated stage than the old zero-sum game. Then, hell was other people's success, as aspirations achieved a brief triumph followed by an agony of despair as one's social competitors leapfrogged one's achievements.

The 1980s are much more fragmented and pluralistic than this, say Henley, as people develop particular fields of expertise which can be more easily defended from social rivals. Instead of buying a whole range of things that are exactly comparable with those owned by their neighbours, they are now focusing on one particular battleground, whether it be audio equipment, wine, cooking, cacti, sports technology, or even toasters, in which they buy the most expensive products on the market. This means that instead of relating themselves merely to their own social world, conspicuous consumers who know what they are doing are now relating to a far more widespread community or network of other experts, and playing out their competitive fantasies with them.

Their neighbours, who are not in the know, will be impressed, but at the cost of a mutual grooming process whereby the wine, cactus and toaster expert has to endure long lectures from her friends about the merits of their remote lighting, word processors, or decorative fish. Henley describes this as 'expertism', a more discriminating form of materialism in which the motive has changed from keeping up with the Joneses to keeping away from them. The theory derives from the theoretical breakdown of authority, due to the fact that politicians are banal, society corrupt and the professions inept. The consumer must find out things for himself and develop his own expertise. Self-respect is enhanced in the process as authority is transferred from external symbols to internal 'savvy' and knowledge.

However, there is one aspect of life where the outer directeds collide painfully with everyone else – that of housing.[11] Now that the East End, and Docklands in particular, has become such a fashionable place to live, a backlash is keenly evident. A group known as Class War is on the march, led by social resister Ian Bone. 'Rich Scum Out!', they chant. Prospective yuppie home owners are promised a 'real East End welcome' if they decide to buy – 'we'll come every night and shout at you'. The locals also scratch the paint on their BMWs and either burgle them or mug them. Class War is a small, eccentric group that maintains a fairly high profile by not only pushing anonymous abuse and other nastiness through the front doors of its new neighbours, but also by various other stunts such as invading Henley during regatta week. But it is to a substantial degree representative.

There can be no going back to the old days, but CW is striking a popular note. Docklands residential land which cost £80,000 an acre in 1981 changes hands for up to £3 million an acre seven years later. For people who have lived and worked in East London all their lives it is a weird and embittering experience, 'like living in the pages of an estate agent's brochure', according to one council house tenant on the Isle of Dogs. Rented accommodation dwindles as houses fall into disrepair and other blocks are sold off to developers who tear them down and rebuild. Increasingly, the elderly, the poor and the unemployed huddle together for warmth, a remnant class which Margaret Thatcher's property-owning democracy has passed by.

The Young Idea

But with such glittering role-models to copy, the younger generation has learned its lesson early. According to a poll undertaken by advertising agency McCann Erickson in November 1987, British teenagers[12] place greater value on cash than either love or friendship. For the time being, their values are absolutely Thatcherite and orientated towards personal success through hard work and money. They have short-term goals and most of them are practical and materialistic. They feel that money is the doorway to modern life and that work is a means of providing status rather than fulfilment. They are determined to become adults as quickly as possible. The fear of unemployment has shaped their lives with an orthodoxy and conformity that seems unreal to their elders who recall their own teenage years as exploratory and rebellious.

In February 1988 the BBC2 programme *Forty Minutes*[13] broadcast a film *Changing Places* about two groups of sixth formers, one from Rugby school and the other from Ruffwood Comprehensive in Liverpool, who each changed places for a week. Both sides found the alternative unpleasant. Gary from Ruffwood was asked by a Rugby housemaster what he thought Rugby would be like: 'There's gonna be toffs', he answered. 'It's going to be tough?' wittered the housemaster, totally losing the point. Groan. After a couple of days at Rugby Gary's friend Gillian phoned her Mum to say 'the lessons are dead boring, the teachers are on another planet, it's all right-wing here'.

In contrast, the Rugbeans found that life in Liverpool really *was* tough. Ruffwood is an area of high unemployment and 100 out of the 160 sixth formers were on maintenance grants. Mark from Rugby was on the lookout for 'pinko leftist gay teachers wearing one earring'. The economics teacher at Ruffwood obliged him in part by launching into a north-south tirade which the visiting toffs politely conceded had been 'very useful'. It was a depressing film, charting two sections of British society apparently programmed from birth to go their separate ways. The Prince of Wales' Clubs in the 1920s enabled young people of all classes to mix much more gregariously together on mutual ground. Maybe they should be revitalised by the present Prince of Wales.

Dr John Rae,[16] till lately headmaster of Westminster School, also confirms that public schoolboys endorse the priorities of the age: every man for himself in the competition for good A-levels, a place at a 'proper' university and a well-paid job at the end of it. The new materialism has a powerful hold on the young. Rae says that the going rate for bribing children not to smoke is around £1,000 if they keep off the habit until they are 21. Some of the more affluent, however, are promised a Porsche.

Younger brothers and sisters[15] are not forgotten, either. They now have their very own department stores. The Toys R Us chain plans 40 stores by 1991, and Hamleys, Woolworths, Boots and Mothercare are enthusiastically joining the trend for children's 'experience shopping', where they are encouraged to play with, try on, explore and climb over everything in sight. Little Samantha can riffle through stylish clothes and accessories, have her hair done, choose bedroom colour coordinates, buy toys, books and videos, and order a birthday cake in the shape of a double-decker bus, then relax at the soda bar and contemplate her purchases. She even has her own line of cosmetics. Harrods is selling a make-up range called Tinkerbell, startlingly 'recommended for ages 4 and above'.

Even pets[16] are in on the act. Coming soon, an American franchise operation 'Lick Your Chops', where the yuppies' yappies can choose from a wide range of de-luxe tinned and fresh food, get kittied out (sic) with a lizardskin collar, consult the resident vet and have their portraits painted.

The First Crack in the Mirror

However, the life of the yuppie may well go down in history as having been rich, nasty, brutish and short, to paraphrase Thomas Hobbes. As expressed in another literary context, Thomas Gray in his 'Ode on a Prospect of Eton College' warned 'Alas, regardless of their fate, the little victims play'.

Everything was wonderful until October 19th 1987, Black Monday,[17] when Wall Street took an awesome purler and dragged down the aspirations of millions with it. The news reverberated round the world that suddenly the ostentatious life-styles of these instant millionaires were at risk, and with them the Vanity Fair of bizarre materialism that had long since broken the incredulity barrier. Just as the market crashed for the first time, the British fashion press was greeting with squeals of delight the unveiling of dress designer Christian Lacroix's new line of off-the-peg clothes at £2,500 a peg. You got to keep the hanger, admittedly.

Outsiders cheered to see the City slickers get their come-yuppance. City workers, previously characterised by the rest of the world as being either bobos (burnt out but opulent) or lombards (lots of money but a right dick), were now labelled puppies (previously upwardly mobile . . .) and otwos (on the way out); but they riposted with another acronym to describe their critics – bleaters (born losers expending all their energy rubbishing success).

In subsequent chapters we will have a closer look at who is likely to turn out right on this one. Meanwhile, conspicuous consumerism still remains exactly that – conspicuous. The phenomenon of overt personal gain therefore attracts more attention than it should in purely numerical terms. It is a media fantasy, though, and the important thing to remember is that there are a great many people who are more altruistic and socially responsible than the reporting of public affairs would suggest, who recognise that the bell does indeed toll for us all, and that if we don't hang together we shall surely hang separately. The concept of interdependence has more support than might be imagined from casual inspection.

Meanwhile at the half-way stage of this analysis of the seven groups, in case any readers are becoming alarmed by its uncompromising tone, let us recall the principles on which it is being conducted –

*   the public figures featured here are, like most individuals, undoubtedly too complex to be categorised under any of a mere seven headings, even though society as a whole can be so divided.

*   however, as described in selected (and itemised) extracts from the press, they each do exhibit strong characteristics of one of them.

*   as will soon be emphasised, each of the groups has its virtues as well as its vices.

The Rich Man in his Castle, the Poor Man at his Gate

In contrast with the United States, in Britain it always used to be slightly shameful to be rich. What was a good deal more fashionable was to be genteel-poor, although fashionable is the wrong word because if you were, you weren't. 'Old money' used to count for everything even if one had none of it. All that was required was to manage poverty with breeding, like the grande but faded dame who was asked by a brash neighbour, 'where did you buy that beautiful furniture?', and was rewarded with the answer 'We didn't buy it, we had it'. The nouveaux pauvres ruled and probably still do. On the subject of rulers, apparently the Queen runs around the Palace turning off the lights. This is the essence of belonger behaviour, in contrast with the conspicuous consumer who leaves the lights blazing away all night, but has to leave the burglar alarm on too.

In days gone by, belongers used to be the largest group in the country. Not just the backbone of England but more or less its entire skeleton. Like the experimentalists they are a transitional group, straddling the sustenance driven and the outer directeds and finding representation among the upper, middle and working classes. The well-heeled variety have more in common with the conspicuous consumers, though in a quieter and more civilised way. Most of the country's 25,000 millionaires are solid belongers, their wealth tied up in property and other tax-efficient long-term investments. The second, belonger sub-group is more closely allied to the survivors in terms of class, core members of the tribe of the sustenance driven at the agrarian end of the philosophical spectrum.

As mentioned in the section devoted to Prince Charles and his self-explorer tendencies, in one sense the Royal Family and the aristocracy very much lead the belonger world. In September 1987 Captain Mark Phillips,[18] husband of the Princess Royal, was fined £120 with £15 costs for driving on the M4 at more than 103mph. The same magistrates on the same day disqualified a driver who had gone beyond the speed limit by 4.4mph. These joint decisions prompted Tony Judge, chairman of the Police Federation, to comment 'all I can say is that one is surprised, isn't one?' The magistrates at Captain Phillips' trial were a retired estate agent, a housewife and a businessman, and they perfectly demonstrated the touching way in which belongers stick together.

Sticking also like leeches to the status quo, their favourite hymn contains the line 'Change and decay in all around I see'. Even so, many aristocratic belongers have had to adapt their ideas to cope with the responsibilities that the latter half of the 20th century has thrust upon them. Responsibility is very much a belonger attribute and it is the one thing that does trigger off some involvement in change – even in their reluctant management of it.

Many owners of stately homes[19] have now transformed them into commercial concerns, employing a substantial staff and playing host to all kinds of events that must have their predecessors revolving in their graves: sales seminars, conferences, weddings, residential parties, shooting and fishing syndicates, hovercraft racing, parascending and war games. Those who regret the passing of the old school of belongers fondly remember the late Duke of Norfolk who, on being chided by his wife that he always wore scruffy clothes around the estate, answered 'If people don't know who I am it doesn't matter what I look like, and if people do know who I am they know that's what I look like.'

Belongers are not in the least bit tolerant of, or interested in, the attitudes, motivation or behaviour of lesser breeds. The writer witnessed a telling scene at the Roxborough Hotel, Charlotte Square, Edinburgh, haunt of the lairds who come in from their outlying estates for an occasional visit to the capital. An elderly belonger couple entered the restaurant and sat down at a table. They ordered 'two large Grouse, one with water', alluding not to the bird but to the whisky. They sipped in total silence for five minutes, after which he observed 'Mrs Mackay's eviction went orf all right, I'm glad to say'. A perfect specimen like this conveys the same exquisite thrill as the sighting of a Death's Head Hawkmoth.

Another supreme belonger conversation, overheard by the writer in the City of London Club, was conducted as follows – 'Hear about my Deputy?' 'No, what?' 'Gave up his perfectly good job, admirable prospects and all that, to go to University as a mature student and get a degree!' 'Can't believe it! At the age of 42 with a wife and two children?' 'I know. Oldest hippy in the business . . .'

Masters and Servants

Daniel Meadows[20] ('Nattering in Paradise') suggests that the community spirit is one of the mainsprings of suburbia. His suburbanites gather together incessantly for a multitude of purposes ranging from tennis tournaments to fuschia growing, but especially for charitable work of all kinds. But there is more than a touch of the Lady Bountiful in its application, and more than a whisper of paternalism about the relationship between giver and receiver. Both sides are generally very conscious of a sense of inequality, though to observe the proprieties, naturally nothing is discussed. Distance lends enchantment to the scene.

But in another exposé of the belonger class, British employees have been found to be significantly more critical of their top managements than are their counterparts in the United States. As reported by the International Survey Research Group,[21] fewer than half of British managers feel that their bosses are doing a good job in a number of important areas. Only 28% think they are providing leadership and only a similar number that they are enabling people to work together as a team. A meagre 25% think they make decisions promptly and just 22% think that they communicate properly to the workforce.

Clearly the top managements of many UK companies still have a long way to go before they win the hearts and minds of their employees. This can be laid at the door of managerial belongers' class consciousness and resistance to change. It has been Britain's belonger managers who in the past have been responsible for the famous 'British disease'. As they now begin to fall like leaves from the tree through redundancy or early retirement, they are at last giving way to either outer or inner directeds who between them are providing our economy with a completely new impetus. At last, and as already mentioned, the British disease is giving way to the British pregnancy, from which something better is going to emerge.

Even now, however, the world's masters are still more often than not belongers by nature, but so also are the world's servants.[22] They partner each other in a never-ending dance of mutual dependence, though it is a dance whose steps are changing. There is a new set of free and confident domestics who inhabit a vastly different world. Butlers demand private health insurance and agencies blacklist unsuitable employers in a world where the upstairs-downstairs image is hopelessly out of date. However, the belonger label is still valid for most who work for a particular family or regularly for a number of households, now in increasing demand as more women want to have both children and careers. These are in distinct contrast to the more varied group who work on an entrepreneurial basis, providing a whole range of services to a wide clientele.

The Church Militant

Where, however, are the classic belongers to be found other than within the master/servant relationship? London's clubland is certainly still a happy hunting ground, but so also are the Civil Service, the Law and indeed many of the other professions (although these do contain a growing number of self-explorers too), the Services and the Church. Basically the establishment is where the breed is best found, but also within the great pyramid of others upon whom the establishment relies, the clerks, yeomen, non-commissioned officers and small artisans.

One delicious clerical example was pinned down by journalist Simon Jenkins,[23] quoting the Bishop of London, Dr Graham Leonard, in an interview on Professor Anthony Clare's BBC series, 'In the Psychiatrist's Chair'. The exchange was conducted as follows –

'Do you fear that our notion of God would be affected by seeing day in day out a lady, a woman up there at the altar?' 'I think it would. When faced with her my impulse would be to take her in my arms – sexuality is built into human life and you cannot get rid of it'. 'That could be said of my being lectured to by a woman professor: my instinct is to take her in my arms and not to listen to her?' 'I am thinking of a specifically religious context, but if you do have a woman lecturing I think we minimise the effect that she has on our actual learning. It's a different relationship from if you have a man lecturing'.

Belongers are capable of dreaming up the most bizarre reasons for resisting change. In this case the logic goes like this, says Jenkins. Men and women were made biologically different, and symbolically it is the male who takes the initiative while the female receives. God is the initiator and the priest is his initiating representative. The ancient professions, the Law, the Church and the Army, have long stood as the defenders of tradition. A threat to them is a threat to the social order and that is the strength of their defence.

However, he then asked, 'what of the converse of this predicament? What of female sexuality? What of the parish spinsters yearning to enfold a dashing young curate in their arms? What of the huggability of male impact – girl students infatuated with male teachers, the millions of women who have to establish an intimate but uncomplicated relationship with a male doctor?' The double standard of Dr Leonard is so archaic, Jenkins concludes, that we have to pinch ourselves to remember that there are a great many people around who still think like this. Oh yes, but there are.

Lord Armstrong[24] – the Civil Servant's Civil Servant

Shaw claimed that 'all professions are conspiracies against the laity'. He was aiming his shaft at doctors, but the same can be said of accountants, lawyers, members of the armed services and particularly the senior ranks of the civil service. Belongers all, these professionals have held us in their sway for long enough. At the time, Shaw was not referring to the conspiratorial camouflage of malpractice. There may be more of that today than in the past, but it is not perhaps as debilitating for society as has been the maintenance of the group's advantageous position by the preservation of professional mystique. Professionals have always duped us into empowering them at our expense, and it is only now that their power is being potentially eroded by the social resister Margaret Thatcher. However, the media would have it that even she fell prey to the suave persuasion of the real life Sir Humphrey Appleby, Lord Armstrong.

As her Cabinet Secretary, Lord Armstrong exerted enormous power, but it was a power virtually invisible to the rest of the country – until, that is, he hit the headlines in the 'Spycatcher' controversy. Compelled to give evidence in Australia, perhaps the single point on the surface of the planet that was least susceptible to belonger fudge, he found himself having to admit in a felicitous phrase that he had been 'economical with the truth'.

The aim of the whole affair was to strangle the publication of the memoirs of Peter Wright, not because they would endanger members of the British security forces, since virtually everything quoted by Wright had been published before by Chapman Pincher and others – but simply as a revenge against one who had broken the code and stood to profit by it. Nobody could have been more representative of the forces of changelessness than the then Sir Robert Armstrong. What he had to defend, to his own personal loss, was the central belonger doctrine that 'for your own good, it would be better if you knew nothing about it and accepted that we know best'.

Peter Hennessy in his *Independent* column 'Whitehall Watch' wrote up Sir Robert on the eve of his retirement. He described his speech to the Royal Institute of Public Administration on a drive for greater efficiency in Whitehall as 'dry and important', which admirably sums up the man himself. A civil servant's civil servant, Armstrong said he always took as his guiding light the demand of Queen Elizabeth I on appointing William Cecil as her Secretary of State – 'this judgement I have of you: that you will not be corrupted with any manner of gifts, and that you will be faithful to the state, and without respect of my private will you will give me the counsel that you think best.'

He is obviously a man for whom honour is paramount. As he said later in his speech, 'the British civil service retains a strong sense of the values of public service and of its importance and worth, which gives civil servants pride in the discharge of their duties and sustains them when the going gets rough.' Certainly during the last years of his tenure of office the going had got exceedingly rough, what with the GCHQ controversy, Clive Ponting, Westland and last of all the 'Spycatcher' disaster itself.

As a very private person, being publicly associated with all these by name must have been appalling for him. For most belongers, ideally one's name appears in the newspapers three times in one's entire life – at birth, on marriage and on death – give or take an award or two in between. In the cosiness of the Lords he doubtless hoped to play out an innings which, though having contained more bouncers than he would have preferred at the time, looked at first as if it was set for a gentler period before close of play.

However, even this was denied him, when the art world was thrown into a turmoil by the forced redundancies of eight senior curators of the Victoria & Albert Museum, soon after his appointment as chairman of trustees. Underneath his public belonger exterior it may well be that he has been directly or indirectly influenced by Mrs Thatcher's sense of priorities. Certainly Professor Martin Kemp, who resigned as a trustee at the time, revealed that the museum's management style changed markedly after Lord Carrington's old fashioned conservatism gave way to a more radical variety.

His public innings had been almost entirely admirable, but then it must be counted as one of the glories of the past. Given the scale of change that we are bound as a nation to have to face in future, at all costs we must shake off the dead hand of the Athenaeum. We will need a new class of civil servant to conjure up the answers to our problems, one who is at ease with the capriciousness of change and the idiosyncricity of events – an idiosyncrat in fact, rather than an autocrat, a technocrat, a bureaucrat or an oligocrat. Whitehall will hate the idea, depend upon it.

The Army[25] and the Immigrants[26]

So much for the Church and the Civil Service; the medical profession we have dealt with already; now it is the turn of the Armed Forces. More than half the cadets at Sandhurst, the Army's officer training academy, now come from state schools. Many may have degrees, but their training is as regimented and snobbish as it was 25 years ago – get stuck into the drill, don't behave like an oik, get rid of your provincial accent, show proper deference to your seniors and find a decent tailor. The Army still feels it needs to teach the 'non traditional' entrants how to fit into its own traditional model, which is determinedly upper and middle class and reflects the origins of the majority of the existing officer corps.

In the past most entrants were ex-public schoolboys who were already moulded the way the Army wanted them. Now it is taking people from different levels of society but argues that if they arrived newly commissioned at their units, they would be embarrassed if they did not know how to conform. Major-General Richard Keightley, the last commandant of Sandhurst, is adamant that the public school way is the right way, stressing the importance of class barriers in running the Army effectively – 'if the soldiers begin to know their officers too well they also begin not to respect them.' This totally disregards the fact that the experience of the SAS has proved that when highly trained and motivated, soldiers can be on far closer terms with their officers without any loss of respect or efficiency.

The assumption still being made by the Army planners of the late 20th century is that men will only respect their officers if they appear to be members of a superior class. 'We're trying to reduce individuality to some extent' says Major Malcolm Flower-Smith, the senior Royal Army Educational Corps officer at Sandhurst. 'It's not really as vicious as brainwashing, it is a form of social engineering. It's uncomfortable, but then there is a great deal of getting together. However one might criticise this approach, it does undeniably weld team spirit and produce strong, often lifelong, bonds of friendship.'

Great belonger stuff, every word of it. The uncomfortable part includes bullying and initiation ceremonies for those who may be excluded from the said bonds of friendship. About these there has been a great deal of recent publicity in terms of the army as a whole. The tendency has an impressive provenance. When a lad at Sandhurst, as narrated by his brother and biographer, Viscount Montgomery of Alamein in prankish mood set fire to the shirt tails of a cadet on the grounds that he was a fearful bounder. This was considered totally reasonable by his fellow students who held the victim at bayonet point while the future Field Marshal lit the match. Doubtless it all still goes on. Boys will be boys; belongers will be belongers.

Nostalgia is one of their very favourite sentiments, and is now enjoying a massive vogue. Georgian, Victorian, Edwardian, no matter which, yesterday is the fashion from costume drama to cookery books, from old-fashioned roses to old-fashioned houses. Heritage is here to stay, classic is more up to date than contemporary. The nostalgia business is basically belonger orientated, and satisfies the needs of those who hanker after the past and its certainties.

Some complain that there is so much nostalgic conservation going on that we have almost reached the point where it is not so much a problem of the past being in danger from the present, but of the present being in danger from the past. There are fears that what began as a step backwards from the anxieties of social change may have become a retreat into an unreal fantasy of yesterday that renders the present even more unattractive. Britain may be in danger of ending up as 'the land that's trapped in time', to quote the slogan of Peter de Savary's heritage theme park at Littlecote in Wiltshire.

One group of people whose land is trapped in time is the strongly belonger section of the Afro-Caribbean and Asian immigrant population which arrived in this country in the 50s and 60s. They came here carrying with them the absolute belief that the mother country would provide everything that they stood for. Alas, in the period between their colonial dreams and their fully conscious experiences, everything had changed here. What they had been celebrating at a distance of thousands of miles was more British than the British themselves.

According to management expert Hari Bedi, writing in *Asia Week*, Asian men and women in international or British national businesses are often working under intense personal pressures that are unrecognised by their western counterparts. 'The family is the dominant social and spiritual force in Asia, and the motivation to succeed at work often derives from family pride and family needs. An Asian manager may decline a promotion if it means moving away from an aged father. Success in Asia's traditional societies is still measured by how well one has looked after one's family. Even in purely financial terms, the Asian manager often has to endure greater pressures, because his higher standard of living raises the expectations of his relatives.'

Family concern is a fundamental belonger trait, but in the case of Asian immigrants it can often bring added stresses with it. The cosmopolitan lifestyle that accompanies a position in a British company can also take its toll on wives and children. Asian women tend to be less worldly than their western counterparts, frequently don't speak good English, are shy with strangers and find it impossible to make small-talk. Meanwhile their children with their British education tend to distance themselves from old ways and customs. While traditional belongers are diminishing in many of the country's walks of life, ironically the people we have attracted to live within our shores because of what we have stood for in the past are now disappointed because our own current reality does not reflect these ideals. Like every belonger's, such ideals are under threat from all sides –

from the survivors underneath them, from the conspicuous consumers alongside them and from the inner directeds beyond them.

Once again, however, it does not do to be too categorical. First, the Asian population exhibits a strong conspicuous consumer tendency – specifically as regards education. According to the ILEA's Research and Statistics Branch, Asian children, including Bangladeshi pupils who have to be taught English before they can perform at all, do considerably better than white working class and West Indian children since in Asian families, as in Jewish ones, there is a drive and a determination for their children to do well.

Secondly, there is also the fervid social resister quality of Islamic fundamentalism, which first showed itself in Bolton in December 1988 with the publication of Salman Rushdie's 'The Satanic Verses', and erupted generally in March 1989. When the Ayatollah Khomeni put a $3 million price on his head, book burnings, protest marches and chants for Rushdie's death took place among Moslems all over the country. Although there were calls for restraint from a large proportion of the British Moslem community, one leading activist's press comment was, 'Kill Him! Mr Rushdie should die because he is a blasphemer. I would do it myself if I could.'

9

THE SURVIVORS AND THE AIMLESS

The Belonger/Survivor Crunch

As indicated, the survivors are the social value group most closely tied to one particular class, the blue collar C2DEs. They form the core of the working-class labour movement and their motivations are much more tribal than the family orientation of the belongers. This was vividly demonstrated in the 1986 miners' strike, when the essentially survivor Yorkshire miners came into head-on collision with the Nottinghamshire belongers. It will be recalled how the Yorkshire miners emphasised the need for solidarity to the cause and bitterly castigated the Union of Democratic Mineworkers for breaking ranks. The Yorkshiremen were strictly survivor material – 'Ere we go, 'ere we go, 'ere we go!' They believed that the only way to survive was by welding together an armour of resistance against change. Individually they could do nothing, whereas as a union they just might just be able to lie down across the rails of progress and bring the inevitable to a screeching halt for the time being.

The essential defensiveness of the survivors stems from the fact that their experience of having to respond to change imposed by others has often been a highly unpleasant one. For most people, there is nothing wrong with change as long as one is holding the test tube oneself, but in general the sustenance driven don't even want to hold it at all. By channelling energy into fighting change, their response is disastrously misplaced for themselves and everyone else.

The Nottinghamshire miners on the other hand were belongers and had clearly been a different breed from their Yorkshire colleagues for some generations. Their loyalty was not so much to the union as to the family; they were liberally quoted as saying that they put their wives and children overwhelmingly before any concepts of union solidarity. Neither side could understand the other and both hated each other – a sharp lesson in the way these distinctions between the social value groups can cause such pain where nobody's motives are psychologically visible to anybody else. These antagonistic energies need first to be understood and then directed elsewhere.

Meanwhile, however, the trade union movement in this country is programmed for chaos and anguish. Now that the Electrical, Electronic, Telecommunication and Plumbing Union[1] has been stripped of membership of the Trades Union Congress, this could be the first signal for others to join it in a mass uprising. A non-TUC EETPU may soon find allies such as the UDM and possibly the Amalgamated Engineering Union, which has been sorely tried in the past and could easily break away from the TUC as well. In the long term, an 'alternative TUC' embracing belonger values rather than survivor ones could become a substantial, if not *the* most substantial labour group, and every other union would be split down the middle as a result.

The rump of the TUC is based on survivor ideology, i.e. that those bastards out there are going to get us unless we stick together. In contrast the EETPU line is now solid belonger ideology but could also form the potential basis for conspicuous consumerism. Not for nothing is this new wave of trade union philosophy known as the 'new reality'. This is the way most union members want to go, but not being prepared to fight to the death for it they are all too frequently out-manoeuvred by the left wing militants on their unbendable, thousand mile, straight line trip along the trans-Siberian railway. The rigour is impressive, but quite inappropriate to today's conditions since both locomotives and rolling stock are overdue for the scrap heap.

The TUC[2] has conceded that 3–4 million trade unionists now own shares and more want to do so. It cites a survey showing that shareholders under 45 have risen from 33% to 47% of the population since 1983, and that their proportion of the C2DE socio-economic groups has risen from 17% to 35% in the same period. In January 1988 it published a paper charting a new policy endorsing 'popular capitalism', which emphasised that as society becomes more prosperous more people can afford to save.

'The next logical stage is investment in shares', says the confidential policy document. 'Not only will a richer society permit more people to participate in capital growth, but such developments are widely supported by the population . . . If shareholders do not understand the policy provisions of social ownership or think they may be penalised by the re-transfer of utilities to the public sector by a Labour government, they may be disposed to vote against Labour.'

The Ron Todd Disaster – The Derek Jameson Triumph

This welcome recognition of the realities of life had its head smashed against the wall less than two months later, when the Ford proposal to set up a plant in Dundee was wrecked by Ron Todd[3] and his bureaucratic minions of the TGWU. Own-goal Todd demonstrated his self-destructive survivor side with a marked preference for the old union rule book over the possibility of 1500 jobs for Scottish workers in a new £40m high-technology plant. Under his leadership, 10 out of 21 of Britain's trade union leaders refused to back the proposed single-union agreement, and understandably Ford in turn refused to negotiate with this grudging and impractical acceptance of their scheme. Many other employers will now doubtless follow them out of this country in the search for new manufacturing facilities.

Todd's stance, one of the final death spasms of dinosaur unionism, took place at the same time as a sudden momentary wave of shopfloor militancy, and everybody got excited. The health service workers, the coalpit supervisors, the ferry operators, and a number of unions at car plants all started flexing their muscles. However, as it turned out this did not signal a return to the winter of discontent of 1974 or indeed to the spring, summer or autumn either.

Ron Todd is a hero of the far left, but unlike Arthur Scargill, principle rather than power appears to be his prime motivation. He is one of Ken Livingstone's models of a good socialist. One wonders whether the people of Dundee also see him as a good socialist, however, since his action has been so devastating not only for them but for Scotland as a whole. For decades the Scots have suffered from a reputation for poor industrial relations which has hampered the efforts of successive governments to encourage industry to move there. There was a common feeling among industrialists that Scotland was a rotten place for investment. During the '80s however, the picture began to change and Scottish workers and their unions seemed to accept that their best interests depended on showing a positive will to make their industries prosperous. And now there has been this fiasco, reverberating around the world.

Two months later, Todd unapologetically resigned from the government's new Training Commission, successor to the Manpower Services Commission. Bernard Levin depicted him as lurching on towards extinction but agonised over the fact that the dinosaurs themselves took 750,000 years to become extinct – even though the mammals had begun making quite some progress over the period. Warming to his theme, he also described Todd as 'prostrate across the path to the future, like an oak felled by last year's hurricane – though in fact it fell many decades ago, and has now grown roots running fully thirty feet deep, at both ends.'

After the 1988 Labour party conference, one young Labour MP summed up Ron Todd as being 'entirely sincere and entirely confused'. Labelled 'Sweeney Todd' by Eric Hammond of the right-wing Electricians' Union, in the Labour movement he is seen, and heard, as an old-time bandleader conducting a deafeningly loud old-time orchestra. No significant change of position in either the TUC or the Labour party, whether on defence, on proportional representation, on employment training, or on whatever else can occur in the teeth of Todd and his TGWU executive.

He virtually wrecked the 1988 Labour conference by sinking those teeth both into the manipulative and conspiratorial far left and the centre right's movement towards pragmatic change. His class-based traditionalism erupted in his remarks about 'sharp-suited socialists with cordless telephones'. 'Dinosaurs', he sighed in contrast, 'ruled the world for more than 200 million years, and that wasn't bad.'

It is no use telling people like this that Margaret Thatcher has won three general elections in a row and that the number of people in trade unions is now fewer than the number of those who have bought shares in the government's privatisation issues, while both the TUC and Neil Kinnock have agreed that there is nothing wrong with working class affluence. Ron Todd will continue the way he is as long as there is breath in his body, even though he may increasingly find himself . . . on his tod.

That is somewhere Derek Jameson[4] will never find himself. Though labelled 'East End Boy Made Bad' by Radio 4's satirical programme Week-Ending ('. . . Jameson is to journalism what lockjaw is to conversation'), he is a show business celebrity through and through, beloved by millions. A complex and many-faceted character, it is nevertheless the warmth and common touch of his survivor mentality that shines through to the public. On the day that there was a fever of speculation as to who would be George Bush's running mate in the 1988 US presidential election, Jameson announced on his Radio 2 programme, '. . . not much in the papers today. The Sun have found a human sponge . . .'

He earned the Private Eye sobriquet of Sid Yobbo, by becoming 'the man who introduced nipples to the North', while Northern editor of the Daily Mirror. When switched to preside over the down market Daily Star, in order to halt the advance of The Sun, he pioneered bingo in newspapers and took The Star's circulation to 1.25 million in twelve months. His third marriage in Arundel cathedral was attended among others by the winners of a *Woman's Own* competition who wrote the best letter saying why going to the Jameson wedding would be the greatest day of their lives. He will probably be the last of the survivors to survive.

Survival . . . of the Fittest?

Unlike Jameson, survivors as a whole are an endangered species. 1987 marked the 125th anniversary of the working man's clubs,[5] whose six million members down an annual £750 million in beer sales, collectively own premises valued at £2 billion and constitute the largest single consumer group in Europe. Years ago the rules stated that three-quarters of a club committee had to be '*bona fide* working men'. This regulation has, however, been gently dropped because nobody can agree on what a *bona fide* working man is any more.

Those who do still qualify as *bona fide* have woken to a cruel dawn, in which many of their old labouring jobs have already gone for good while technology is eroding the rest. For years they have been protected from this reality by their leaders who insisted that they were the only essential group in society. They were quite unprepared for a world in which their work was suddenly of no more than marginal significance. Not only has their work disappeared, moreover, but their whole smokestack way of life now appears pointless. The culture of the factory is in decline and the close communities that clustered round its gates are changing fundamentally.

Survivors have always displayed a rock-like communal strength and a welcome sense of the interdependence which is so essential for all our futures, but their particular brand of it was restricted entirely to their own group and largely also to their own gender. On the other side of the historical coin, these old sustenance-driven communities that are now passing away were male-dominated, narrow-minded, restrictive and chauvinistic, notwithstanding any romantic ideas to the contrary.

Anne Robinson, the *Daily Mirror* columnist, pleaded that on Mothering Sunday she and her kind did not want grandiose cards, overpriced flowers or a plastic pinny, 'but if at any time over the weekend we came across a pile of freshly ironed clothes, a bath without a tidemark, a school satchel hung on a peg, best of all a stew in the oven, most of us would be pathetically grateful.' There speaks the wife of the modern Andy Capp — chance would be a fine thing.

Only 17 of British Rail's 19,300 train drivers are women and all of them have vivid stories of sexual discrimination on the railways, ranging from promotion barriers to verbal harassment and physical abuse. BR and the Rail unions are still operating what is virtually a closed shop for men, and in spite of their claims of equal opportunity there is a maze of discrimination involving outdated attitudes on the part of officialdom, macho attitudes on the part of colleagues and restrictive practices on the part of unions.

Female drivers complain of being treated like dirt and that neither management nor unions want to know about the problems. One woman driver revealed at the 1988 Blackpool Women's TUC Conference how she had been sexually assaulted by a male colleague while driving a passenger train at 50mph. The complainant, Karen Harrison, said spiritedly that both unions and management needed 'a sharp elbow in the beer gut of male domination', which could also apply to the status quo still pertaining in sustenance driven smokestack communities of all types and descriptions.

Being a survivor is also bad for the health, ironically.[8] At a conference on inner city medicine sponsored by the Royal Colleges of Physicians and of General Practitioners in July 1987, it was revealed how the health of those living in deprived urban areas is affected throughout their lives. As babies they are born into poorer families in overcrowded and decaying housing. Their childhood is blighted by accidents, vandalism and violence, and they struggle as adults against high unemployment, neighbourhood crime and the stress of a whole chain of social problems. In old age they are increasingly isolated and vulnerable. Partly, as we have seen, however, their problems derive from the fact that they are unprepared to look after themselves. What first needs to be broken down is the dire combination of short-sightedness, self-pity and stubborn ignorance that keeps so many of them resentfully chained to a life without prospects. Conversely, what the survivor group can teach us is an incredible sense of interdependence and closeness. How the rest of us can help them in return is by awakening them to their own true value, their ability to work for themselves and their huge potential.

This is a matter of empowerment. How wrong it is to imagine that this group can do nothing for itself! For either authorities or individuals to ladle out paternalism from a moral soup kitchen is absolutely not the answer. But many survivors are now so alienated that they deliberately halt progress for others with self-defeating acts of defiant pride. These in turn induce rejection by the rest of society and the bitterest of social divisions. It is a problem that requires the most sensitive possible handling.

North, South, North, South

Already the polarisation between north and south is as acute as it has ever been. Young families or sometimes just their breadwinning males are being drawn southwards in search of work, leaving the elderly, the unemployed and the unadventurous trapped in northern depression. The 1981 population census pinpointed Newcastle-on-Tyne as having one of the highest concentrations of old people in the country: 50,000 pensioners, of whom 20,000 were aged over 75. They cannot afford to come down south and live closer to their families; the city is therefore in danger of becoming a backwater of lonely old people, many of them frail and handicapped. It is yet a further example of the destruction of the survivor family network.

Survivors are normally characterised as essentially part of the industrial inner city scene, but country people[9] left stranded amid a sea of affluence also fall into this category. Villages in the south-east have become the new suburbia for many whose work is unrelated to agriculture and whose rich lifestyles are heavily dependent on the motor car, not to say on two or three of them per family.

However, many of their neighbours are still traditional village residents, agricultural workers, local service workers, those employed in small industries and many elderly people, who find it impossible to compete with the rocketing local house market and the gentrification of the local shops. They are contained within this new category in the social vocabulary, the underclass. 'Working class' is out of date because everybody works – that is, all except the unemployed, most of whom, ironically, constitute what used to be called 'working class'. The new word is a necessary evil.

Robert Chesshyre[10] in 'The Return of a Native Reporter' quotes Gordon Chopping, manager of Durham's Easington Unemployment Centre – 'There is a new proletariat, it doesn't wear suits; it doesn't *have* suits; it doesn't buy consumer durables. Any work it does is in the black economy. Its members are a million miles away from people who watch ads on TV and can say – oh yes, we'll go and get one of those'. Chopping tells of a young man of 20 with one A-level and nine O-levels which would have guaranteed him a job in the south without any trouble, but who had not secured a single interview from 70 applications to local offices and banks. But most Durham people would rather stay close to home and be out of work than gainfully employed down south where it is rumoured that people scarcely know their next-door neighbours.

[153]

At 3am on June 12th 1987 Margaret Thatcher,[11] having won her third electoral term, immediately announced to her supporters from the steps of Conservative Central Office 'We must do something about the inner cities'. So saying, she embarked on her already described mission to change the political and social landscape by eradicating these strongholds of socialism. She now utterly believes that her next task is to ensure that everybody shares in what she is convinced is the beginning of Britain's economic miracle, by providing a self-help rescue package to break the cycle of urban decay.

This involves a whole avalanche of legislation: enabling council tenants to opt out and choose private landlords; forcing councils to put out services to competitive tender; boosting crime prevention; providing inner city pupils with high-tech education at the 20 city technology colleges. The reader will be familiar with the list. All of these moves are aimed at the conversion of the entire survivor group into good little belongers or conspicuous consumers in a breathtaking experiment in social engineering.

There will be much resistance. The survivor tradition has always bred a collective identity rather than a spirit of property-owning entrepreneurship. But the old cloth cap arguments have been roundly defeated by the experience of the National Freight Corporation[12] (now NFC), born from the marriage of British Road Services and Pickfords. Here at least, Thatcher is on the right track. Sold off to its employees in 1982 for a mere £60 million, in February 1988 the company was valued at £450 million, and a cool £814 million on its introduction to the Stock Market a year later. The average stake held by the company's employee shareholders is now worth around £40,000, and more than 500 of the company's secretaries, tea-ladies, lorry drivers, clerks and managers now each own more than £250,000 worth. No wonder that the Labour Party is reviewing its philosophy of envy and state control.

Housing – The New Approach

Meanwhile the Thatcher aim is to attract the better-off to the inner cities, for example in London's Docklands[13] where, although there is this initial clash of cultures, the new people moving in should ultimately bring in welcome money, decision-making power and further investment. The idea is for the country's inner cities to appeal to medium-sized businesses that want to expand, but are under pressure from rising costs and a shortage of appropriate labour in their traditional south-east stamping-grounds. Low cost housing, a cheaper lifestyle, less traffic and access to beautiful countryside and natural amenities comprise the rest of the package. The cure depends on the self-reliant and self-developmental thrust that can be provided by both individual and corporate initiatives, giving people the responsibility and opportunity to solve their own problems and make the industrial deserts bloom again in the process.

Glasgow[14] is one of the inner cities that has led this move towards positive self-help. In contrast to Liverpool's slogan, 'stop rubbishing Merseyside', their's declaims 'Glasgow's miles better' with a picture of a smiley face. And it is. After ten years of restoration and more than £500m in public and private investment, it now provides a shining example of what can be achieved in this current surge of inner city revivalism, with sound evidence that even the most run down areas can be transformed into green and pleasant places where people will happily pay to live.

Once labelled the workshop of the Empire, the city's manufacturing base had collapsed, taking with it scores of thousands of jobs. Whole communities had been moved out from areas like the Gorbals to deadly housing estates such as the already featured Easterhouse on the city's edge, creating a new variety of slum. The most talented and determined packed their bags and sought their fortunes elsewhere; the east end of Glasgow was left with what was bureaucratically descibed as a 'residual population' living in conditions that ranked with Sicily at the bottom of the European deprivation league.

Glasgow pulled itself together in terms of looks, learning and culture, like a neglected wife determined to recapture her errant husband. It transformed decaying tenements into handsome desirable sandstone properties. It provided the Burrell Collection with its own museum, opened a huge exhibition centre, mounted a garden festival, committed itself to building a 2,500-seat concert hall to house the Scottish National Orchestra and, much to the chagrin of Edinburgh, its toffee-nosed neighbour, was elected by the European Community as the European City of Culture for 1990. But amid all this new elegance, there are still plenty of survivors who detest the change and argue fiercely that the transformation has totally robbed the place of its old character.

All over the country, however, more and more people are beginning to live contentedly in refurbished local authority housing.[15] On the south bank of the Thames is a council-owned tower block, the 18th floor of which contains a two-bedroomed flat rented at £69.35 per week. Exactly opposite, on the other side of the river, is the Belvedere, focal point of the new exclusive Chelsea Harbour development, of which the 18th floor penthouse is soon scheduled to go on the market at £3 million.

A proponent of the hidden value of shabby council property and its potential in a private sector context is David Goldstone, managing director of Regalian plc. Goldstone's first important achievement came in 1980 when his company broke new ground with the refurbishment of Battersea Village. The company successfully tendered to the Borough of Wandsworth for the purchase of five dilapidated blocks of 1930s council flats, vandalised and neglected, a Saturday night no-go area for the local police. Instead of merely slapping on a coat of paint and selling the units off cheaply, it opted for the more adventurous course of creating something with positive long- term social implications, 300 carefully rehabilitated flats with landscaped courtyards that actually fostered a sense of communal pride in their residents. Battersea Village suddenly became a prime example of what could and should be done to stem the tide of violence and deprivation.

Regalian now works closely with local authorities, sometimes buying property for refurbishment with the agreement that it reserves say 30% of the new units for people on the council's existing housing list, selling to them at a 30% discount. The hallmarks of Regalian property are magnificent siting, up-to-date kitchens and bathrooms, landscaping and architectural enhancement to soften the generally rectilinear outlines of the building's structure, security in the form of entry-phones with television monitoring or porterage, reliable lifts and frequently a package of other scarce local amenities which may include shops, a laundry-room, a gymnasium, recreation room, sauna and swimming pool, and libraries of books, records and video films. Ever since this first experiment, it has combined a truly caring sense of social responsibility with enormous commercial success.

The net result has been to engineer an entire social change. Gradually in these and similar ways, the survivor mentality will dwindle away over the years, as long as there is enough money to keep up the momentum of improvement. Unless we are faced with a global economic crash (over a period of decades), once the younger generation overtakes the old the last remnants of the survivor ethos will disappear. However, one region where its divisive tribalism still exists to a formidable degree, and where it would be unreasonably optimistic to expect its disappearance, is of course Northern Ireland. There, the survivors will survive in their antagonistic misery for many years to come.

The Aimless – Both Ends Of The Life-Cycle

The aimless social value group is, as we have seen, primarily divided into two major sub-divisions, the very old and the very young, although of course there are also middle-aged aimless who have reached this condition, having mostly been unemployed survivors for so long that their instinct for any positive activity has disappeared.

In practice it is difficult to establish what is the proportion of aimless in the population, and the Taylor Nelson/Applied Futures estimates may well err on the low side. The reason is that by definition it is quite a feat to get aimless people to answer one questionnaire for an hour and then to fill in another one in an hour-and-a-half of their spare time. The Taylor Nelson team laboured long over this problem and ultimately came up with an alternative method of questioning which involved group discussions, as an adjunct to the sampling itself.

They eventually managed to recruit 35 aimless of various ages to attend a group discussion and share their views on life. They were encouraged to participate by expansive promises of food and drink at the meeting, plus a £10 note or a bottle of whisky at the end of it. Came the evening of the party and the researchers surrounded the groaning board with their clipboards and sharpened pencils at the ready, but in vain. Not a single recruit actually turned up. There's aimless for you.

Although a significant proportion of old people[16] over the age of 75 belong to this group, it must by no means be thought that they do so automatically. Plenty of people are staying young until their 80s and indeed their 90s, in all senses except for the number of birthdays they have aggregated; all of us know old people with enough energy to light up a small town. Nowadays more and more retire from 50 upwards, and it is likely that this trend towards early retirement will mean that they embark on second careers, engage in voluntary activities, or pursue hobbies with such vigour that they postpone almost indefinitely the onset of senility.

Interest is the key factor. Some old people keep on skiing into their seventies, others turn their efforts to nature and its conservation; yet more discover a keen affinity for politics, while many involve themselves more deeply with bridge parties or their grandchildren. Elderly people, with either a wide range of interests and social contacts or one absorbing pastime which they pursue relentlessly, can thus stimulate their own mental processes in exactly the same way that exercise stimulates their bodily processes. They keep in mental trim.

However, for more than a few, the advantages of a continued active life are passed up and the result is a loss of concern and a decline into apathy. These are not necessarily in worse health than others, but they eventually find themselves out on a cold and lonely limb, talking only about people who have died and refusing to make new friends. A Punch cartoon depicts an old man sitting in a marriage bureau being inspected by a prospective partner. Round his neck is a card with the message 'Batteries Supplied'.

With the increased ability of medicine to prolong the lives of the elderly, this section of the aimless population is bound to increase due simply to demographic and techno-medical changes. In 2015, it is estimated that our population will include 4 million people of 75 or over, double the 1961 level, while 13% of pensioners will be over 85 as opposed to 8% in 1985. The old aimless are bound to constitute an increasing problem unless as a society we are determined to find ways of galvanising them.

But will society be prepared to do this? The elderly are now the group most vulnerable to incompetent and neglectful institutional treatment. There are 120,000 old people in local authority and privately run homes in Britain, and some of the conditions they live in vary from shocking cruelty to stultifying indifference ignored by the younger members of their families. In David Cohen's *Observer* article 'The Home of the Zombies', a worker in a private home said of the atmosphere that 'people spend all day sat in their chair, they are existing not living, so they start giving up and they die'.

Research and common sense both suggest that people become apathetic and depressed if they are inactive. This particular home, and indeed undoubtedly many others, actually encouraged inertia. Often if residents wanted to get up and walk around they were told they could not do so. A cook in one particular home described the atmosphere as like a morgue, claiming that old people were told they could not get up from their chairs, and that one particular staff member restrained them by sitting on their laps.

Certainly we need more and better old age homes which must be properly supervised, but some new government bureaucracy set up to raise the consciousness of and about the elderly will do no good at all. This is outmoded dependency all over again. What would be genuinely effective is for there to be more volunteer workers who really understand, maybe from the ranks of the recently retired whose time to be on the receiving end of the process will soon come, entailing a kind of inter-dependent old age care insurance contract of 'protection and indemnity'.

Putting The Boot In – England's National Game

The other major sub-group of the aimless category is the aimless young; under-educated, frequently unemployed, resentful and despairing, they represent an easy target for manipulation by social resisters who often recruit them as an army of mercenary thugs to fight their particular causes.

November 1987 saw the publication of a disturbing report compiled by English and Belgian academics that detailed how Britain is now exporting football hooliganism[17] to Europe. English hooligans, linked with the National Front, combined with Belgian, Dutch and German fans connected with European nationalist groups to take part in gratuitous violence at continental matches. Scenes during the 1988 European Cup were particularly loathsome, and the trouble has grown to the stage where it has of course now become a political issue.

In his contribution to the above report, Lode Walgrave, professor of the Belgian University of Louvain said, 'the British are seen as the true professionals (in hooliganism) . . . what we see now is only the tip of the iceberg . . . under the surface there are complex social problems'. The report went on to show that most came from unstable working class families and that almost none had held down a regular job. And the vast majority of them were, in *Private Eye*'s phraseology, tired and emotional as a newt.

There is an elaborate sub-culture of lawlessness surrounding certain clubs; as Sports Minister Colin Moynihan put it, 'we are aware that this hooliganism is now a far more sophisticated and organised criminal problem than ever before'. During the past few years this kind of violence has spread, both on and off the field, to rugby, cricket, racing, snooker, tennis and golf. Sportsmen no longer see themselves as possessing free will, but as violent elemental forces that can be temporarily channelled but never permanently controlled. The expression of this self-indulgent attitude inflames the yobbo spectators into ever more violent excesses.

Jack Crawford, the Football Association's anti-hooligan officer and former Chief Constable of Merseyside, introduces a note of interdependence as a solution to the problem. 'This is everyone's responsibility and it really has to be the terraces that clear up the trouble. In parts of Europe the supporters have a major say in the running of their clubs. That is the key. The fans must get more involved with their clubs. We must develop fan clubs in England, and in particular football in the community. The clubs with the all-weather pitches provide an invaluable service. This is more important than banning supporters and making matches all-ticket events. Ultimately we must give the game to the fans.'

Meanwhile some of the worst of Chelsea's hooligans, frustrated by the banning of English clubs from Europe, duly switched their particularly nasty breed of collective violence to the support of Glasgow Rangers, since Scottish clubs are still *persona grata* on the continent – for the time being. Britain may have joined the Common Market, but could yet find herself permanently blackballed from European football.

The government's response has been the new Football Spectators Bill, heralding compulsory identity cards for almost all supporters, cancellation of licences for uncooperative clubs, and a new quango to administer the scheme. But in spite of 6,147 arrests at football matches in 1988, 6,542 expulsions from grounds, and 5,000 police officers tied up each weekend, it may be that the violent aimless have scented trouble and evaporated, to condense malevolently again somewhere else in due course.

John Stalker, former Deputy Chief Constable of Manchester, suspects that 'the people who did the damage in football have already moved on. Football was only a vehicle. There was never such a thing as a football hooligan. They were violent people who found their easiest outlet in football.' Certainly the end of the 1988/89 season seemed mostly quieter, and it just may be that the Government has moved too late and punished the wrong people – although a full analysis of the Hillsborough disaster may prove such a judgement to be altogether too sanguine.

Drugs, Crime, Race and Alienation

Next stop, drugs and crime.[18] According to a report published by the Centre for Criminology at Middlesex Polytechnic in mid-1987, serious crime in England and Wales could rise to nearly 6 million offences by 1992. Based on the number of these offences per 100,000 of the population, the last time figures were so high was in the 1880s, a paradoxical return to Victorian values, if you like.

In sharp relief, of course, are the predominantly black areas like Brixton, Toxteth, St Paul's, Bristol and Broadwater Farm, Tottenham, to which most people's minds automatically repair when the problem is mentioned. However, a more recent phenomenon has been the white riot. According to the Police Federation these are now common in many areas and consist of gangs of sometimes hundreds of white youths wielding knives and machetes rampaging through peaceful towns and deliberately seeking battle with the outnumbered police.

Quiet backwaters like Stroud, Mansfield, Shrewsbury, Banbury, Chertsey, Llanelly are involved, not to mention seaside holiday resorts such as Bournemouth, Weston-super-Mare, Morecambe and Brighton. And Crowborough, where in June 1988 200 youths fought police for three hours in what Home Office Minister John Patten described as 'white collar yobbery'. Other ministers, including Margaret Thatcher herself, have been equally outspoken.

The phenomenon has its City of London counterparts as well. The Stock Exchange determinedly refuses to acknowledge its existence, with its chairman Sir Nicholas Goodison murmuring about 'an element of high spiritedness among young men'. But the staff at Liverpool Street station and the police who are responsible for it have another story – one of 'urinating in public, pushing elderly passengers about and even attacking staff with broken bottles and glasses', according to Det. Constable Sean Burke of British Transport Police. Said Mr Rob Newell of the Institute of Psychology, 'these are the kind of men who if it had not been for Big Bang would still be thumbing lifts home from building sites.'

This unattractive product is also being exported to Portugal and Spain and selected parts of Greece such as Corfu. The tourist authorities in these countries are now reserving the right to put incoming troublemakers straight back on their planes again and return them to their original point of exit. The carriers themselves are now also prepared to refuse people on their aircraft if they are in no condition to travel.

Deprivation, homelessness, unemployment – none of these seem to be to blame here. From what are these people then alienated? Drinking appears to play a considerable part, for sure, particularly under-age drinking, and most incidents occur on Friday and Saturday nights at pub-closing time. Drugs are certainly an increasing factor too, and more seriously so, among both casual muggers and the more professional armed robbers. The former include a growing number of addicts needing money to support their habit, while the latter use proceeds from their raids to buy their way into the more lucrative drug dealing and smuggling rackets.

The fashion in drugs comes and goes as supply and demand factors affect the market, just as with any other. Cannabis, heroin, cocaine we know about already, but there are two others that are potentially even more virulent because of their relative cheapness and ease of manufacture – crack, a smokable combination of cocaine and baking powder capable of giving an immediate high; and MDMA, also known as 'ecstacy', a grade 1 prescribed drug that causes brain damage in monkeys and severe psychological disturbance in humans, and has entered the yuppie culture at 'Acid House' parties all over the South-East.

Closely connected to all this is the new practice of 'steaming',[18] a vicious brand of street crime which involves gangs of up to 30 who swarm into a shop, a bus or a tube train and steal *en masse*. They rely on sheer weight of numbers to engulf their victims, and to ensure that other members of the public are unable to stop them or get help from outside. Small shops and passengers on buses without conductors are especially vulnerable to this modern equivalent of robbing a stagecoach. There is a kind of carefree arrogance about it that is new and alarming. The most dramatic example took place on an early morning train between Bedford and Kings Cross, when a gang of two dozen young men snatched money, jewellery and other valuables from at least thirteen passengers, assaulted those who resisted, and slashed one man across the face. Your sophisticated steamer now uses a Stanley knife with two blades prised apart with a coin, making a double cut which is impossible to stitch. Shattering for its victims, steaming is also a difficult crime to prevent and highly expensive in both manpower and financial terms to stamp out. The crime first appeared in the deprived urban areas of Los Angeles and New York in the early 1980s. In August 1987 the police announced that at least 12 gangs were operating during the Notting Hill street carnival but it is now also widespread in the five-mile 'corridor of crime' between Lewisham and Peckham. It has occurred in Bristol, Birmingham and Liverpool and seems to be reaching out everywhere on a copycat basis.

In February 1988 figures for street robberies showed a 13% monthly increase in London alone, where they were running at an average of 400 a week. On the London Underground in the first six weeks of the year muggings were up by 100% compared to 1987. But a few months later, passengers were bewildered to see platforms and carriages being patrolled by Guardian Angels from the New York subway, kitted out in Rambo-style uniforms and scarlet berets. This spurred Public Transport Minister, Michael Portillo, into posting an extra 80 police officers to the Underground. Moreover, in other areas suffering unduly from burglaries and muggings, householders, shop proprietors and business people have since begun to form vigilante groups or hired security firms to protect their personal and commercial property.

In March 1988, Education Secretary Kenneth Baker announced an enquiry into the upsurge of violence by pupils against teachers in schools, but there is now a related but less well-known issue of violence by children against parents. Parents' problems used to centre round screaming babies, rumbustious 8-year olds and sulky teenagers; now, many calls to an East Midlands 24-hour helpline are from parents who have been mentally or physically abused and cannot bear to talk to anyone else about it.

The helpline is called Parents Anonymous and comes under the umbrella of OPUS (Organisation of Parents Under Stress). There is a great taboo against parents telling the police that they are being assaulted by their children and enduring the shame of having the child appear in court. The front door closes behind this violence, projected mostly against mothers but also against fathers and grandparents. Worryingly, it is increasing.

Much of today's gang violence is quite different from old patterns and the random rowdiness of the past has little to do with it. The perpetrators of this new violence enjoy its media value and carry it out with premeditated malice and intent. As Tony Blair, Labour MP for Sedgefield wrote in *The Times*, what is new is for youths to beat up an old age pensioner as a form of initiation rite to prove their fitness for membership of a local gang. Thus the term 'football hooliganism' is misleading since it has little to do with football or football supporters; it is simply naked gang warfare.

This has been going on since the days of the Caesars, but have we not developed since then? Blair considers that its new emergence is something to do with the decline in the notion of community, of the idea that we have obligations to our neighbours and society as well as to ourselves. These gang members have not been taught the discipline that derives from recognising that one's own value is in some way related to the value given to others. They therefore feel that they have to prove their worth and power by inflicting fear upon somebody else. Blair rightly describes it as 'a profound and corrosive form of alienation'.

He argues that none of us can escape responsibility because collectively we determine the values of society. When a sense of community is strong this adds its own special pressure against antisocial behaviour. The non-communal but dependent society brings with it the understandable resentment that 'they' are patronising, hence the vandalism of local authority tower blocks. The independent society brings with it the resentment that 'they' couldn't give a damn about you anyway – 'they' often including parents and teachers. This breeds a more frightening vandalism against people as opposed to property.

It is only where and when the interdependent society of the millennium is actually in place – as with the example of the Easterhouse mosaic

– that people who have before felt themselves deprived and alienated have enough sense of community and of their own value to encourage them to exhibit sociable behaviour. In an I'm-all-right-Jack society where social responsibility is seen as a drag anchor on private pleasure, we have all learned to tolerate what should not be tolerated. We avoid and evade; we do not want to become involved. As Blair affirms, some of us may appear to be secure, but we will pay an ever increasing price for our security from the victims of the world outside unless we learn this lesson.

This is because behind this there also simmers the far deeper potential for racial unrest.[19] Militant black activists have set up a group to develop links with Sinn Fein, the political wing of the IRA. The organisation is called the Black and Green Committee and it aims to organise meetings between Republican groups and the black community, to raise funds, and to coordinate demonstrations in support of Irish nationalism in black areas. A London-based activist group, the Black Liberation Front, has distributed a document which states 'We are proposing that we meet to look into practical measures which can be taken to express this solidarity. These might include the sponsoring of public meetings, organising a black delegation to visit the Six Counties, or the formation of a broad-based black committee in support of the Irish struggle.'

This is the echo of the aimless cry of anguish. Often the right-wing football hooligan element adopts a racialist stance, in response to which aimless members of the victim groups combine to retaliate. Pakistanis and Bengalis are especially subject to this kind of persecution, but large sections of the Afro-Caribbean population also suffer physical assaults, damage to property and other offensive unpleasantness. In parts of the East End of London the growth of abuse particularly relates to the erosion of traditional local values through a combination of high unemployment, housing deterioration and the influx of ethnic minority immigrants. All this exacerbates an already highly dangerous situation.

Happily, Broadwater Farm Estate in Tottenham, the scene of the October 1985 riots in which PC Keith Blakelock was killed, is now being transformed into a safe place to live. The key, as in Easterhouse, is self-help. At Broadwater, a string of cooperative enterprises has been started and run by local people; these include a sewing workshop, computer centre, creche, greengrocer's, hairdresser's, and youth and pensioners clubs – all of which provide some support, work and training for the 3,000 residents of whom 80% of the young people are jobless. As a result the crime rate has dropped by 80% to one sixth of that of the surrounding area. There are hundreds of other places where such

improvements could be paralleled, but they are not celebrated or recognised, and some kind of explosion may have to occur before they are.

The reason for all this disturbance among young people is a matter of
hot debate. Some say that it is a matter of discipline, others that it is a
matter of unfulfillable expectations being artificially raised by television
and advertising. Other theories focus on diet and the ingestion of damaging additives, from lead in petrol or from the occurrence of an extra (XYY)
male chromosome. Under-education, child-abuse, and the repression of
people by a system which does not want to own them, are also blamed.
Probably the answer is a combination of most if not all of these – perm any
six from seven – once again illuminating the principle that no one aspect is
absolute and that all problems, all situations, are most rewardingly considered in a holistic and balanced manner.

10

THE STATUS QUO

Where does that leave us, then? How, in other words, can this analysis of the country's seven social value groups help us look towards the future, the next century, the millennium itself, with any greater sense of understanding and clarity? How can it help us create a society we really want? To answer this question, we first have to consider where we stand now. Can we 'rightly get there from here', or will we have to go via somewhere pretty nasty first?

Britain On The Brink[1]

The spring of 1988 had seen the Conservative government in a self-congratulatory mood. Triumphalist was the adjective used by its enemies to describe it. It had smashed them to the boundary in the election of June 1987, and had enjoyed a rapturous party conference in October, setting the scene for a Queen's Speech that presented a delicious menu of radical reforms. Legislation had proceeded relatively smoothly in the face of a lacklustre opposition performance, and the tax concessions of Nigel Lawson's budget had gilded the political gingerbread. The Labour party was beset by its usual internal squabblings and by a leadership contest that diverted the attention of its front bench from day-to-day parliamentary matters. At the same time, the fog of selfish incompetence that surrounded the reshuffle of the Alliance parties had disorientated all those concerned and their possible supporters.

The spring of 1989 was rather different. There was no longer that air of total self confidence, and for the first time the government began to look mortal. A number of issues were proving simultaneously unpopular with the public, to a greater or lesser degree. The mishandling of the food scares, consumer resistance to water and electricity privatisation, the poll tax, lack of investment in the infrastructure, concern about the National Health Service and the first rumblings over the Official Secrets Act – all these combined to demolish the government lead over Labour, at the same time that the economy, previously the strongest card in its hand, began to look as if problems could be in store.

Moreover, the spate of disasters over a short period of 18 months had been almost unprecedented. The Zeebrugge ferry sinking, the destruction of the Piper Alpha drilling platform, the King's Cross underground fire, three fatal rail accidents at Clapham, Purley and Glasgow, the salmonella egg drama and the contamination by cryptosporidia of the Oxford/ Swindon water supply – the litany of danger to life and health had a thread of greed running through it. The greed might be indirectly responsible, camouflaged in the name of efficiency, or in causing human error among employees suffering from the strain of overwork; but the corner-cutting in safety that did result from it in these and other cases was a poor advertisement for the market economy and the unrestricted domination of the outer directed ethos.

In consequence, what people were beginning to require of Mrs Thatcher was a better society, not just a sounder economy – an inner, as well as an outer directed agenda. They were uneasy about the social consequences of her obsession with the market alone, and the new inequalities that gave rise to the emergence of an underclass and had contributed to a wave of such anti-social behaviour. They wanted a climate of peace and openness between East and West. And above all, they wanted something done about the protection of the environment.

In an attempt to break out of her defensive position on these issues, she first used the 1988 party conference to launch the concept of 'active citizens', a prosperous and beneficent bunch of helpers who put something back into the community by dutifully engaging in Neighbourhood Watch, parents' associations, school governerships, charitable work and the like. This cosmetic response made little impact, but on the second item she scored a notable public relations triumph over the Gorbachev visit, even though her attitude on disarmament was less than lukewarm. On the third public concern, that of the environment, the jury is still out.

Enter The Green Goddess[2]

Certainly the historical evidence is not helpful to the defence. In 1985 Thatcher bracketed environmentalists and peace groups as 'the enemy within'; and during the Falklands campaign she declared, 'it is exciting to have a real crisis on your hands when you have spent half your political life dealing with humdrum issues like the environment'. But having read a short sharp paper by Britain's Ambassador to the United Nations, Sir Crispin Tickell, entitled 'Rapid Global Warming – Worse With Neglect', based on data from the prestigious Woods Hole Research Center, she underwent a Damascus Rd (S.W.1) conversion.

It manifested itself at a speech to the Royal Society in September 1988, in which she described the protection of the environment and the balance of nature as 'one of the great challenges of the late 20th century', an issue she then went on to amplify at the Tory Party conference. The opposition parties had been taking a more cramped and localised view of the issue, so in warning that mankind may have 'unwittingly begun a massive experiment with the system of this planet itself', she effectively cut the ground from under their feet.

She went on to consolidate her statesmanlike approach by hosting the Saving the Ozone Layer conference in March 1989, and hinting at the future presentation of a Green Bill which would tighten up on pollution of all kinds. Tax concessions of lead-free petrol in the 1989 Budget underlined the message that environmental concerns were not peripheral any more, but mainstream.

But people were suspicious. 'Blimey!', commented Jonathon Porritt, lately Director of Friends of the Earth, wisely reserving further judgement. The Conservative party's record to date had been abysmal, after all. Britain had been the only major European country to refuse to make a 30% reduction in the power station sulphur emissions that cause acid rain; had held up for many months an international treaty to control ozone destructive chemicals; had opposed EEC wildlife and countryside protection legislation; and had dragged its feet on vehicle exhaust fumes. The retiring Euro-Commissioner for the Environment, Stanley Clinton-Davies, complained, 'Any excuse to avoid or delay progress would be deployed – more research, more studies are needed – the scientific case has not been fully established – industry is not ready – market forces must be allowed to set the pace – and, of course, it impairs national sovereignty'.

The results? Much British drinking water was failing to reach minimum EEC standards, and a February 1989 Greenpeace report showed that

Britain's rivers were being polluted at a faster rate than at any time since records began. The number of pollution incidents had risen from 12,500 in 1980/81 to 23,250 in 1987/88, and in two years over 450 miles of clean rivers had been poisoned, since for industry and agriculture it was infinitely cheaper to pay a minuscule fine than to take proper care. Concerned more with efficiency than with public health, the government had allowed 1,800 of the country's 6,000 sewage works to break the law and pump filthy water into our rivers and seas – resulting in revolting beaches and in serious skin disease among inshore fishermen.

Leakage of methane and toxic wastes from former rubbish dumps comprised another hazard, compounded by excessive secrecy on the part of the authorities. And it was a firmly held public view that the Ministry of Agriculture, Fisheries and Food was very much more on the side of the producer than the consumer, who did not like the idea of lavish grants to Farmers to spread pesticides and nitrates, and to crowd animals and poultry together in dark, miserable, drugged conditions.

Nicholas Ridley, Secretary of State for the Environment, represented the traditional Tory view of these matters, making statements that were at odds with his leader's new theoretically radical approach, and declaring that as far as he was concerned, there was no crisis on the planet and that green people exhibited an attitude that was more religious than scientific. He was clearly not capable of demonstrating any serious commitment to the overall issue, either intellectually or temperamentally.

Margaret Thatcher herself, however, saw in the movement not only the possibility of electoral advantage, but a means of reducing the country's dependence on coal and hence of further weakening the National Union of Mineworkers. This apart, the subject had gripped her attention as a trained chemist – but the shift in values behind it still seemed to be far beyond her. She appeared not to have come to terms with the fact that it was unrestrained individual self-advancement and economic growth that were leading to the environment's destruction.

In this, moreover, she had provided a hostage to fortune. Either she would have to fudge the issue and concentrate merely on cosmetic measures such as the control of litter; or she would have to recognise and communicate the fact that green might be beautiful but it certainly was not going to be cheap – and that the consumer and/or the taxpayer would have to foot the bill. Coming from her, neither approach was likely to be popular. As stated, the jury is still out.

All these issues are more part of the natural stamping ground of the opposition than that of the government, but on peace and the environment, at least, she seemed to have established an ostensible lead, cynical and opportunistic though her approach may have been. If she had devised the perfect opposition from her own point of view, it would have been hard for her to come up with anything better than what she had already. The centre parties were absorbed with scoring points off each other and their combined poll ratings had slumped to some 10% less than at the general election by mid-1989. The Labour party possessed many attractive and gifted young front benchers, and in Neil Kinnock a leader who was performing more confidently, and fully understood the virtues of pragmatism and moderation embodied in the party's major policy review. But it was still lumbered with the hard constituency left and the leaden Tolpuddle TUC, forming an effective coalition against any real progress.

In summary, Margaret Thatcher had always sensed a burning mission to roll back the socialisation programme of the 1945 Labour government for good and all. Her mandate to do this rested on the thrice recorded approval of the electorate; nobody could say that what she did was without popular consent. A right wing Roundhead, she brilliantly managed to provide the individual elector with a sense of personal economic wellbeing, and her support among trade unionists and members of the skilled working class had grown steadily enough to melt Labour's power base away. The survivor working class was breaking up according to plan, with the most competent and determined among its ranks defecting to the belonger middle classes, leaving merely a demoralised rump in the dying heartlands of old-fashioned industry. Meanwhile the self-explorers and experimentalists, nature's floating voters, had picked up the Thatcherite message of autonomy, honesty, integrity, self-responsibility – and success.

Voters are generally selfish when it comes to the bottom line. The reality is that if in 1991 the average voter is still definitely better off and feels definitely better off, then regardless of other considerations the Conservative government will probably be re-elected. If not, then not, since in that case other considerations will also be weighed against it. As long as her policies are able to release a further surge of entrepreneurial and innovative talent, then the trickle down effect could come to benefit virtually everybody. On the other hand, if not, the divisions between the middle class and the residual underclass will grow so acute as seriously to threaten the very fabric of society.

Furthermore, she will also have to work creatively with the wider cultural changes whereby social responsibility and public service are once again becoming reputable values. She is a populist, and not only shares but personifies the values of a vast number of people; but she may well find herself out of tune with the new mood. If so, the public will sense it, and should she be simultaneously beset with other difficulties, she may lose her touch just at the time when Labour is getting some kind of a sensible act together. Thatcher's grip on the political crown could well become weaker, and she may end by being seen as a creature of the 80s (or that the 80s were a creature of herself), rather than of the 90s.

The Economic Outlook – Making Waves[3]

However, other challenges to her vision come from the world outside, and particularly from across the Atlantic. With all her money staked on stimulating growth and curbing inflation, should either fail to occur – for any reason – then her position would be hopelessly compromised. If the spectre of an American recession were to solidify into the shape of a world depression, with or without hyperinflation in the interim, she would be lucky to escape with her skin, as the outer directed surge finally collapsed.

Given this kind of a crash, she would probably crash with it however blameless – following the well known engineers' 'six stages of a project': enthusiasm; disillusionment; panic; search for the guilty; punishment of the innocent; reward of the uninvolved. . . . All the reservations of the caring self-explorers and experimentalists would come seething to the surface if the British economic miracle for some reason proved unsustainable.

Most people are familiar with the theory of the trade cycle in which economic bust follows economic boom, to be followed in turn by the development of yet another economic boom at the centre of which are the seeds of its own eventual destruction. Less familiar perhaps – and indeed unacceptable to many traditionalists – is the long wave economic cycle, first postulated by the Russian economist Kondratieff and subsequently modified by Elliott, Schumpeter, Cogan and Beckman among others. This also follows a predictable course but one that, because of its scale, is easier to see in retrospect than in advance.

Indeed, with hindsight it is possible to chart an elegant pattern in the rises and falls of socio-economic activity, stretching back to the very beginning of the industrial revolution. Nikolai Kondratieff believed that all economic activity moves in these long predictable waves, each of which lasts for something in the region of 57 years, more or less the maximum period of individual economic awareness, so that each person experiences each stage of the cycle at some time in his or her life.

The theory was published in the 1920s and ran counter to the Stalinist thinking of the time. Any conception that the capitalist world was expected to suffer an imminent crash was a popular one, but what was impossible for the Soviet authorities to swallow was the idea that this would eventually give way to a period of growing western prosperity. Poor Kondratieff was interned in solitary confinement in a labour camp, went mad and died. His theory that capitalism moved in predictable rhythmic cycles was deemed 'wrong and reactionary' and for many years his work was neglected. However, under the investigatory scholarship of such as Professor Peter Hall of Reading University, it has now resurfaced.

Kondratieff's view, as modified and extended since his death, perceives four great waves of economic activity each of which peaked in a froth of glory, to be followed by a savage depression, in the years 1816, 1873, 1929 and now maybe, God help us, 1987. The first wave encapsulated the industrial revolution itself. 57 years back from the peak year of 1816 was 1759, during which the Bridgewater canal was begun between Liverpool and Leeds, the threshing machine was invented, Wedgewood established his Staffordshire pottery works, the British Museum was opened and the first daily newspaper, *The Public Ledger*, was founded.

Months later Watt invented the condenser, the first step towards his steam engine, and Hargreaves the spinning jenny. This wave broke after the Napoleonic wars and was followed by collapse into the trough of the 'hungry forties'. During this period land in Hampshire fell in value by almost two hundredfold, for example. It was followed however by the upsurge of creative and innovative activity that marked the early second half of the 19th century – basically stemming from the Great Exhibition onwards.

The excesses of the late 1920s have been well chronicled but it is instructive to look at those of the late 1860s and early 1870s to see what was happening to the Cambridge University[4] yuppies of that period just before the crash. It was not until 1866 that the week of the boat races occasioned any social activity when the Trinity First Boat held a ball in a local hotel with '300 guests, numerous ladies and a handsome supper'. This was the first May Ball. In 1868 Charles Dickens sent his son to next door Trinity Hall, equipped with three dozen bottles of claret, three dozen of sherry, two dozen of port, three bottles of brandy and personal pocket money that equated in modern values to £6,000 per year.

By the 1870s things had become even more hectic. In 1874 Henry Latham, Master of Trinity Hall, expressed much concern about the new and remarkably expensive style of undergraduate life. He linked this with what he termed 'the general increase in the scale of living in the upper and middle ranks of society, the emphasis on enjoyment and amusement and the desire to consume animal food. At the present time', he went on, 'the general style of living in England is more luxurious than it has ever been, and children are brought up in habits which would formerly have been considered self indulgent. These habits tend to make young people easygoing in money matters and careful of personal comfort . . . the gaieties lately introduced in the Easter term have largely increased the expenditure of a considerable number of men.'

The crunch came when the second wave broke in the early 1870s, ushering in the economic depression of the century's end, as described by Trollope in his bitterly savage novel 'The Way We Live Now'. Things began to pick up again in the early 1900s but, following the war-induced armaments boom of the years from 1913 onwards, there came the most spectacular crash of all in 1929, which led to the Great Depression and lasted on and off till the next armaments boom prior to World War II.

It is not however so much war, as technological innovation which triggers off the upwave and releases us from penury every time around. Entrepreneurs flourish when there is a breaking up of traditional economic bonds and they can fish for opportunities in the muddied waters of confusion, revelling in being ahead of the game within the dynamics of change. It almost seems as if the cycle needs to impose a dark winter in order to stimulate this springtime of innovatory and entrepreneurial progress. As soon as a new breed of entrepreneurs starts to create the basis of the next technological wave, things begin to move. These innovative products are based on the bundling together of technologies, leading to a different industrial paradigm in which a swarm of new applications is introduced.

The first Kondratieff wave of the industrial revolution rode on the back of the technology of cotton, wool, wrought iron and steam power. After the 1820s crash, the building of the railways hauled the economy up to a new peak of prosperity. Then the 1870s and 1880s saw the application of electricity, telephones and motor cars. Between the wars came the first glimmerings of electronic innovation, talking films, TV, the earliest computers – and the jet engine. Communication of all types was the powerhouse of this phase in which the concept of the global village first surfaced.

[173]

The smart money is now on the myriad applications of the micro-processor to pull us out of trouble eventually, by harnessing information technology to miniaturise, quicken, cheapen and encourage lateral thinking in the transformation of existing products, methods, processes and occupations – not to mention the creation of a myriad new ones and the salvation of the earth itself. We are moving from the industrial tangibility of the blast furnace to the trans-industrial intangibility of inter-dependent information.

At the dawning of the new century, the new technological infrastruc-ture will emerge in parallel with this other whole philosophy – a totally different prevailing attitude of inner directedness and interdependence. The secret is that we are witnessing the phenomenon of two waves in phase with each other – Kondratieff's with its four peaks from the begin-ning of the industrial revolution and Maslow's which heralds the trans-industrial revolution as a new millennium, absolutely unique and unprecedented.

Kondratieff's theory, taken to its limit, would have the crash of '87 leading ultimately to the war of '97. But with an international climate which is month by month accelerating us away from the very idea of global war, we may find ourselves in the thick of a different kind of millennial war – a war against want, a war against fear, a war against misery and a war against all the excesses of the past that could culminate in the victorious peace of the future. If we collectively decide that is what we want to do, that is.

The Social Implications Of Economic Disruption

The birthpangs of this event may well be prolonged and unpleasant, if the Thatcherite dream of prosperous independence actually turns to night-mare. In the event of an international economic collapse, the resulting social upheavals are liable to be so intense that it is now vital for us to identify the issues clearly, and create a common fund of experience as a blueprint for the future. ·

We have to recognise that we may at any moment be engulfed by an economic blizzard. One morning we could wake up and find ourselves metaphorically snowed in with the electricity lines down and the tele-phone on the blink. When this happens in real life there are two ways of tackling it. The first is to fret, fume, curse and expend a lot of energy trying to get out of a situation which has wrecked our preconceived and important plans.

The second is to abandon any plans for the time being and concentrate on doing the smaller individual things that are suddenly more crucial – like clearing a path to the woodshed, listening to the radio for the latest information, checking up on the neighbours, venturing forth and stocking up with food in any way that presents itself, snowballing and toboganning with children, or curling up with one's partner in front of a blazing fire and listening to Mozart. Making the best of a bad job, in other words, going with the flow and helping other people out where we can; this will be the best answer if and when the roof falls in.

Faced with chaos we will have to accept it and share with others what we have each discovered are the best ways of tackling its implications. When established methods are clearly not working any more, individuals will have to become more individualised and less institutionalised. We will need to decolonise ourselves once it is clear that money, laws, morals, education and government can no longer be passed down to us by outmoded authority figures. We have abdicated our individual power for too long and have become dependent on institutions instead.

We thus need to go through a renaissance of true independence before we recognise the abiding necessity for human interdependence. In the face of this recognition, the underlying power of many institutions will crumble and individuals will be forced to act for themselves and for each other. We will learn that we can do nothing about our economic environment in the traditional sense, so we might as well enjoy ourselves in creating new perspectives that turn our problems into solutions. Amazingly, this is already happening in tiny grassroots initiatives all over the place, and some examples of the process will be described later. The individual blades of grass are forcing their way up through the cracks in the concrete. It will not be long before, instead of a desert, we have a meadow.

The path towards this millennium may possibly be smooth, or it may be about the roughest thing the human race has encountered since the Black Death. Because of the nature of current change, whatever the intervening years may hold for us it does seem from the evidence that ultimately the inner directed philosophy will prevail. What, however, of these intervening years? What of the valley that now separates us from the shining peaks of the future? There are three alternative routes across it and their maps are outlined in the chapter that follows. But before that let us look again for a moment at our starting point – Black Monday, October 19th 1987.

Black Monday[5]

JK Galbraith, author of 'The Great Crash, 1929' and an esteemed expert in these matters, has held the Reagan administration substantially responsible for what happened that day. First he blamed it for reducing taxes and thus increasing income, which jacked up the already alarming public budget deficit and transferred a good deal of speculative money into the hands of people who promptly put it into the stock market.

Secondly, Galbraith complained that its monetarist programme of the early 1980s had resulted in high interest rates, a dollar that was too strong on the world's exchange markets and a flood of subsidised imports – especially from Japan and other south-east Asian countries – which compounded the deteriorating situation by accelerating the American balance of payments deficit. The dollars the Japanese and others earned in the process were largely invested in American securities and thus became subject to a double uncertainty – that of the market and that of the dollar itself. As a consequence, both were seriously over-priced, and the whole world economy began to resemble a snake that was swallowing its own tail.

The Sunday Times economic commentator Brian Reading described the US and Japan as being like two drunks leaning against each other for support. The Americans had been spending too much; the Japanese had been saving too much, so the Japanese lent their excess savings to the Americans who obligingly spent them on Japanese goods. As long as both continued like this, all was well, but as soon as one sobered up the other was bound to fall flat on his face.

In an election year the American government was unwilling or unable to tackle the country's budget and trade deficits in any way that would have persuaded the rest of the world that it meant business. The crash might have been delayed if the Japanese and West German central banks had agreed to lower interest rates to stimulate their own economies. Instead they told the Americans in no uncertain terms that they weren't going to go on playing their silly game any more, and perversely raised their interest rates instead.

James Baker, Secretary to the Treasury, blandly informed the world that the dollar could be allowed to fall even further, and there was a rush to liquidate holdings. The biggest spender of them all, the borrower of last resort, the mighty United States, had run out of credit and would have to contract. In round figures, the 1987 US trade deficit was set to stand at $180 billion and the budget deficit at $160 billion.

And so to Black Monday itself. Described by Chairman of the New York Stock Exchange, John Phelan, as 'a financial melt-down', it saw the Dow Jones Index drop 22%, having already fallen 18% from its peak at the end of August. Buyers suddenly vanished and a rush of sale orders from institutions, speculators and computerised trading programmes were triggered off. As the Dow fell below the critical 2300 level, Wall Street's panic chased the sun from one stock market to another and reflected the brutal reality of 24-hour world markets and push-button world communications. As Sir Kit McMahon, Chairman of Midland Bank, put it 'they have let the genie out of the bottle and onto the VDU'.

The entire global village rapidly succumbed to the virus as markets in Paris, Frankfurt, Hong Kong, Sydney and Tokyo all collapsed and lay writhing. This was a pandemic, and the City of London was not immune. Everyone there had known that a Wall Street correction was long overdue, but nobody thought it would be quite as shattering as that. Every market was looking over its shoulder at the next, and though governments could take some action to stabilise their own national exchanges, no one could stop this universal vortex of deterioration.

At the time of the 1929 crash, US President Hoover stated that 'the fundamental business of the country is sound', a sentiment ominously echoed by all the western leaders in 1987. How precise this echo was to be no one could tell at the time. Was it possible to learn from the lessons of exactly 57 years before – to the very week?

In 1929 share prices on Wall Street had fallen an average of 40% in four weeks, though bouncing back by 15% immediately after the end of the first phase. After little change for the rest of the year, prices then recovered steadily until April 1930, by which time they had regained half their losses. Thereafter the chain of misfortune and default took hold, and prices did not bottom out until the middle of 1932 when they were just about 15% of their 1929 peak. In contrast, the early summer of 1988 had begun to show signs of a tentative recovery which gradually strengthened throughout the year and spilled over into 1989. Tokyo bounded ahead even more vigorously, reflecting the burst of confidence that suffused Japan – now unassailably the world's leading economic power. Markets everywhere responded; but how long could it last?

The 1929 crash had been preceded by a five or six year period of dazzling economic activity, underpinned by a social climate with remarkable similarities to our own. Speculation was omnipresent and there was also a substantial underground economy – fed by alcohol in the 1920s prohibition, and cocaine, heroin and soft drugs in the 1980s. In both periods there was also acute competitive pressure to appear to be doing very well, and to this end people acquired considerable debts. The engine for creating more apparent wealth was the stock market in 1929 and the housing mortgage and other credit markets in the 1980s. Remember how a notorious broom cupboard opposite Harrods was offered by estate agents for £35,000?

Both periods also saw a number of banking and fiduciary scandals. Unemployment was high at both times, even though union membership was declining. In each case there were strident cries for protectionism in the United States, particularly among farmers. Bad loans to South American countries were sold to unwitting investors as bonds in the 1920s and to unwitting banks in the 1970s and 1980s. There was the same polarisation of rich and poor. Both economies were in unbalanced and eccentric orbit, and the only real difference was that in 1987 people were unable to throw themselves out of the windows because of the double-glazing.

Most important of all was the level of personal debt which was growing far faster than real income. In the 1980s the drive to achieve short-term satisfaction was lowering the credit rating not only of the United States but of all Americans, and fuelled by their example, the individual debt levels of virtually everybody in the western world. There was much wailing and gnashing of teeth about the unbalanced federal budget and the US negative balance of payments, not to mention the profligacy of third world countries which had accepted tempting loans during the 1970s when the banks were desperately looking for a home for all those OPEC petrodollars. However, few people worried about their own individual debts, based on bank overdrafts and loans, credit cards, and above all house mortgages.

In the period between 1929 and 1933, due to falling prices, personal debts were left seriously uncovered by the value of their underlying assets – these fell overall by about 75% while actual debts declined only by 20%. In real terms debt had therefore not been reduced and a deflationary correction was inevitable. The 1980s had the same smell about them, even though to some it was not identifiable. Like The Bank for International Settlements which encapsulated the events of October 1987 in the masterly statement – 'there is a widespread feeling that lessons should be drawn, but it is not easy to see what those lessons are.' At present it seems all quiet on the Western Front, but one should watch.

The London Scene[6]

Meanwhile, in the City of London the October crash had initially been followed by an uneasy lull. Apart from being boosted by the international bull market, the place had had its own artificial build-up over the previous months. A year before, The Big Bang had launched a once-for-all period of deregulation and reconstruction. The traditional 'single capacity' arrangement, whereby stockjobbers and stockbrokers respectively made the markets and bought and sold on behalf of investors, was replaced by a 'dual capacity' system where anyone could do anything, as long as he had the money and had joined the club. Investment houses were allowed to make markets in securities, to buy and sell them for clients, and also to raise capital for industry, commerce and public bodies both British and foreign.

For years inefficient stockbrokers had hidden behind a cartel of fixed commissions, but this was also abolished and replaced by a market ruled by competitive pricing. In the wake of such radical reform the whole shape of the securities market was transformed by a stream of takeovers as the big British, European, American and Japanese financial organisations all jockeyed for position to snatch up the most talented investment operators.

The Stock Exchange, till then an exclusive belongers' freemasonry whose partnership structure made rapid expansion impossible, had been in danger from the powerful foreign financial institutions which were threatening to create their own stock market and bypass it completely. Only through enormous injections of outside capital would its firms be able to afford the necessary market risks, the highly sophisticated computer technology and the increasingly inflated salaries being offered to the sharpest market minds; only then could the City of London take its place alongside New York and Tokyo as the third leg in what was already becoming a 24-hour world securities market.

In the twelve months that followed, a series of financial scandals rocked New York, London and Hong Kong. It became apparent that of those two warring elements that comprise market sentiment, greed and fear, greed was now the prime mover. Still not satisfied by the awesome salaries that they could command, the bonuses that sometimes doubled them, the 'golden hellos' for highflyers poached from other firms and the loyalty increments for those who promised to stay on − on top of all this, more than a few decided that they could dispense with the rulebook. The conspicuous consumer and the outer directed experimentalist ruled the roost, and in a pretty arbitrary manner. As one weary belonger complained, 'it isn't like it used to be. Thank God I am retiring early next month. There'll be blood running in the gutters soon and I'd rather none of it was mine'.

How wise he was to get out in time. The mood was dangerously optimistic and the competition ruthless. Commissions were slashed for the big institutional bargains, which meant that private investors began to be fobbed off with a considerably diminished service — but the wave of privatisation issues continued to enrapture them as the government continued to flog off the family silver with unabated enthusiasm. There were a few Cassandras who pointed out, for example, that with no less than 27 market makers in gilt-edged government securities some of them must be losing money, but the scramble to recruit the best people and to maintain the top teams in any specialist field at any price went on.

Like the South Sea Bubble, the party couldn't last for ever. By August 1987 the consensus was that The Big Bang had been an overall success, but its related problems were becoming more evident. Two clearing banks had retired hurt from certain aspects of market making; brokers' back offices were awash with months of unsettled bargains; and the new computer technology was subject to breakdown at times of peak trading volume.

On the other hand electronic dealing had clearly won substantial support, and the floor of the Stock Exchange, where bargains had always been struck on a face-to-face basis, was virtually deserted except for the mice. Just as the market was congratulating itself on its robustness, however, came the first tremor, as news of a sharp rise in bank lending knocked share prices by 3% in a single day. It was as if the water levels had inexplicably fallen in all the wells, and suddenly the birds and animals became restless. Institutional investors began to pay attention to the rumbles, creaks and groans of a shuddering market.

A week after the Wall Street earthquake eventually occurred, 22% had been slashed off the value of quoted UK shares. In four weeks the slide had cost Barclays de Zoete Wedd over £50 million. A 15-year-old schoolboy ran up a £60,000 market loss unknown to either his broker or his parents, and a 23-year-old trainee accountant took the wooden spoon with personal debts of more than £1 million owed to the investment arm of the National Westminster Bank. A 24-year-old options dealer, hooked on a lethal cocktail of greed, fear and ego, was single-handedly responsible for a £3m loss for his employers, Smith New Court.

City operators, accustomed to the merry jingling of bonuses at Christmas, were soon listening to a very different tune. NatWest cut the salaries of its top investment managers – all earning over £150,000 – by a fifth. Market makers were not only losing money on their portfolios but the volume of equity trading had slumped month after month, and expensive people, offices and equipment were quite unable to earn their keep. A miasma of redundancy suddenly wreathed itself around the City dealers. Firms no longer asked themselves whether they were performing but whether they were surviving at all, and many of them withdrew from or cut down on parts of their operations. As share trading shrank month by month, fancy offices and fancy salaries became impossible to justify, and more and more found themselves on the street.

Some allowed themselves the luxury of a little watery optimism during the spring and early summer of 1988, as the British economy appeared on the face of it to hold out more promise than those of its competitors. But its relative health had also strengthened the pound, which had the effect of sucking in a flood of imports at the same time that it rendered British exporters less competitive. At the end of June, a record monthly balance of payments deficit of £1.2bn was announced. Chancellor Nigel Lawson allowed himself the use of only one weapon with which to stave off a sterling crisis, a step by step rise in interest rates to almost double their lowest levels in the summer of 1988. A year later, base rate stood at 14%, and seemed set to rise further.

There was much debate as to whether these savage measures would result in a soft or a hard landing for the economy. Certainly retail sales fell as planned, but both industrialists and houseowners with mortgages voiced bitter complaints. Month after month saw appalling trade figures, once reaching a record deficit of over £2 billion. The stock market took fright, but then decided in January 1989 that it would catch up with the ¬est of the world's regained optimism and staggered up to an FT 100 level of 2200 – from which, ominously, it staggered back again.

Brokers and market makers were still cutting costs and pulling out of unprofitable areas, as competitive price cutting meant that few firms were even covering their overheads, let alone making an adequate return on capital. Many old and respected names had disappeared completely. Sheer size had also lost its attraction, due to unwieldly structures, bitter internal rivalries and huge problems of information control. It was estimated that 12,000 people had been sacked out of a total of 250,000 whose salaries depended on the City's prosperity, and pessimists were talking about 30% of the City's workforce melting away over the next few years. The bear market was still alive.

There were several sound economic reasons for this, close to home, apart from the technical and political ones already mentioned –

* however brave the talk, UK inflation was on the rise already, and with falling unemployment, so were wage demands as well.

* at the same time, forecasts for growth were being adjusted downwards, reducing the chances of floating off any rocks we might .hit.

* the huge and burgeoning current account deficit, caused both by consistently high consumer spending on imports and by uncompetitive exports, was bound to mean ultimately higher interest rates if a sterling crisis was to be avoided.

* probable result – the entire credit balloon would explode, with appalling results for debtors, bankers, spenders, retailers, houseowners, and all who depended on them.

* so the likely denouement was thus a relapse into stop-go policies and/or that unlovely state known as stagflation – high inflation plus low growth – resulting in a stock market collapse.

Stop The World

But there were other and larger factors in the equation.

An eerie calm suffused the world in mid-1989. Politically, the most remarkable thing about it was the universal realisation that after over 40 years, the Cold War was finally melting away. The common need for fuller, happier and safer lives, the common recognition of a shared humanity, had suddenly flipped a switch and bathed the ordinary people of both East and West in a common light. In practical terms, almost everything else needed to be done, but the vision itself was there.

Environmentally, the same applied. People everywhere began to perceive the effects of their collective behaviour, and the desperate danger we were imposing on ourselves and future generations, not to mention all the other forms of life with which we shared the planet. Toxic waste ships, seal slaughter, whales trapped in the ice, the rape of the Amazon rainforests, serious public alarm about the content of the food we eat and the water we drink, and above all the clinical scientific data of the diminishing ozone layer and the greenhouse effect – all these combined to fuse together into a critical mass of world opinion that could no longer be ignored.

Time Magazine[7] made 'Our Endangered Earth' the 'planet of the year' in its first issue of 1989. In Britain, according to a MORI poll, those registering unprompted concern about the environment as an important national issue jumped from 9% in November 1988 to 22%, third highest of all issues, in February 1989. Vision, yes – actual solutions, not a lot as yet. Those who held the purse-strings mouthed a few platitudes but were not especially inclined to practical remedies. For a start, the possible switch of resources from outdated nuclear capability to blindingly essential help for the Third World and the ecosystem of the planet was quite beyond their imaginations.

Economically, however, there was not even a world vision; just the same old mixture of self-interested greed and fear. After the shattering experience of Black Monday and the months that followed, the global economy had gradually recovered its nerve. Whether it had any right to do so was another matter. Because apart from the little local difficulties that were beginning to affect the British economy, there were four salient features of the world scene that gave reason for extreme concern – economic imbalance in the US, political and stock market imbalance in Japan, the rebirth of international protectionism and the maturity of international debt.

President Bush[8] had painted himself into a corner during the 1988 election campaign by repeatedly pledging that he would neither raise taxes nor cut major weapons programmes, and nobody in the US quite understood the implications of a 'flexible freeze' on spending as a means of squaring the economic circle. Nobody seemed to care much at the time, either. Life and liberty could be taken for granted and America seemed hell-bent on the pursuit of happiness, as Mr Bush's unofficial campaign theme, 'Don't Worry, Be Happy!' won the Grammy award for best song. As *Newsweek* magazine commented, 'America is getting a little too cheerful for its own good'.

However, the voters' opinions of Bush were lightly held and unlike the outgoing President, he did not have a solid ideological foundation of support. His rambling press conferences, his initial inability to put an administration together, his manifest lack of world stature compared to the brilliantly charismatic Gorbachev,[9] his apparently reactive rather than proactive style, all led commentators to draw unkind comparisons with Jimmy Carter. Frittering away his most exclusive asset of presidential prestige, he was described as having 'hit the ground crawling' in the early days of his presidency.

Meanwhile, JK Galbraith's pre-crash analysis, summarised in the previous section, still held good. The fever might have temporarily broken, but the underlying symptoms of the disease were quite evident. Inflamed budget and trade deficits, a flaccid dollar, rising inflation and interest rates, swollen corporate and personal debt (the former associated with a rash of highly contagious 'leveraged buy-outs'), and gangrene apparent in nearly one third of the nation's savings-and-loan associations had together induced a sense of mild delirium in the patient. The last thing it needed was to be under a doctor who didn't know what he was doing.

Meanwhile, by the spring of 1989, the Japanese[10] stock market was, appropriately, suffering from a sort of tulip-mania. Economic miracle or no economic miracle, it seemed astounding, almost irrational for the Nikkei Index to stand at 34,000, having moved up from a mere 6000 in 1980. In the aggregate, the companies that made up the index were selling at over 60 times their reported earnings, compared to equivalent ratios of 15 and 11 for American and British securities respectively. Admittedly, after October 1987, Japan had taken over the leadership of the world economy from the US, and now stood as creditor nation to the entire world, besides being far and away its most successful in terms of productivity and growth. But at the time of writing the degree of imbalance is so ostentatious, the hubris so unthinking and the defiance of gravity so gross, that one shudders in anticipation of the inevitable correction.

One possible crack in the edifice could be the market behaviour of Nippon Telegraph and Telephone, the giant of the Tokyo stock exchange, worth more than half the gross national product of Switzerland, and with shares priced around £7,000 each. Scandal surrounded the colossus due to suspected bribe-taking by the former chairman and another director from The Recruit Co, an employment agency and financial conglomerate which also rocked the political scene with its indiscriminate handouts. Three cabinet ministers and two senior civil servants had been forced to resign, the previous prime minister was under investigation and the current one, Noboru Takeshita, was deeply implicated. Opinion poll support collapsed to 5%, and finally unable to govern, he resigned also.

Between the three power blocks of Japan, America and the EEC, there was a real danger of a steady increase in protectionism, moreover President Bush, though a free trader at heart, was vulnerable to considerable pressure from a Democrat congress to go along with protectionist legislation in return for their supporting his efforts to reduce the budget deficit.

Japan-bashing was acquiring the status of a national sport, at the same time as American consumers kept right on buying Japanese goods.

Two out of three Americans surveyed wanted their government to curtail Japanese investment in American companies and property. An element of hurt pride was involved here, but there was also a widespread feeling that Japan was prospering by exploiting the vast and relatively open US market, while at the same time keeping its own markets closed to American goods. US farming products were systematically excluded, and other goods often arbitrarily classified by Japanese customs officials into categories that were ineligible for import licences. Domestic calls for retaliation were getting louder.

If the EEC were to adopt a fortress posture and construct trade barriers to keep out American goods after 1992, looking possibly into Eastern Europe rather than to the United States as its most important economic partner, the nail in the coffin of world trade would be dealt another hammer-blow. Seeing the danger, the US administration sounded warnings to this effect, but it is as yet too early to determine whether or not they will be heeded. In the immediate short term, however, concern is less about a trade war, as about an interest rate war, with inflation edging upwards particularly in the US and the UK. This has profound implications for the developed world, but horrendous ones for those countries saddled with virtually irredeemable debt.

According to the World Bank, Third World debt stood at $1,300 billion at the end of 1988, 70% of which had been lent by the ordinary banking system. One third of the total was owed by Latin American countries, which over the 80s had suffered from plunging terms of trade, sluggish economies, rising urban crime, social and political discontent, rocketing populations, lost opportunities and dashed hopes. The strategy of solving the problem through growth had not worked.

South America's politicians, both in and out of office, told the US that they could not afford to meet their existing obligations. The Baker Plan, offering debtors new loans and easier terms in return for financial rectitude on the part of the sovereign states, was dismissed out of hand by them as being far too onerous. Debt forgiveness or even debt reduction was dismissed out of hand by the creditor nations as being far too lax. The emperor's clothes were becoming increasingly transparent.

Where Do We Go from Here?

So was Monday October 19th the dress rehearsal for the end of the world, or an isolated aberration? This is the absolute question at the time of writing, with the answer still hidden in the future. As it appears at the time, and as described in the following chapter, there are three possible paths we can now follow in the immediate years to come; or more probably meander from one to another, progressing bumpily along a combination of all three. However, two facts seem clear.

The first is that we have not a lot of choice as to which route we start out on – this will much depend on the economic climate that prevails – recessionary, expansionary, or moderated. The second is that however tortuous the journey, we do have a lot of choice as to our final destination in the early years of the next millennium. It is within our capabilities to choose a future which, though primarily inner directed, also contains the positive elements of the sustenance driven and the outer directed, the agrarian and the industrial cultures, the earth and the intellect.

The short term, however, is much trickier. No one who watches the financial and economic gurus with even half an eye could possibly imagine that they have got it right yet. At some time or other in the reasonably near future the wheel will turn and a recession will confront us – whether deep or shallow, sooner or later no one knows, though the writer's bet is on the deep and soon variety. This will be the moment of complete change.

There is as yet little genuine sense of interdependence among the great and the good in their self-important international world, compared to what seems to be quietly happening on the micro-level. But human institutions, like human beings, tend to change only when forced by pain to do so – when the pain of carrying on, inappropriately, in the same way they have always done is greater and more frightening than the pain of changing their habits. We are therefore likely to need a collective kick in the teeth before we voluntarily abandon our old industrial age attitudes and replace them with trans-industrial ones. Any psychotherapist would confirm that. One hesitates to chill the blood, but it could take a combination of economic collapse and resultant social collapse to bring us all to our senses.

The self-destructive elements that could combine to scupper us are formidable. But HG Wells described life as a race between education and catastrophe, and our present need is for a true process of education to reveal the possibilities and alternatives open to us. Fortunately, all over the world, but especially in this country, there are small and localised experiments being carried out to establish new principles and fashion new tools with which to create this new and more holistic society – in education, in health, in art, in work and business and in human relationships. It is all there for the taking.

The last chapters will embody some of this theory and practice – physical, philosophical, psychological, managerial and economic – that is now being built up as the foundation of a demonstrably new order of thought. The final one gives specific examples of the role models who are now working on its blueprints, and demonstrates the principles behind their efforts.

But first – our three possible futures.

11

THREE SCENARIOS FOR THE FUTURE

Why Alternative Scenarios?

Forecasters have never enjoyed a very good press. Joseph was one of the most successful in biblical times, but even he revealed a flair for alienating his public in the early days of his career. Some seers and prophets met a sticky end because they bore good tidings and got it wrong, and others because they bore bad tidings and got it right. Indeed it is recognised by futurists that the telling of bad tidings automatically loses 70% of one's audience, who are followed hot on their heels by the other 30% when the tidings come true. No wonder then that it was the custom of the ancients from Pythia to Paracelsus to wrap up their prophecies so that they could be interpreted at the whim of the recipient, a practice not only enshrined in ancient custom but still devotedly followed by economic forecasters today.

Pursuing the biblical theme, however, when the writer complained to a colleague that forecasting was as uncomfortable as being an Old Testament prophet but without the luxury of being able to call down fire and brimstone on the unbeliever, he received the retort 'It's worse than that. We are more like New Testament prophets – us they crucify'. Because forecasting implies the recognition of potential change it goes right against the establishment grain and the orthodox in every sphere. Many Christian fundamentalists hold that the future is something it is better to know nothing about, the Roman Catholic church is certainly not too keen on the crystal ball department in any shape or form, and the Holy Koran abjures the reader that he who foretells the future is a liar even if he proves to be right in the end.

In this matter the average person does not go quite as far as the average Ayatollah, but nevertheless reserves a healthy scepticism for those who claim to be able to forecast what is going to happen with any degree of accuracy. In 1972, when the writer was interviewing economist and ex-ambassador Peter Jay on a futures project, his classic opening put-down was, 'to look at the future, you can either take the present and extrapolate it rigorously, in which case you get rigorous nonsense; or you can make a great leap in the imagination, in which case you get imaginative nonsense . . .'

When examining the future and its possibilities, a more respectable approach is therefore necessary in order to assess the current situation and its emerging trends as closely as possible. The best way to do this is to try and gauge the impact of these trends, both patent and latent, upon each other in the form of a range of alternative scenarios. The time between creation and publication is an uneasy one for the futurist writer, since some extraneous event, some unexpected discontinuity like a Martian invasion, may blunder into his carefully circumscribed scheme of things and make a mockery of all his forecasts. The scenario method also has the added advantage of making possible an each-way bet and narrowing the overall odds.

What are scenarios? Basically they are devices for ordering one's perception about a range of possible operating environments in which individual decisions can be played out. What they are not is predictive; they illuminate rather than reduce risk. In a business sense they are used for setting corporate objectives in the planning process; for individuals they represent a series of alternative possibilities, some of which will be more advantageous and some less.

Provided with these varied visions of the future, it is up to the individual or the institution to choose the most attractive permutation and then to strive mightily to bring it about, at the same time hedging the bet with a range of fall-back contingency plans. If enough people agree, the futurist could then be in the pig-in-clover self-fulfilling prophecy business.

There is always an essential artistic relationship between creation and interpretation. In music, in theatre, this is the chronological order in which it occurs. But when it comes to the future, the process is reversed – interpretation does not follow creation, it must precede it. It is only by interpreting the present correctly that one can ride change as it gallops along and steer it to reach the palace of the desirable future at the end of the journey.

However, the interpretation of the present first requires the correct interpretation of the past, in which the lens of history has filtered out the extraneous, focusing only its appropriate wavebands to illuminate the here and now. When looking at the future, the what-next is thus always subject to the why. The answer to the why is only visible when this special lens is used to examine the roots of the past and the germinating seeds of the present.

The approach evaluates risks, clarifies the rules of the game, and anticipates key moments of change and major leverage points at which the informed individual and the informed organisation can make his, her or its presence felt. It identifies trade-offs between narrow short-term needs and broader long-term goals, in other words it helps people to look at the future in the capacity of an informed gambler.

The cast of mind required is one that is happy to work on a 'what if' basis, in rewriting history or biology, say. For example, what would Europe be like today if Napoleon had won the Battle of Waterloo? What would the United States be like today if the South had won the Civil War? What would a rabbit or a buttercup be like today if they had evolved under conditions of half-gravity, a mean temperature of 50°C, an average rainfall of 100 inches a year and a prevailing wind of 50mph?

To arrive at a credible picture which is neither over-rigorous nor over-imaginative and contains as little nonsense as possible, the scenario approach is best. One can tackle it in various ways, alone or in combination. One is to construct a computer model or a dust-dry series of projected statistical features such as demographic profiles, crime and housing figures and the like. Another is to take an imaginary group of people and project their lives onto the screen of one's creativity, given various different sets of environmental circumstances. A third – the method that has been chosen here – is by the use of imaginary future headlines.

For long enough, economists and technologists have insisted that the most important trends, the prime movers of the future, were bound to be products of their respective fields of economics and technology. The effective counter to this is that we have for too long been obsessed with figures and measurements and they have been found wanting. Quantity is after all only one of the qualities, and the expert in the white coat is all too frequently confounded by pure human cussedness. Our whole society is undergoing this millennial period of unprecedented change, and it is under the stress of this that social factors may well backfire and perversely turn out in the long run to be more influential than economic, political, or even technological ones, confounding the out of date experts.

Holding this view, Taylor Nelson/Applied Futures have adopted the alternative scenario approach. Working for the National Economic Development Office on the official publication 'IT Futures . . . It Can Work' they created three distinct models of the future, which we can conveniently label 'Retrenchment', 'Assertive Materialism' and 'Caring Autonomy'. In each of these one of our three core philosophies predominates, respectively sustenance driven, outer directed and inner directed; or agrarian, industrial and trans-industrial, if you prefer.[1]

However, the likelihood is that reality will unfold for us as a mixture of all three, oscillating between them and maintaining components of each instead of extrapolating neatly in a straight line in any given direction. The scenarios must therefore be regarded as artificially pure, but they do reveal a vivid picture of what various aspects of life could be like in part. The research suggests that whichever is the short term alternative, both the inner and outer directed groups will probably show overall growth at the expense of the sustenance driven in the early years of the next century, even though there could well be a serious reversal en route.

This is likely to produce a period of short term turbulence, as the sustenance driven group feels increasingly threatened and one of the other two takes off to become the predominant force in society, ushering in either the Caring Autonomy or the Assertive Materialism scenario. It is quite possible, however, that in an intervening period of Retrenchment, sustenance driven values will reassert themselves more than just temporarily. The main determinant here will be the political and economic climate in which the world in general and the UK in particular then finds itself.

However, by the year 2020, inner directed attitudes are likely to have predominated, while outer directeds will be seeking esteem by exhibiting these values and positively vying with each other as to the extent of their fashionable inner directedness. The reasoning behind this view relies much on the fact that not only is there in any case a recognisable social shift in this direction, but that information technology will eventually make possible the combination of autonomy and interconnectedness – the dream of the inner directed – no matter what outside economic forces prevail.

Table 3 shows the 1987 and forecast percentages of the three major groups in the UK – as reflecting all the foregoing arguments and given the conditions of the three alternative scenarios. It signifies that, whatever the circumstances, by the year 2020 the inner directeds will be the country's largest group; and it is worth re-emphasising here that this trend is currently growing more exuberantly in the UK than anywhere in the world outside the Netherlands, Scandinavia and the West Coast of the USA. Remember, too, that the ebb and flow between outer directed and sustenance driven is highly susceptible to outside economic conditions, whereas the constant recruitment to the ranks of the inner directeds is slower but relentless.

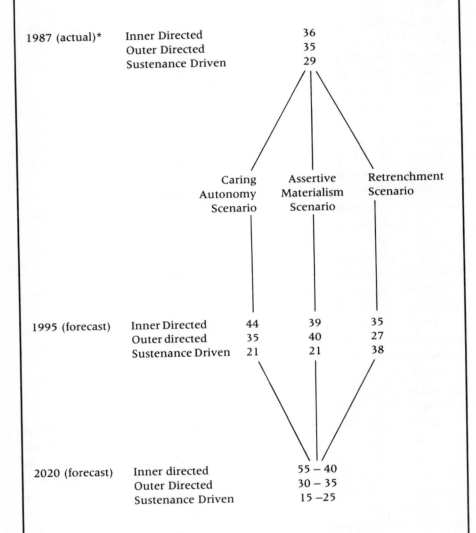

TABLE 3. PERCENTAGES OF SOCIAL GROUPINGS UNDER THREE ALTERNATIVE SCENARIOS

1987 (actual)*	Inner Directed	36
	Outer Directed	35
	Sustenance Driven	29

	Caring Autonomy Scenario	Assertive Materialism Scenario	Retrenchment Scenario
1995 (forecast)			
Inner Directed	44	39	35
Outer directed	35	40	27
Sustenance Driven	21	21	38

2020 (forecast)	Inner directed	55 – 40
	Outer Directed	30 – 35
	Sustenance Driven	15 –25

*The 1988 survey was never carried out, as the Applied Futures management buy-out was taking place at the time; the 1989 survey, by NOP Limited, occurred too late for its results to be included here.

The Retrenchment Scenario

Kondratieff may or may not be on the button but if he is, then in the immortal words of Bette Davies, 'Fasten your seatbelts, everybody – it's going to be a bumpy night'. In this event, the bear market continues its progress of deep downturns interspersed with shallow upturns. This will eventuate into an American-led or Japan-led recession which will ultimately be so severe that even in the short term it leads to a sickening collapse in the other industrialised countries of the west and almost more importantly, to an even steeper slump in commodity prices.

This has its most damaging effect on the Third World producer countries that rely on them for the servicing of their colossal overhang of international debt. In the past their defaults or potential defaults have been countered by what is politely termed 'rescheduling'. This process entails the rolling up of interest which is added to the capital sums outstanding, and combined with the lending of additional money in order to afford the new and larger payments. When you boil this down, it has amounted to a hope that continued inflation would mean that neither banks nor governments would have to write off these debts. With the old loans being paid in new money, equal in nominal terms but considerably less in real terms, the emperor's clothes might still be thought to keep him sufficiently decent.

However, this concept has always relied on the ability and willingness of lender governments, lender banks and global lenders of last resort like the World Bank and the International Monetary Fund to play along with the fabrication. But if suddenly they themselves are subjected to a squeeze so that they need the money back – at the same time as the ultimate provider, the United States, is bust both internally and externally – we are all in considerable trouble.

The international currency crash that could follow the recognition of this reality would leave 1929 et seq. looking like a parachute drop as compared to a free-fall. It would usher in a period of intense depression during which greedy outer directed values would be at a serious discount and where the call would be for revenge against all those who had contributed to this disaster or might conceivably have benefited from it. Sustenance driven values would pertain, for a while at any rate, and the price of turnips would be a more significant news item than the level of the FT All Share Index.

Under such conditions the whole economic and social climate reverts to the dire characteristics of the sustenance driven philosophy, as more and more outer directeds abandon the competitive struggle and slink into their ranks – both these groups being of course more influenced in their behaviour by outside economic circumstances than are the inner directeds. In this scenario, there are loud wails for Daddy. Absolutely any Daddy, as long as he can persuade enough people that He Knows Best. Hence a greater reliance on large organisations, both public and private, which project an image of stability and security. But here, given the overwhelming sense of economic drabness and panic, the collectivist approach is favoured, particularly in the shape of multinational or state-owned nationalised enterprises.

The intent of the majority is to keep their heads down till the trouble blows over, while the powers that be sort out the mess, any way they want. Though at each other's throats, the establishment at the top and the masses at the bottom are both averse to change, and traditional or authoritarian remedies are at a heavy premium over liberal and imaginative solutions. Threatening or unusual messages of any kind incite sudden and violent unrest. It is a world that combines the worst aspects of *1984*, *Rollerball*, and *A Clockwork Orange*. Belongers, Survivors and Aimless rule the roost.

These conditions could become too acute for any of the traditional political parties to provide effective leadership, so an authoritarian, either extreme left or right wing, regime might well result. A new government of this sort could well start by instituting measures to protect the public from the violence of the young unemployed. As these measures intensify, the regime becomes more despotic and adopts an increasingly nationalistic and protectionist posture. Appeals to tradition, duty, sacrifice and service abound. This scenario would of course be facilitated by the emergence of a charismatic leader.

As regards work and employment, in some sectors there would be an increase in trade union influence and muscle, with a strong token belief in the 'right to work' which it is up to society or the state to fulfil. But, in its turn, management is bureaucratic, hierarchical, authoritarian and rigid. Unemployment is widespread and scores of applicants fight for every job in Haywards Heath. Because the majority still aspires to unfulfilled material consumption, people are highly susceptible to a feeling of rejection if unemployed, but a generally strong commitment to the status quo ante and the family/community ethos make it difficult for them to flush out alternative employment opportunities.

So, these are the circumstances brought about by a monumental stock market and international currency crash followed by an agonising depression. Virtually no-one is free from it and almost everyone is on the floor. Those who have conserved their resources by judicious manipulation are still at the mercy of the vast army of have-nots who unrestrainedly harass them, steal from them, defraud them and even threaten them with bodily violence. Regarded as parasites, they are mercilessly parasitised.

Many inner directeds accept this whole situation as a passing phase which may affect them temporarily but has no permanent result on their overall philosophy. A few outer directeds are still twisting and flailing about to avoid the inevitability of a sickening drop in their standard of living; the majority of people have by now accepted the sustenance driven philosophy and see circumstances as wholly depressing and malevolent. Toads under the harrow, they sit and quiver, waiting for the final squelch. These are the things they will be reading about in the papers.

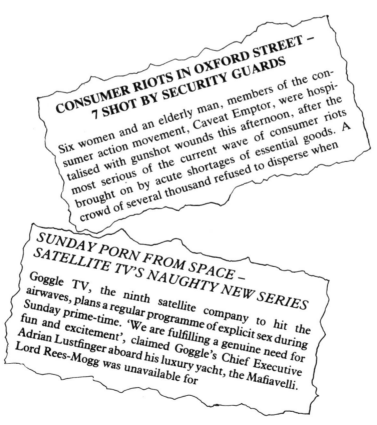

CONSUMER RIOTS IN OXFORD STREET – 7 SHOT BY SECURITY GUARDS

Six women and an elderly man, members of the consumer action movement, Caveat Emptor, were hospitalised with gunshot wounds this afternoon, after the most serious of the current wave of consumer riots brought on by acute shortages of essential goods. A crowd of several thousand refused to disperse when

SUNDAY PORN FROM SPACE – SATELLITE TV'S NAUGHTY NEW SERIES

Goggle TV, the ninth satellite company to hit the airwaves, plans a regular programme of explicit sex during Sunday prime-time. 'We are fulfilling a genuine need for fun and excitement', claimed Goggle's Chief Executive Adrian Lustfinger aboard his luxury yacht, the Mafiavelli. Lord Rees-Mogg was unavailable for

NHS COLLAPSE – 5 YEAR WAIT FOR HERNIAS

Sir Harry Half-Staggers, President of the Patients Association, has called upon the Department of Health to alleviate the suffering of those in the ever-lengthening queues for treatment. Hip operations, hernias, cataracts, and other

CRACK RING CRACKED – TOP BANKER IN MAYFAIR DRUGS PROBE

Saturnine playboy and financial mogul, Carlos Paragon, refused to comment on rumours that his affairs are under investigation by Drug Squad officers and that his South Audley Street penthouse contains a fully equipped chemical labora-tory. Meanwhile, in a midnight swoop, houses in Worthing, Cheltenham and Harrogate were raided and samples of substances taken away

ELEVEN WAYS OF COOKING TURNIPS

The humble root, when treated with imagination and resource, can be orchestrated to tempt even the most demanding palate. Turnips à la mode d'Orléans are by no means, as has been rumoured, St Joan's final revenge against the English. Prepare a marinade of vinegar, garlic, white pepper, black pepper, red pepper, and tabasco

RATS INVADE WHITEHALL

The collapse of the main sewer under Parliament Square has thrown the process of government into confusion as hundreds of rats, released from the confines of their environment, seethed upwards into offices, terrified typists and bit clerical staff.

WIN A MILLION ON TELEPHONE BINGO!

Cuddly Daisy Glovetrot never guessed she would end up . . . a millionairess! But our Telephone Bingo made her wildest dreams come true. 'It was all a bit of a lark, really', she laughed. 'Wayne, my boyfriend, kept on at me to have a go with him for months. In the end I said yes, so now we can buy the video recorder we've always wanted, and take a luxury holiday for two in Torremolinos. Hasta la pasta, that's what I say'.

WOKING'S CARDBOARD CITY

Homelessness, the scourge of the 90's, is making itself evident in some surprising locations. Woking's main shopping precinct is now home for 38 freebies taking advantage of the warm summer nights to occupy a remarkable variety of cardboard boxes there. Police are carefully keeping a low profile. 'These people have no alternative,' admits Chief Superintendent Harvey Third. 'It would be quite wrong to

"WE'VE NEVER HAD IT SO BAD"

The Opposition mounted a concerted attack on the Government's economic strategy, adapting the MacMillan motto of the 60's to today's crisis conditions. As the world's major economies founder, the UK's political climate is hotting up. Commenting

ONE IN FOUR JOBLESS – COMPUTER REVOLUTION BLAMED

Mr Amrit Patel, Shadow Employment Secretary, has hit out at the substitution of the microchip for the man at the workbench. On the day that the seasonally adjusted unemployment figure soared to over 6,700,000, senior trade unionists and politicians are getting together to re-plan Britain's future. About time, too, says some. Certainly in Hayward's Heath, things have never been like this.

PETROL COUPON LORRY HIJACK

An armed securi-van, carrying two months supply of petrol coupons to Aberdeen, was held up at gun-point yesterday on the hard shoulder of the M1 near Rugby. The five members of the gang got away with a haul having an estimated black-market value of £1¾ million. In an appeal to the public, Inspector Jim Boloney

SCUM-BASHERS EXPEL DOCKLANDS TRENDIES

Scum-Bashers, the working-class malcontent group, is bent on making life increasingly undesirable for the rich and rare of Dockland's Yuppieville. Architect-designed res's are the targets of these antis who exhibit a militant tendency to plaster them with aerosol graffitti, superglue and 'Human Liberation' stickers. Now, the beleaguered well-heeled are beginning to fight back, but almost too late. Samantha Thoroughgood-Jolly, a resident since 1987, has

The Assertive Materialism Scenario

An aggressively materialistic stance is the flavour of the month here, as long as the economic clouds somehow roll by and the world in general and Britain in particular turn out to be on the threshold of a prolonged period of Thatcherite growth, underpinned by the view that science and technology have finally delivered all the answers.

In the sagacious James Robertson's[2] phraseology, this is a HE (Hyper-Expansionary) world, as compared to the SHE (Sane, Humane and Ecological) alternative depicted next in the Caring Autonomy scenario. In this event, Margaret Thatcher's experiment will have succeeded in doing all that she hopes for it, setting us all up for a continuing period of increased material prosperity. This would be based on a fundamentally sound British industry which will have used the past few years to shake out manpower, improve its finances and galvanise its management into a mood which is assertive and wedded to the concepts of excellence, hard work and results.

This scenario constitutes the final flowering of the outer directed, competitive industrial revolution ethos, where Britain is one more great due to a return to the values that originally earned it that adjective. Selfish they may call it, but what the hell − nice guys always lose. The thrust is towards the full rich life, with an emphasis on living for today and escaping from any whisper of an unpleasant reality of social and global problems. The dynamic is derived from the paramount importance of economic concerns. People group together to beat any threat of an economic crisis by the old-fashioned means of grind, efficiency and productivity.

They believe that economic growth will solve all problems, yet some also use work as a means of avoiding the personal and societal problems they cannot face. The key words are prestige, status, power and success. Large, successful multinational organisations and strong central governments are applauded for their efforts to develop the economy. Duty is accepted as a norm; people ache to be respected, to be successful and (to appear to be) well off.

They are therefore concerned with appearance, fashion and technology. In a sense they hark back to the good old days of economic growth in the 60s. They also have never had it so good, even though times have moved on, and with them the status symbols, needs, attitudes and beliefs now current. Society backs traditional organisations, institutions and methods of operation, believing in hierarchies and well proven rigid command structures.

[199]

People accept change, as long as it brings growth in its train and is gradual, controlled and orderly. Economic concerns provide the means for improved efficiency and greater competitiveness between organisations. Social and environmental problems are ignored and single-issue groups encounter stiff opposition. Authorities are required to provide greater protection for individuals and properties, and policing is intensified.

Organisations grow to even greater size, sometimes organically but more often by merger, until a small number of them dominate the world economy. The outer directeds who call the shots are organisation men who seek the status and rewards which these large prestigious enterprises can provide. They tend to favour mammoth, privately-owned economic enterprises, but many also have a burning wish to start their own businesses.

However for most of them the motivation is to make money and to show they have made it, unlike the inner directed entrepreneur whose motivation is to create something valuable and fulfil a personal vision. The outer directed woman is the power behind the throne, supporting her man in every activity to boost his success and basking as the eye-catching status symbol on whom he showers his material achievement.

Within organisations the marketing, sales and financial functions become even more influential. Work has two purposes here; to enhance position as an indication of status, and to produce income to support the outer directed lifestyle. People look for the 'right sort of job' at a good salary. Employees stay in rewarding jobs if the pay is good enough but more commonly seek advancement for themselves in both aspects. There is a close relationship between contribution and responsibility on the one hand and salary on the other, so that people are prepared to work exceptionally hard to enhance their own qualifications in order to get ahead. Unemployment has by now been markedly reduced by the high level of economic activity, but not for those with the wrong skills or who live in the wrong geographical location. This is how it feels.

IBM LAUNCHES BRAIN – LINKED COMPUTER

Real and artificial intelligence have been harnessed together in a commercial product for the first time. IBM's Polymath 2001 electronically matches the beta waves of the user's brain, making direct contact between thought process and floppy disc.

CBI CHIEF SLAMS GREEN WALLIES

Industrial leader Sir Jasper Thunderblast used the CBI conference platform to mount a blistering attack on 'limp environmentalists' who are trying to hold back progress. 'People want jobs; people want money; people want success. The natterjack toad and the lesser spotted woodpecker come pretty low down on their list of priorities.'

GLAMOUR GRANNIES ON THE PILL

Yesterday's little old lady is more likely to be tomorrow's model girl, thanks to the youth-restoring effects of new wonder drug, PDQ. Para-dichloro-quinine, extracted from the bark of the silver eucalyptus by Nobel Prizewinner Prof. Nostrodamus van Tromp,

MIRACLE BOOM SURGES ON

Treasury figures released today show that after four years of unchecked economic growth, there is still plenty of steam left in Great Britain plc. Discounting the effects of inflation, in real terms output last year leaped a massive 7.1%, while exports hit a record high at

TOP OF THE FORM FOR CUTH'S

St Cuthbert's Primary School, Chelmsford is the country's best – and that's official. Announcing the winners in the National Examination Finals, Education Secretary Lavinia Nutt praised the keenness and dedication of both pupils and staff. 'Winning is about beating failure', she insisted,

IDENTITY CARD SCHEME MOOTED

Plans for a National Identity Card system are to be set out in a Government Green Paper due for publication next month. The recent inner city crime wave has alarmed ministers, who are also under pressure from Brussels to bring British practice into line with her Common Market partners. Scotland Yard's Chief Commissioner Bernard Lash welcomed the news. 'Only those who have something to hide have anything to fear', he told

SKIN IS IN!

Flash the flesh – that's today's fashion must. Gaps, flaps and panels show a peep of thigh here, a glimpse of shoulder there, a revealing cleft, an uncompromising curve. Daring skin paints and glitters are essential, the dazzlier the better, if you are going to feel at your most alluring.

TAX-EFFICIENCY: TOP PRIORITY

Nowadays so many people are making so much money that there is a natural desire to hang on to what they have earned by the sweat of the brow. At a well-attended conference in Douglas, Isle of Man, delegates heard about the numerous new ways one can avoid, perfectly legally, having to fork out

STRESS – THE PRICE TO BE PAID

Leading cardiologists are concerned about the ever-growing numbers of heart attack victims in our competitive society. Luxury lifestyles, long hours, and high performance demands are taking their toll of those at the top. But increasingly the economic explosion is detonating people up and down the whole social scale. Norman, 49, a clerk in an insurance

JUDGE SUES SCANDAL-SHEET

'Show-Off', the celebrity magazine, is at the centre of a new row over the power game currently being played out within the legal profession. Lord Justice Munge, hot tip for the top job of Master of the Rolls, has filed a libel writ against

SELF-STARTERS FOR SELF-STARTERS

Entrepreneurship is no longer just confined to business. It is now a force to be reckoned with in the dining-room, too. Guests are getting more and more carried away with the idea of doing-it-themselves. Of course, crudité dips and fondues have been around for years, but with the new range of individual battery-driven microwaves from Kamakaze, so many more dishes can be precisely engineered to suit everyone's personal taste. Wild Boar with Palm Hearts and Calvados is always a favorite

The Caring Autonomy Scenario

This scenario is more likely to pertain if the UK economy is neither in a severe recessionary nor a broad expansionary phase, and possibly somewhat less buoyant than the rest of the world. Under these conditions, a large number of individuals are gradually turning towards the inner directed philosophy, many of them in positions of leadership within industry and government. The economic emphasis is on 'good growth' and 'sustainable development', a steady improvement in the quality of life rather than a hectic boom that carries with it the seeds of a subsequent bust.

It is a more caring world with a safety net for those who are genuinely deprived, but at the same time there is a strong reaction against any collective organisation of welfare, since individual freedom and individual responsibility are so highly valued. Implicit within this responsibility, however, is the demand that people involve themselves with others who are less fortunate, and help to bring them to their own fulfilment.

In the political arena there are two new movements. The old polarisation is giving way to consensus and compromise among the small cells and local networks that are springing up all over the place; secondly, the process of government is moving from top down to bottom up, with the interaction of local and nationwide groups in this highly pluralistic society. The message to leaders is that they can no longer rely on the 'trickle down' effects of fiscal or financial regulation from above. The new mood is one of 'trickle up' from the grass roots to the stem, the leaves and eventually the flower itself.

There is a growing emphasis on the understanding of inter-personal processes, compromise, tolerance and empathy. In the planning sphere citizens are constructing new, small, interrelated institutions for themselves. There is a great sense of urgency for people to become involved in the life of their own neighbourhood and community; single issue groups proliferate. There is pressure for more decisions to be taken at local level rather than in Whitehall and indeed for central government's role to diminish to that of an overall coordinator and representative in global matters.

The working society has become highly complex with new forms of organisational structure, reflecting the predisposition of inner directeds towards small-scale institutions and activities in which they can do things their own way. Consultancies, open networks and overlapping cells flourish rather than hierarchies and bureaucracies. Large organisations

[203]

show a tendency to split down into federalised and project-based units, human factors in business are emphasised and interrelatedness, openness and trust are demanded of managements.

Flexibility, innovation and responsiveness are the determinants of business success. Professional functions, planning, creative IT application and research and development are where the action is. Unemployment is less of a stigma among the majority and people are thus not so suceptible to feelings of rejection and better able to find or create new innovative opportunities for themselves. In addition there is a sense of active concern for the plight of those sustenance driven who still do suffer in this way.

HOW GREEN IS MY VALLEY

End Farm, Notover, Norfolk was till five years ago an 800-acre agribusiness. Massive injections of drugs, hormones and fertilisers were required to keep up animal and crop production. Quality was another matter, however, until farmer Gordon Thursday went organic. 'It was a dramatic change for both me and for the land itself, but

SOLAR POWER BOOSTS ENERGY SUPPLY

In spite of the vagaries of the English climate, solar panels are invading the nation's houses. The purchase price of the newly developed germanium sulphide panels is falling rapidly, and the Department of Energy estimates that already 12% of homeowners

THE DOLE – A STATE SALARY

The unemployed are beginning to treat their benefit as something they can pass on to benefit the community as a whole. BURN, the British Unemployment Resource Network, cities the case of painter and decorator, Scott Oldcastle, 29, who having been twice made redundant, has now set up a free service for old-age pensioners in his native Sheffield. 'The dole makes it possible for me to help out with

PARENT POWER: THE ADDED VALUE IN OUR SCHOOLS

Parents are getting their act together to influence school gover-
nors and teachers to provide the kind of education they want for
their children. As the official curriculum requirements become
more specific, parents are also demanding a broader
approach. Already, the GCSE Exam has led to a more cooperative, project-led relationship between teachers and pupils,
in which parents can particip

ETHNIC FOODS – PART 6: THE SOUTH AMERICAN TASTE

Argentina, Brazil and Uruguay are the places for meat
dishes, but now that red meat has declined in popularity
due to both health and environmental considerations,
the fishy delicacies of the West coast countries – Chile,
Peru and Equador – are very much on the menu. Spicy
prawns and oyster

SKILLS EXCHANGES REVITALISE RURAL COMMUNITIES

A swop-shop of skills has brought about a wave of communal involvement in West Suffolk, and similar skills
exchanges are now planned for Avon, Dorset,
Derbyshire, North Yorkshire and Powys. The barter
system is based on earning points for providing goods and
services, which can then be spent on those provided by
others. It is, however, already attracting sidelong glances
from the Inland Revenue, which yesterday initiated a

BISHOP SOUNDS ALERT ON SCHISM THREAT

'In essentials, unity; in non-essentials, liberty; in
all things, charity', quoted the Right Rev. David
Mostly, Bishop of Lincoln and leader of the Church
of England's mystical reform group, New Reve-
lation. Addressing a crowd of over 20,000 in
Tottenham Hotspur's White Hart Lane Stadium,

THE KNOWLEDGE INDUSTRY – BRITAIN'S POWERBASE

As manufacturing industry and technology are increasingly being transferred to developing countries like Taiwan, Mexico and Nigeria, the export of knowledge, training and education is being recognised as the key to Britain's steady progress. Blessed by the fact that English is the world language of business, commerce and science, British information exporters

IT'S ALL IN THE MIND

Last night, I went to a concert at the Festival Hall. Entering the auditorium beside me walked two men in late middle age. Merchant bankers, I thought, or possibly Harley Street consultants. 'Yes, as a matter of fact I meditate for twenty minutes every day', said one to the other. 'Interesting, isn't it?', came the reply. Such an exchange would have been unthinkable even two or three years

CHARITY BEGINS AT HOME

Last year, Britain's charities collected a record £3 billion in donations from the public, over 10% more than ever before. The annual report of the Charity Commissioners emphasises the trend towards personal commitment in charitable concern. 'Just signing a cheque is no longer enough', says the report's introduction, 'people now want to get involved as well; and they

ACUPUNCTURE BREAKTHROUGH

For years, traditional medics have derided claims that acupuncture can have any beneficial effect at all. 'Anatomy is anatomy', they have intoned, 'and that is that'. Now researchers at Southampton University's Department of Physiology have detected small electromagnetic force-fields within the human body that correspond to the 'meridians' known to Chinese acupuncturists for over a thousand years.

WHISTLE WHILE YOU WORK

Consultancies, cooperatives and part-time jobs are the most attractive sorts of work, admits the Department of Employment. These three working modes have recorded the highest growth rates over the past four years, and now account for over 20% of all

Which then of these alternatives do you prefer? Probably none of them, because they are all exaggerated. But the point is that it is possible to pick out aspects of them all from which to create our own ideal futures. And there is nothing wrong with that. Given the best of all three, we have a good world to go for. In the longer term, society seems to be moving more strongly in the direction of the caring autonomy scenario, but spiced with the best elements of the other two. There are already examples about, but before we investigate them, as promised a short philosophical and psychological interlude comes next.

12

THE HIGHER SYNTHESIS

Virtues and Vices

Critics may complain that the analysis so far has been somewhat divisive in that it has laid bare the imperfect and disadvantageous qualities of each social value group. An American hostess called Alice Roosevelt Longworth[1] was wont to command her guests 'if you can't say anything nice about anyone, come and sit next to me'. We would all undoubtedly be better people if we laid off this kind of thing, but it is irresistible. Even Confucius declared that there was nothing more pleasant in life than to see an old friend fall off a rooftop. It is more fun to dwell on the bad points. On the other hand, having done so it is only fair to dwell on the good points for a while, as well as being practical and constructive.

As among the three broad social value clusters, it can however be said that five of the seven deadly sins are focused fairly specifically. Anger and lust in their different manifestations are pretty well spread. But sloth and envy fall into the sustenance-driven slot; gluttony and avarice are the stamping grounds of the outer directeds, and while pride in its ostentatious form also constellates around this group, the more insidiously damaging moral variety is the downfall of the inner directeds.

Yes, the self-explorers are priggish, the social resisters are bigoted, the experimentalists are sybaritic, the conspicuous consumers are selfish, the belongers are boring, the survivors are bolshie and the aimless are – well, aimless. But if you took the human vices of the twelve apostles and aggregated them together, it would make a fairly unattractive combination too. In contrast, imagine a team comprising the *virtues* of Prince Charles, Margaret Thatcher, Richard Branson, Robert Maxwell, Lord Armstrong, Ron Todd and an old woman on her deathbed.

Imagine a world where the seven groups' respective virtues are given full rein and where their positive potential is unlocked: the self-image and dignity of the aimless is enhanced, and the grit of the survivor, the stability of the belonger, the thrust of the conspicuous consumer, the verve of the experimentalist, the determination of the social resister and the freedom and care of the self-explorer are plaited together into a rope so strong that it is capable of pulling the human race through the millennial barrier into an altogether different dimension. Laughably idealistic? Millennial, in the dismissive sense? We shall see. There are those who would argue that the old realists are merely trying to hang on to an outmoded ideal, while the old idealists are in fact the new realists.

Their approach is that we are each born with a certain set of attributes both positive and negative, which develop partly through our genetic heritage and partly through our environmental upbringing. There are others who would add another dimension, the karmic or astrological one: whether or not the reader agrees with that detail is of little consequence because the principle remains the same – we are each given a hand of cards and we have to play them to make as many tricks as possible. We know at the very depths of our beings exactly how many tricks we are likely to win or lose, based on our personal circumstances. What we must do is to win in this lifetime, some would say in each lifetime, at least one more trick than the cards would merit. How amazing if the whole world, the whole human race was successful in this principle! Not that it is likely to happen any time soon, but that is not the point. Once you are awake enough, enlightened enough, you have a duty to play the tables in the casino of life with that purpose in mind.

Certainly the transformation cannot happen overnight, but nowadays there are plenty of aids on the market to help us improve our game; books, tapes, seminars, workshops, self-development courses, counselling, therapy, even board games and packs of cards. Harley Miller,[2] the lovable eccentric who initiated the Spirit of Europe Foundation, has developed what he terms 'A Scale of Qualities as a Guide to Self-Acceptance'. He has scaled a number of psychological qualities from one to ten, printed on the cards so that the lower the number the more the state of pain; the higher the number, the more the state of fulfilment. As one example –

10	Liberated	5	Disheartened
9	Free	4	Dejected
8	Unrestricted	3	Gloomy
7	Unsupported	2	Depressed
6	Discouraged	1	Despairing

These all represent grades of the same essential quality, just like the grades of the same hue on a decorators' colour chart. At the lowest level a despairing person may feel utterly alone in the dark night of her soul. In this condition it is of no use for the helpful bystander to tell her to snap out of it – 'you are like *this* but you should really be like *that*' – since this amounts to a pressure from society to become what she is not, hopeful instead of despairing. It is simply not possible for her to conjure up an entire opposite out of the air and don it like a magic cloak.

It is however very possible for her to haul herself up the ladder one rung at a time, inching towards the positive aspect of the negative psychological quality that she is feeling at the moment. Note that there is a neutral area around the seventh rung of the ladder, 'unsupported', which can mean either lacking support or not needing support. It is at this stage of mental attitude about one's condition that the flipover from negative to positive takes place.

The pack consists of 22 of these scales, from Arrogant to Truthful; from Threatening to Creative; from Enslaved to Devoted, and so on. They are intended to act as self-assessment and self-supporting mechanisms, but can also be used by a teacher to encourage a pupil, a counsellor to encourage a client, an employer an employee or a friend a friend. They are the very stuff of the way we have to move together in understanding if we are ever to harvest the combined talents of our group, our school, our business, our society, our species.

The East-West Divide

Miller has himself used these to extraordinarily potent effect for some years now, on his own private diplomatic crusade to promote understanding among the countries of Europe, and between East and West in particular. Like all pioneers, he has had to suffer the quizzical raised eyebrow in the past, but now enjoys the satisfaction of an unofficial but instrumental role in the burgeoning glasnost industry. This, the first sunrise in the East for long enough, may or may not prove to be a false dawn, but cannot and must not be dismissed out of hand.

We are all beginning to acknowledge our essential oneness, apparent ever since both American astronauts and Russian cosmonauts first saw the world from outside its gravitational field, hanging in space as a precious and shimmering pearl of wholeness undivided by mankind's artificial barriers. Professor Stephen Salter[3] of the University of Edinburgh has examined in his paper 'Some Ideas to Help Stop World War III' just how artificial and counter-productive these barriers have become. He quotes Samuel Gorovitz, Professor of Philosophy at the University of Maryland – 'Gorovitz describes an auction. As in a normal auction the goods are sold to the highest bidder. The difference is that the second-highest bidder also has to pay his bid but gets nothing. Let us suppose that the article for sale is a dollar bill and the auctioneer invites an opening bid of ten cents. The profit margin appears very attractive and plenty of people will be found willing to make a small bid for such a handsome return. Unfortunately there will be others willing to raise the bid to fifteen cents. While it is splendid to buy a dollar bill for only ten cents it is not good to pay ten cents and get nothing. The sensible step for the opening bidder is clearly to raise the bid to twenty cents.

'The two bidders are now locked into the fiendish trap devised by the rules of the auction. As bidding proceeds their possible profit steadily declines while the penalty for coming second steadily rises. A smile appears on the face of the auctioneer as the bids pass fifty cents. The smile gets wider as each victim tries to force the other into second place and the bids get bigger. In psychological experiments it has been shown that people will bid up to five times the value of the article which they were originally tempted to buy for a tenth of its value, a fifty to one change. The auctioneer wins ten times his risk capital.

'We should note that it is only the rivalry between the bidders that gives the auctioneer his chance. If they could have been persuaded into cooperating by making a joint single ten cent bid they could have shared the dollar and put the auctioneer out of business. There is no record of experimental subjects falling for the trick twice but presumably a sufficiently dogmatic insistence on out-bidding a competitor would lead to this result.'

Despite the simplicity of its rule, the Gorovitz auction is an acutely accurate model of the progress of an arms race. In 1945 it seemed as though nuclear weapons would give everlasting peace. There need be no more military service or dead young men. The initial bid was low. A very few bombs would do. But neither super-power could allow the other to make the higher bid. Each increase had to be matched. Inevitably, as time has gone on, the size of the bids has risen. We keep hoping that each new one will provide the longed-for security but each in turn proves inadequate. It is most interesting to retrieve from the archives the proposals for yesterday's weapons, now claimed to be insufficient, and to predict the inadequacies of the ever more expensive weapons proposed for tomorrow.'

Thank heavens this impasse now appears to be dissolving. But as Salter puts it we are still childishly sensitive to the division of the cake. 'Given that a child is not suffering from malnutrition, its absolute happiness is not much affected by whether or not there is cake for tea. But children are acutely sensitive to relative benefits. If there is cake for tea then it is distressing to feel that somebody else is getting more. Children have devised an elegant solution to the difficulty, based on the 'I cut, you choose' rule.

'Mathematicians like cake as much as anyone else and have found rules to share cakes between more than two people. They have also been able to prove the intriguing fact that if there are irregularities in the cake, such as more icing in one place or more cherries in another, and if the opinions of the sharers about the relative values of icing and cherry are different, then all the parties to the division can feel sure that they have come off best. This assurance is exactly what we need for nuclear disarmament.'

Except we become as little children . . . There is still fear on both sides and it is letting go of that fear that is the task for all of us today. Soviet Ambassador at large, Vladimir Lomeiko,[4] tells the following story: 'A woman in New York has a dream. She is walking home at night when she hears heavy footsteps close behind her. She walks faster, then runs. The footsteps come pounding after her until she reaches her flat, slams and locks the door and falls on her bed in breathless relief. Then she hears the footsteps advancing through the hall and entering the bedroom."What do you want of *me*?", she screams. A voice replies "What do you want of *me*? After all, this is *your* dream".'

For in that dream of death what sleep may come? The sage Krishnamurti taught us that there are two attitudes that keep us 'asleep' to our potential, fear and desire, parallelling the economic theory that markets are controlled by fear and greed. If fear has characterised the relationship between East and West to date, it is desire and greed that have been the cause of contention between North and South. The drama of Third World debt has many sorry acts and few heroes, but a large cast of villains, fools and unfortunates drawn variously from the developed world, the oil-rich states and the underdeveloped countries. The Toronto economic summit in June 1988 travelled a few inches towards a solution. We must simply pray that it soon accelerates if our consciousness of the real need for interdependence is going to be a peaceful process rather than a rude awakening, as we tumble out of bed on to the stone floor. Krishnamurti has it both ways in any event.

Psychosynthesis and Society

Society, the human species as a whole, is now clearly exhibiting the same symptoms as an individual in the throes of crisis. The Chinese pictogram for crisis is a combination of two others, 'wei', danger, and 'ji', opportunity. The danger is that we sink; the opportunity is that we swim to somewhere better. Ambassador Lomeiko's story is particularly apt in that it involves a dream. It is so often through dreams that we each play out our deepest mysteries, and if we can master their language or imagery and symbolism we have a key to unlock the door of crisis that keeps us in danger, so that we can pass through it into the garden of opportunity.

This involves recognising and redeeming, i.e. accepting as a valuable, all the different parts of ourselves so that we can reassemble them in a higher synthesis. It was another of Carl Jung's followers, Roberto Assagioli, who elaborated and clarified the concept that every individual's psyche contains a number of sub-personalities, just as every individual's body contains a number of organs. These must work in harmony together if the whole is to function properly, but most of us seem to have more trouble achieving this aim in the psychological than in the bodily sense. For the psyche to become whole and untroubled by conflicts between its constituent parts, we each need to go through the process of what Jung called individuation, the awareness of the Higher Self, which was described by Assagioli in his 'Psychosynthesis'[5] as consisting of four steps –

* *Thorough knowledge of the personality.* Generally known as psychoanalysis, this is the courageous journey into the lower unconsciousness to discover the dark forces that ensnare and menace us, the images that obsess or dominate us, the fears that paralyse us and the conflicts that waste our energies. At the same time we also discover the treasure within: our hitherto unknown abilities, true vocations and higher potential, which we have repressed through lack of understanding, prejudice or fear. This positive process reveals the deep reservoirs of energy that lie beneath the surface of every one of us, however ruffled, cloudy or calm that surface may be.

* *Control of the various elements of the personality.* This procedure is divided in two – first the disintegration of the harmful images or complexes, and secondly the control and utilisation of the energies that are thereby set free. In other words we *redeem* our weaknesses by first recognising them; and then by recognising also their corresponding strengths that are revealed on the obverse, golden side of these tarnished coins of ours. Rather than projecting our faults on to somebody else or some other class or group and blaming them for everything that goes wrong, we understand that the solution lies within ourselves.

* *Recognition of the Higher Self.* This is generally a long, arduous and heroic endeavour, the discovery of a unifying centre. It involves either the deliberate creation of an ideal model of oneself or, as a minor variation on this major theme, the projection of our idealism outside the self and onto some external cause. Social resisters, beware the trap of thinking that causes alone are enough, however.

* *Psychosynthesis.* This final stage consists of the reconstruction of the personality around the new centre, and the lifelong struggle towards the actualisation and realisation of the creative model.

This accurately describes the experience of the individual, as all those individuals who have been valiant enough to undertake the journey will testify. It is also, collectively true of organisations, of societies and indeed of humanity. As Assagioli expressed it 'this ordering presents interesting and suggestive analogies with that of a modern state with the various groupings of its citizens into communities, social classes, professions and trades, and the different grades of human activity.'

We have here, in other words, nothing less than a holistic vision whereby the characteristics of the whole society, the organisation and the team are echoed, but more visibly and approachably so, within the holon individual. The term holon, which has been introduced here before, was coined by Arthur Koestler,[6] whose notion it was that everything is a whole entity but at the same time part of a bigger holon; an autonomous part within a greater participative whole. Whatever is common to the individual holons at one level will be so of the next. Whatever is common to him and her or to me and you will be common to them or to us, and ultimately to all.

Acting on this premise, the hidden purpose of the text so far has been to explore Assagioli's 'thorough knowledge of the personality' of our entire society; from now on it will try to illuminate the path towards the 'control of the various elements of the (collective) personality'. The analysis may have pained, angered or embarrassed some of its readers, but pain, anger and embarrassment are all part of the normal therapeutic experience, and steps along the way to deeper self-knowledge. They teach us much about our real selves if only we listen to them. Meanwhile the final two Assagioli stages must be left for resolution over the next centuries, the early portion of the new millennium, and this is the task that will face our successors.

A bold claim, no doubt, but as Assagioli himself insisted, 'it is only by individuals attempting this voyage of exploration that they will be able to work harmoniously together – first in a team or an organisation, then in the larger sense within the state of society as a whole.' The teachings of Assagioli, and indeed of Jungian and humanistic psychology in general, represent an advance over mere behaviourism and Freudian psycho-analysis, in that his major concern is less with repression and control than with developing the whole personality in a healthful way. However threatening these present suggestions may seem, they do represent a means of escape, of release and of fulfilment for us.

Towards the end of his life, his colleague Maslow looked beyond even these concerns to the small minority of individuals who had passed through self-actualisation and self-realisation to self-transcendence, from personal and egoistic concerns to universal and transpersonal ones. One might perhaps call them the 'meta-directeds.' These are the growing numbers of people who are beginning to think in terms of planetary humankind; compulsive innovators and discoverers of the new, shunning luxury, possessions, honour and privilege in so doing. A viable, sustainable and convivial future is now within our reach as these people harness their capacity for deep internal development.

A major feature of such a world will be that the deleterious effects of the military ego and the hi-tech revolution will begin to move away from the centre where they have been masters, towards the periphery where they will be servants. And today's emphasis on mere cleverness, of which we now certainly have an abundance, will therefore ultimately be reinforced by wisdom, of which we currently have far too little. 'Where is the wisdom we have lost in knowledge; where is the knowledge we have lost in information?', asked T S Eliot.[7] All the wisdom we have at our command will need to be exercised should we soon be faced, as seems more than possible, with the pain and suffering of unprecedented economic chaos in humanity's own mid-life crisis.

Looking back in history, humankind can perhaps be seen as having lived through its childhood in the period before Christianity and other organised religions, during which the purely physical and bodily aspects of existence were emphasised. The early organisation of religion brought with it an adolescent emotional dimension, and the flowering of the intellect occurred with the dawn of the Renaissance and the marvel of Newtonian thought, which ushered in the Industrial Revolution. In such earlier eras the propensity to exercise these later faculties was present but largely dormant, though very much in evidence among a few individuals.

Now in the autumn of the industrial age another apple is falling – a golden apple this time. Humanity is almost ready to fuse the three manifest aspects of itself into a single whole and crown it with the gifts of intuition and true spiritual awareness. But, as is frequently the case with the individual, it may take a global crisis of awesome proportions to persuade us all of the need for this. Its infinite benefits may only be apparent at the end of a dark night of the collective soul.

He, She and It

The deeper causes of this crisis are apparent when one returns to a more detailed consideration of Assagioli's theory. Each individual's make-up comprises a rich variety of archetypes and images, but there are three that are common to everyone. Two of them are the real and ghostly sexual sides of our personalities. Jung[8] had discovered that each of us carries within our psyches what he called a contra-sexual element. Thus every man holds deep within himself a feminine aspect which Jung termed the anima, and every woman correspondingly bears inside herself an animus or masculine principle.

These hidden parts of the personality manifest themselves to a greater or lesser degree – in the form of directed, assertive, competitive, mind-orientated traits in the case of a woman, and as diffuse, reflective, cooperative and intuitive traits in the case of a man. They must be reconciled with the main driving force of each of our psyches, feminine or masculine respectively. The third, omnipresent and particularly sensitive subpersonality is what is termed the shadow, the unlovely side of each of our natures which remains dark and hidden and of which we are most frightened and ashamed, preferring to bury it deep down rather than to examine it, befriend it and redeem it as we should.

[216]

Discovering all this within ourselves, however, is often so painfully difficult that we try to pin down these mysterious inner forces in a guise where we may relate to them in more solid form, by investing other people with our own graces and our own faults. A man's quest for his anima is therefore subsumed into a quest for his ideal woman, while his shameful shadow is projected with all its horrors on to some convenient scapegoat outside in society as a whole – the reds, the bosses, the Jews, the blacks or the next-door neighbour. As far as the outside world is concerned, what goes on at an individual level – this self-misunderstanding and frustration repeated dozens, hundreds, thousands and millions of times – is what then goes on in the collective of the team, the organisation and the nation state.

In conditions of crisis, which as already mentioned frequently occur in mid-life, there is effectively a break-up of the psychological status quo. These unexamined polarities that have long existed within a person's psychological make-up now have to be faced, once the protection of life's comfortable assumptions has been savagely ripped away by reality. The danger side of this spiritual break-*up* can be a break-*down* into collapse – whether it be a nervous breakdown, a physical breakdown or an emotional breadown. However at the same time the twin opportunity of a break*through* is always at hand; the discovery of a new way ahead in synthesising the transformed elements of what has gone before, after they have been purged of the conflict and polarity that divided them.

This process of individuation is always a difficult and sometimes agonising journey. Even though the ultimate achievement of harmony and balance is immeasurably worth this Odyssey, people are only capable of embarking on the commitment if the crisis provides them with nothing else but an alternative too terrible to contemplate. Just as today's individual suffers this crisis, intensified by the acceleration of change that we are now experiencing, so also as a macrocosm of what is occurring to the men and women in it, today's society is crisis-ridden. The individual, unable to face the, to him, hideous shadow side of his own psyche, projects what he hates so much onto society which, likewise inflamed by the pace of change, spits its collective agony back into his face.

Since 20th century society is so demonstrably dominated by the masculine values of achievement, logic, science, competition, leadership and material success, we can consider it in parallel terms to a man in his mid-life crisis struggling to come to a reapprochement with his own anima. Neither the individual nor the collective will be able to proceed until they have done this and accepted not only both the masculine and the feminine sides of their nature, but also the neglected shadow, which is repressed, deprived and always seething there, waiting to rise up and mindlessly destroy as a sop for its frustration.

It is only by also facing the shadow, recognising it, accepting it, loving it and transforming it, that the individual and society will be able to become whole. Today it is the deprived and the repressed of the world who constitute the collective shadow, with South African apartheid representing perhaps the starkest example of its dangerous neglect. However, in Afghanistan, Cyprus, Armenia, Cambodia, Northern Ireland, Nicaragua, Iran, The Falklands, Ethiopia and countless other places in the world there is evidence of its fearsome potency.

The anima of society only really began to assert itself at the beginning of the century with the suffragettes. The seed they planted has germinated, as we are well aware, into the dramatic upshoot of the feminist movement. Dramatic, and understandably so, because in world military, intellectual, scientific, technological, legal and sociological terms we have had a masculine-led hierarchical system for around 3,000 years now, and many women are getting fed up with it. Quite why this replaced the matriarchal nature worship that preceded it is lost in history, but in view of the violence with which the remnants of that earlier culture were repressed, it must in its heyday have been just as unattractive as the excesses of male domination are today.

However it can easily be argued that if modern women had the power that men have now, though there would doubtless still be competition, war would be less likely. The sense of inter-connectedness, of generality, of common purpose and interest, is more characteristic of the feminine principle than of the masculine, which favours specialisation and the protection of its value by competitive means. In a sense, one can also distinguish between masculine and feminine in terms of the difference between the love of power and the power of love.

The attributes of the masculine principle are those of intellect, competition, science, analysis, direction, promotion and quantity. The corresponding attributes of the feminine principle are those of feeling, cooperation, spirituality, synthesis, coordination, attraction and quality. But both are necessary and it is heresy to over-emphasise the feminine qualities just as it has been heresy for so long to have over-emphasised the masculine ones. It is now to be hoped that the next millennium will help us conceive a sense of balance. The two hemispheres of the brain of humankind must work together for its body to function properly.

Some of today's more strident feminists might resist this assertion. They would be wrong, but it must be remembered that they have fulfilled a valuable function. It is symptomatic of many revolutions that the attitudes of the vanguard have to be exaggerated if the apathetic mass of society is ever to be moved towards the middle ground. There would never have been any change at all without the example of the stormtroops battling through and beyond the real objective of harmony and balance, which could then safely be occupied and consolidated by the remainder of the army following on behind.

In summary then, it is like this. Conflict within the individual is projected as conflict in society, not only in the form of the antisocial behaviour of the criminal statistics, but also because individual stress and crisis is at the same time both fed by and a creator of the increasing pace of social change. The crisis spirals to and fro between the individual and the collective, awaiting the realisation of wholeness at all levels through a resolution of the polarities of the masculine, the feminine and the shadow. The organisation, sited between the individual and society, is no exception to the rule, as will be demonstrated in a particularly vivid example in the next chapter. The organisation can only exist if it responds correctly to outside circumstances, and circumstantial evidence in support of this entire argument is provided by the fact that some organisations are already responding to it. It is at this level that a few of the necessary breakthroughs are quietly being made.

Science Fact and Fiction

In our present model, the inner directeds, outer directeds and sustenance driven could be said to represent the embodiments of the individual's feminine and masculine principles and the neuter shadow side, writ large. In an organisation these might also be equated with the design, marketing and administration departments. One can travel even further afield and still find attractive allegories – the world of atomic physics is dominated by the feminine, stable, and inner directed proton; the masculine, urgent, outer directed electron; and the neuter, passive and sustenance-driven neutron.

Interestingly, the cosmic building block of hydrogen, consisting only of one proton and one electron, the masculine and the feminine, is incapable of doing anything else except produce yet more hydrogen, until the creation (redemption) of the third particle, the (shadow) neutron. The introduction (acceptance) of the (shadow) neutron makes possible the conversion of hydrogen – via its isotopes – into helium, and thence the manufacture of all the other elements in their various complexities. It is, in other words, a new recipe for fundamental change and the gateway to evolutionary diversification. As a powerful metaphor it is also – this jump from a two-particle to a three-particle atom – what actually happens at the core of our very sun, the nuclear fusion process at the heart of every star which represents the entire source of power and light in the universe.

Only then, once this magic has been accomplished, can the wonders of the Mendeleev Atomic Table be realised, with its harmonic progression that orders the rhythmic creation and transformation of each chemical element in turn, born into one of a series of families like the notes of a scale and their octaves, the notes from which the music of the spheres has been composed. So, the universe repeats itself, exquisitely, in every one of its myriad dimensions, but can only do so once the masculine and the feminine are combined in balance and the transformative value of the neuter shadow has been recognised.

Is it too absurd to conjecture that in both the atomic and the cosmic process there exists an eternal truth that rings and resonates around every harmonic in between? Including, and in particular, humankind, set so significantly just in the middle of the scale? And that at every level – individual, organisational and societal; the masculine, the feminine and the neuter; the outer directed, the inner directed and the sustenance-drive; the proton, the electron and the neutron – all have their parts to play. Just as Kondratieff shouts for us into the echo gorge of economics, so Mendeleev gives an insight into another aspect of nature's wonderful integration. Everything relates to everything else. And surely the same can be said of everybody.

The idea of wholeness is very much alive in our times and nowhere more so than within the scientific community. It is inspiring people to construct an outer world that reflects their inner sense of it. In ecology, in politics, in religion, in psychology and indeed in all disciplines, new schools of thought are emerging that emphasise the interrelatedness and the interdependence of life. Touch it here, and it trembles there.

In the past there have always been poets and visionaries who have known in their hearts that life is one, while groups of people have often bound themselves together by a common belief in the unity of creation. Now however the intuitive, often vague and idealistic notion of oneness is shown to have solid basis in fact. Many scientists are declaring that their observations of the physical world reveal to them that everything is held together in an unbroken wholeness. It is the marriage of the feminine and the masculine revelations, the intuitive-poetic and the intellectual-concrete, which is today bringing these images of unity into such sharp focus.

The scientific community has the task of observing nature as she really is and, through rigorous intellectual struggle, revealing the realms of the unknown. Max Planck,[9] one of the pioneers of modern physics, said of science that it 'means unresting endeavour and continually progressing development toward an aim which the poetic intuition may apprehend but which the intellect can never fully grasp.'

Great physicists of this century – Einstein, Bohr, Planck and Heisenberg – have looked deep into the heart of matter in search of the ultimate constituents of the material world, the separate parts from which every-thing is made. What they discovered was that the material world is not made up of separate parts at all. In the words of physicist Fritjof Capra,[9] modern physics 'shows that we cannot decompose the world into independently existing smallest units. As we penetrate into matter, nature does not show us any isolated building blocks, but rather appears as a complicated web of relations between the various parts of a unified whole . . . sub-atomic particles – and therefore ultimately all parts of the universe – cannot be understood as isolated entities but must be defined through their interrelations'. Physics and metaphysics are suddenly veering closer together after a schism of 500 years.

In 'Clairvoyant Reality', Lawrence Le Shan[10] describes an experiment in which he took sixty-two statements of 'how-the-world-works', half of them written by physicists and half by mystics down the ages. He then mixed them up in unattributed form to see if people could tell which persuasion the author of each statement belonged to. His respondents were of three kinds, those trained in physics, those trained in philosophi-cal and mystic disciplines, and a third control group of lay people. No group did particularly well, and all found it difficult to distinguish accur-ately between the statements, so consistent were the conclusions of both sides. Mystic subjects tended to guess with 60%–70% accuracy and physi-cists with 50%–60%, while the lay respondents were left at the post.

We have moved from sociology and diplomacy, through psychology to physics. Let us now go mad and irresponsible and enter the world of science fiction. Not quite mad though; *Futures* magazine, one of the world's most prestigious forecasting journals, has a regular science fiction section which serves to explode the minds and preconceptions of its erudite readers by introducing them to the way-out possibilities of the far future so that they can think laterally about the present. There are lessons to be learned here, in the world of the imagination.

In 'The Gods Themselves', Isaac Asimov,[11] a maestro of science fiction, tells of a planet in another universe similar to earth but where there are not two sexes but three, known collectively as the Soft Ones, to distinguish them from the Hard Ones, altogether higher forms of benevolent and powerful being. In this parallel universe, the Soft Ones are divided equally between Parentals ('right-lings') who are the grounding force of the group of three, stubborn, practical and occupied with the day-to-day business of keeping the triad together; Rationals ('left-lings') who are the intellectuals and exploratory minded ones; and Emotionals ('mid-lings') who as their name suggests live primarily in and for the realm of feelings.

They could be respectively described as earth, air and water; as body, mind and emotions; or in our own in-house vernacular as sustenance-driven, outer directed and inner directed. As a triad, they generally live harmoniously and unexcitingly together. But occasionally if they exhibit a very high form of interdependence through a sexual act known as 'melting', they are transformed over the process of time into a single Hard One, only then capable of taking on higher powers and responsibilities.

It is a fanciful concept and entertainingly told, but it is also wise and significant. Even more fanciful, maybe, to take it as another parallel of what we have been considering here, but Asimov's dedication of the book 'To mankind and the hope that the war against folly may some day be won after all' indicates that he had something more than mere storytelling in his mind when he wrote it. The book is a parable of the truth that it is only when people are capable of coordinating, balancing and developing to the full all the different sides of their natures that the need for interdependence will be clear. First, though, we must value and accept the strengths and talents of others as having equal validity with our own, and see our weaknesses as neither more nor less worthy and capable of redemption than our neighbour's.

The Philosophy of Interdependence

It now seems clear that the atomic, the ecological, and the cosmic thrust is towards interdependence as a general scientific principle of the universe itself – of which we are a part and in no possible way immune from its laws. It is also a concept that has an admirable philosophical provenance. As the true Renaissance Man, Leonardo da Vinci said: 'To develop a complete mind – study the science of art; study the art of science; learn how to "see"; realise that everything connects to everything else'.

Bertrand Russell, describing the work of Georg Wilhelm Hegel in 'A History of Western Philosophy',[12] stated that 'He retained a belief in the unreality of separateness. The world in his view was not a collection of hard units, whether atoms or souls, each completely self-subsistent. The apparent self-subsistence of finite things appeared to him to be an illusion; nothing, he held, is ultimately and completely real except the whole.' He illustrated this by examining the metaphorical statement, 'reality is an uncle'. But if reality is an uncle, this presupposes the existence of a nephew. So perhaps reality is a nephew. But no, because this in turn presupposes the existence of a brother and a sister, a mother and a father, and a whole gaggle of in-laws and cousins constituting an entire family.

From this thought, Hegel conceived a dialectic consisting of what he called thesis, antithesis and synthesis – in other words a current mode of thought or conventional wisdom (uncle), which is challenged by another opposing concept (nephew), until ultimately the two fuse together. This then forms a synthesis (family), which becomes the thesis of the next stage of philosophical development, to be challenged by the next antithesis that somebody dreams up. This constant onward flow of evolutionary thought, this developmental striving towards an unattainable infinity, is almost Taoist in its conception –

> 'Therefore having and not having arise together.
> Difficult and easy complement each other.
> High and low rest upon each other.
> Voice and sound harmonise each other.
> Front and back follow one another.'
> (from 'Tao Te Ching', by the 6th century BC sage Lao Tsu)

Brian Magee in his 'Popper', describes philosopher Sir Karl Popper's[13] attack on the utopian society in 'The Open Society and Its Enemies'. Here he warns against the temptation to return to the womb-like security of a pre-critical or tribal situation, a nostalgically agrarian or sustenance-driven one in other words. This, Popper insists, means arresting the processes of change by the rigid social control of stopping people doing anything on their own initiative, leading inevitably into totalitarianism.

The supposed Utopia of a particular political and social philosophy must eventually be superseded by a change to an alternative Utopia, which then becomes the conventional wisdom and which in turn is challenged by a further alternative development. Here we are travelling in parallel with Hegel's concepts. Popper concludes that we are powerless to make a perfect society which will continue to be perfect for evermore. Anything we construct will only be a stepping stone towards the formulation of an improved model to be developed by our successors.

What we may perceive as the longed-for ultimate is simply another, even though possibly a somewhat more elaborate aspect of the whole. This is a valuable lesson for the inner directeds who are, as we know, prone to elitism and intellectual or psychological snobbery. It once again underlines the fact that everyone has their virtues and their vices but that all have their limitless potential. The position of the self-explorer is not the terminus at the end of the line, but simply a small village station on it. As the Taoists put it, 'before enlightenment, chop wood, carry water – after enlightenment, chop wood, carry water'. The simplicity and inevitability of wood and water underline the essential truth and wholeness of the Gaia concept. First of all we thought the earth was flat. Then we realised it was round. Now James Lovelock[14] is persuading us that it is alive. Lovelock has created a theory that overturns conventional biology and classical evolutionary thought in that it postulates that the earth is simply a single organism on the surface of which life-forms and the physical environment continually interact to maintain a life-preserving equilibrium. With the birth of the idea in 1972 we were at last offered the wholesome possibility of natural harmony rather than the old guilt-ridden view of mankind as a thoughtless looter and pillager of the innocent land. Values of cooperation and restraint were suddenly not only justified but vital, in the root sense of the word.

The theory, based originally on exceedingly sensitive testing of the earth's atmosphere for chemicals characteristic of life, is that some primitive organisms established themselves on earth at just the moment when the atmosphere happened to be favourable for their development. This was so successful that it was able to change the entire global climate by means of an increasingly elaborate series of feedback loops between the environment and the life it supported. It now makes sense, the theory continues, to regard the entire planet as a single system – a system which has properties that are shared with things we know to be alive, and which thus embraces rocks, seas, plants and animals as a single functioning life-form.

Subjected to the sun's energy, the gases nitrogen, oxygen, carbon dioxide, water vapour and methane that formed the earth's only atmosphere could have interacted to create a dead environment similar to those of our two nearest planetary neighbours, Mars and Venus; but in contrast our own atmosphere has remained constant and supportive since life started. So indeed has our prevailing temperature, more or less, even though when life began the sun was emitting only about two thirds of the energy it does now.

The heat must therefore have been trapped extremely efficiently, probably by carbon dioxide, but as this began to be taken up by plants the earth could have become fatally cooler as a result. What must have happened, then, was that life at that time produced an abundance of ammonia and other 'greenhouse' gases in compensation. Further natural mechanisms such as forest fires, the saltness of the sea and the relationship between green plankton and the formation of clouds – all these and a hundred others combine to explain the otherwise inexplicable – that Gaia, the earth goddess of the ancient Greeks, is actually alive.

In Gaia's current struggle for survival, the deforestation of the tropics is to Lovelock far more dangerous than CFCs or methane pollution, or indeed even than nuclear power – 'the three big enemies of the world are cars, cattle and chainsaws', he insists. He is an unapologetic believer in technology as the only thing that will help us through our present eco-crisis, however. If we fail to harness our inventiveness appropriately, the overheated and polluted seas and the widening ozone holes will overwhelm us, before some process inherent in the system can absorb these harmful changes that we ourselves have wrought. Without the help of human ingenuity, Gaia may not be able to react quickly enough to preserve many of the more complex forms of life that cannot stand this much variation in their environment – such as, alas, the human species itself.

Fanciful? Possibly. Well, think about it. And consider also a rounded statement[15] that has been circulating secretly for a number of years now, on cards and posters and stickers, spreading anarchically through networks of kindred spirits, with nobody able to find out where it began or who created it. Its origin is indiscernible but it is expressed in the suffusing, haunting Lovelock language of the inner directeds –

If the Earth
were only a few feet in
diameter, floating a few feet above
a field somewhere, people would come
from everywhere to marvel at it. People would
walk around it, marvelling at its big pools of water,
its little pools and the water flowing between the pools.
People would marvel at the bumps on it, and the holes in it,
and they would marvel at the very thin layer of gas surrounding
it and the water suspended in the gas. The people would
marvel at all the creatures walking around the surface of the ball,
and at the creatures in the water. The people would declare it
as sacred because it was the only one, and they would protect
it so that it would not be hurt. The ball would be the
greatest wonder known, and people would come to
pray to it, to be healed, to gain knowledge, to know
beauty and to wonder how it could be. People
would love it, and defend it with their lives
because they would somehow know that
their lives, their own roundness, could
be nothing without it. If the
Earth were only a few
feet in diameter.

Leadership and the Team

Enlightenment has been described as 'licking honey off a razor'. Its rewards and its responsibilities are both intense. Among these responsibilites is the cultivation of a fraternal rather than the old paternal style of leadership – leadership in the widest sense – that comes from alongside rather than from above, and empowers rather than instructs. But this is also important in the narrower and more technical sense of leadership, since our present concern is not only with the holon individual but also with the team, the organisation and society.

If we take the rallying cry of the French Revolution – *Liberté, Egalité, Fraternité* – it can be said that the 19th century was largely taken up with the attainment of Liberty, and the 20th with that of Equality, leading one

[226]

to hope that Fraternity will be the characteristic of the Millennium. If so, it must initially come from the top as an admission of the essential nature of inter-connectedness and interdependence in our new world.

A team leader who represents a demanding, critical or authoritarian parent, rather as does the Prime Minister herself, is of no help at all to the underdog. Harking back to Harley Miller's quality scales, when because of circumstances of deprivation, unemployment, poverty and depression, the people concerned are ground down by the weight of their problems and have simply lost their self-respect – as many members of the survivor and aimless groups now have – they are unable to make the vital leap from dependence to interdependence. Their will has been sapped and however gently it is put, the message 'you must pull yourself together' is at best inaudible to them and at worst counterproductive.

What is needed in its place is the empowerment of an encouraging parent who stands beside them and understands empathetically where they are and how it is. This parent helps them tackle the long and painful climb up Miller's scales, until their egos are strong enough to believe that they have it in them to develop their talents. This ideal of holistic politics may now seem implausible, but it will be as necessary and relevant to tomorrow's people as holistic medicine will be to them as patients, and holistic business will be to them as consumers and employees.

Observer columnist Katharine Whitehorn[16] has written movingly of the human value of praise and thanks. She took as an example the man who failed to shut the great sea doors of the ferry which caused the Zeebrugge disaster, quoting a sentence in the subsequent enquiry – 'He knew his job was important, though nobody had told him so'. She contrasted this with the World Health Organisation's health manual for Nigeria which read 'If you have one child that seems less bright than the other, try to reward his effort, not his achievement'. She concludes admirably, that in that sense, we are all backward children and all wish that someone would reward or even notice our effort. Let us celebrate our sameness in that.

Around the same time she also wrote how she had attended an American conference 'Agenda 2000', the purpose of which was to outline the reasonable goals that should be set for the next century. It was evidently a gloomy occasion, but she must have caught a whisper of Something Else. She admitted that in the 'real' world of balance sheets and arms races people would never change the way they live, or be intellectually persuaded to have cooler rooms, stop eating beef, walk rather than take the car, or care remotely what happens on the other side of the world. 'In cold, rational terms, it simply cannot be done.'

But she went on to insist that there are considerations other than the merely cold and rational, and stronger ones too. 'I don't personally think that any restraints that do not have the irrational force of religion will save us; the impulse will have to come from the unconscious will of the species to survive. I am only guessing about this and I won't be there to see it, but my ghost will not be astonished if the end of the 21st century has seen the rise of a new and overwhelming Green religion.'

She is too pessimistic. Millions of tiny individual blades of grass are already forcing their way up through the desert surface. And one of the most unlikely but fertile seedbeds is, as we shall see, the world of business.

13

BACK TO BUSINESS

Teamwork and The Drive of Market Forces

'We shall not cease from exploration, and the end of all our exploring will be to arrive where we started and know the place for the first time'
(T S Eliot.)[1]

The exploration undertaken in this book started with business and will end with business, the argument being that if a change of approach from the separative to the holistic, from the competitive towards the cooperative, is seen to be profitable then that change will occur and business will be the driving force behind it. The market indeed exerts a relentless leverage. If the People who Matter Most – the individual consumers, employees, shareholders, colleagues, pensioners, suppliers and onlookers – all begin singing the same song, it will not be long before business joins in the chorus.

We have already seen examples of large companies gradually feeling their way towards a more inner directed position in parallel with and in response to the movement among their customers, their employees and the public as a whole. And the New Testament of management practice, Tom Peters'[2] 'In Search of Excellence', besides emphasising the outer directed imperatives of business success, notably balances this with a strong undertone of the value of inner directed qualities in a combination of passion and humanity directed towards a business goal.

Both elements are necessary and it is wrong for the over-enthusiastic self-explorer to denigrate the competitive outer direction of much of business. Holism must be appreciated in this respect, too. It is impossible to argue that competition is bad as such, because without it there would be no yardstick by which the comparative usefulness of new ideas could be measured. This is true of business, of science, education, the arts, whatever one may think of. There are however three important points to be made here. First, competition must be fair; secondly, competition must be balanced with cooperation; thirdly, competition must stem from pure motives.

The examples of a new approach given in the first chapter were of isolated instances in large companies. They are echoed however by the Institute of Directors[3] which, under the leadership of Director-General Sir John Hoskins, launched in September 1987 a long-term strategy document for the nation's business leaders urging them to 'make the enterprise culture an enduring reality'. This document, 'A New Agenda for Business', called on members of the Institute to embrace a five-point plan. For us here, the interesting part is that of those five points two are distinctly inner directed in nature –

* to show greater readiness to 'put something back' by using financial and managerial strength to help solve public problems

* to treat employees as individuals and participants in enterprises, moving away from the traditional collectivist view of employees as factors of production

A similar attitude exists at the Confederation of British Industries which also issued a strategic document to its members along the same lines. And when researchers Margerison and Dawes, investigating the role and development of senior managers, asked of their elite panel 'What have been the most important things you have had to learn in order to perform your role as a senior manager?', the most frequent answers were –

* patience and understanding, listening, tact and tolerance

* how to motivate people, to understand what motivates people, to encourage teamwork, to get the best out of people

Sir John Harvey-Jones[4] in his book 'Making it Happen' declares that the role of management is to identify the direction of change and then to bring about the conditions in which it can occur positively, primarily involving what he calls 'headroom', giving people all down the line the opportunity to realise their abilities by cutting the hierarchical layers which stop messages from getting through. 'I wanted our executive team to operate as a band of brothers, where discussion was free and uninhibited'. This is very close to the Japanese recipe for success as identified by Pascale and Athos[5] in 'The Art of Japanese Management' with its Seven Ss that have already been described above.

Teamwork yet again, you see. One proven way of building up a team ethos is through the egalitarian feeling of sharing both responsibility and rewards. Japanese companies coming to this country and working with employees in what have been regarded by British managements as black-spot areas like South Wales or Tyneside have found that by emphasising the contribution that each employee makes to the whole and avoiding the dread feudalism of the British class system, prevalent for so long in so many businesses, amazing results can be achieved.

There is no company song at Nissan's highly successful car factory in Sunderland, but all workers gather in groups for five minutes every morning to discuss the projects and tasks of the day ahead. No one clocks on or off, there is one style of uniform, one canteen and one shared car park. 3,500 workers will build 200,000 cars a year in 1992, double the productivity of some rival British plants. On the other hand, the Nissan and the Japanese approach in general is not sexless and it is not ageless. In this culture, men rule and old men rule absolutely. Furthermore the absolute subjection of the individual to the group is not always acceptable to the British mentality, which in its purest form prefers to balance the demands of each.

The Archetypal Approach to Teams

The emphasis on effective teamwork is gaining ground in modern business, as is the recognition that the team should be multivariate. Charles Handy[6] in 'Gods of Management' described the disastrous results of recruiting team members who were all clones of each other. He illustrated four such types of organisation, governed respectively by the gods Zeus, archetype of the club-culture and famed for the power of his presence; Apollo, supporter of rules and order and of the role culture; Athena, protectress of problem-solvers and the task culture; and Dionysius, the existential and supreme individualist. The real way to run a railway is to have some of each, even though this can make for a greater danger of misunderstandings in relationships. But you would never pick a football side consisting only of brilliant goalkeepers or brilliant strikers, after all. This view is endorsed by Sir Robert Haslam,[7] chairman of British Coal —

[231]

'The team should have compatibility but complete consensus can be overdone. A team member should not be so aggressive that he does not fit, but having too comfortable bedfellows is bad as well. The team must be broad in the sense of getting people together who have different views, but its leader must not allow the development of different groups and cliques who wage civil war on each other. What is wholly good is to have individual views and talents'.

Steve Shirley[7] of FI Group, the computer software house that is staffed mainly by remote-working housewives who telecommute electronically from home, enlarges this to require a mutual determination for openness among her team members and a willingness to sit down and debate personal attributes unthreateningly.

'I have a gut feel about people and I will back it. But in recent years I have looked for theoretical reasons to show why I am right and have used personality testing such as the Luscher colour test and Myers-Briggs. Everybody in my top team is given these tests, including myself, and we all see our own and each others' results. This accelerates the understanding by team members of each others' capabilities. People now appreciate that when there are differences the other person is not being stupid or obstreperous but just seeing the problem from a completely different viewpoint. This illuminates the problem and makes the ultimate team solution better than could have been devised by any one individual alone.'

This is similar to the theories of Dr Meredith Belbin[8] as expressed in his book 'Management Teams: Why They Succeed or Fail'. Here he analyses the behaviour of teams in both executive management exercises and in real life business situations. From this, disregarding their technical functions, Belbin classifies team members into eight different psychological categories, their typical features, strengths and weaknesses being illustrated in Table 4.

Belbin's hypothesis echoes Steve Shirley's experience that successful business teams need a mix of different types of people who are not only each aware of who they are but of who everybody else is too – who apportion both their functional and their psychological roles deliberately and openly and who accord value and dignity to each others' contributions to the whole. He concludes by identifying the main contributing factors of a good team by further defining the optimum relationships between these various types. We are in Assagioli country again here, and these individuals can be represented as the sub-personalities of the team. At the same time the teams themselves can frequently be identified as the

TABLE 4. IDEAL MANAGEMENT TEAM CONSTITUTION (AFTER BELBIN)

Team Role	Typical Features	Positive Qualities	Negative Qualities
Company Worker	Conservative Dutiful Predictable	Organising ability Practical commonsense Hard-working Self-discipline	Lack of flexibility Unresponsive to unproven ideas
Chairman	Calm Self Confident Controlled	Capacity for treating & welcoming all potential contributors on their merits without prejudice A strong sense of objectives	No more than ordinary in terms of intellect or creative ability
Shaper	Highly-strung Outgoing Dynamic	Drive and a readiness to challenge inertia, ineffectiveness complacency or self-deception	Proneness to provocation, irritation and impatience
Plant	Individualist Serious minded Unorthodox	Genius Imagination Intellect Knowledge	Up in the clouds Inclined to disregard practical details and protocol
Resource Investigator	Extroverted Enthusiastic Curious Communicative	Capacity for contacting people and explaining everything new Ability to respond to challenge	Liable to lose interest once the initial fascination has passed
Monitor/Evaluator	Sober Unemotional Prudent	Judgement Discretion Hard-headedness	Lacks inspiration and the ability to motivate others
Team Worker	Socially orientated Rather mild and sensitive	An ability to respond to people and situations and to promote them	Indecisiveness at moments of crisis
Completer/Finisher	Painstaking Orderly Conscientious Anxious	Capacity to follow through Perfectionism	Tendency to worry about small things Reluctance to let go

sub-personalities of the organisation. Indeed the writer has experienced such a case when working in a consultancy capacity.

The client organisation was a pillar of the financial establishment, which some 50 years after its formation was experiencing a mid-life crisis. It had come seriously unstuck through the marketing of a technically flawed product, which had resulted in a massive collapse in outside confidence. The marketing-orientated managing director, who had been responsible for the decision, was forced to resign and replaced by a colleague from the production side of the business who was very much of the cautious, traditionalist and establishment persuasion.

This brought a revival in support from the organisation's distributors and market-creators, but the long-term effects of the sudden change were critical. There began to be widespread internal complaints that the whole enterprise had lost direction and was 'getting fat and middle-aged', and a sense of introspective malaise suffused the organisation. The writer's task was to find out what the outside world really thought of it, and his response was to ask first what the inside world thought of it. As always happens, these two views coincided – and the philosophical concept 'as above, so below' was transformed into the human concept 'as within, so without'. In other words the organisation, like the individual, is entirely responsible for what happens to it, echoing the pyschotherapist's question to his client 'What is your universe telling you?'

In the case in point the answer depended entirely on whether the particular respondent was employed in or, if an outsider, in primary contact with, the production, the marketing or the administration departments – making it very clear that the enterprise was, in the words of the psalm, divided against itself and could not stand. On further examination however, it exhibited not three of Assagioli's sub-personalities but five, none of which were working harmoniously together.

Clearly, the company needed above all to reconcile the tribal conflicts that were raging among its inner parts, since these were taking up all its energy and had left it unable to compete effectively in outside markets, parallelling the classic problems of the individual racked with inner turmoil. In the process of psychosynthesis the sub-personalities are imaged and then labelled allegorically. Using this technique the writer identified the sub-personalities of the client organisation as under –

* *St George* the production department, was favoured disproportionately by the new managing director who had come up through this route. It was traditionalist, trustworthy, straight, conservative, arid and

boring. The darling of the City establishment, it represented all that is terribly good and all that is terribly bad about the traditional English gentleman. Within the organisation it comprised a blue-blooded elite that had always performed most successfully in the past, but flaunted its 'influence and superiority' and was enormously resented by the less distinguished.

* *The Dragon* was the marketing department, which took a fundamentally different line to the managing director and his production orientation. It had essentially been the marketing department which had perpetuated the earlier major error necessitating the reconstruction of the group. The head of the dragon had been cut off when the then managing director was sacked, but as is the custom of dragons another head had grown to take its place. A sinister figure in Christian lore, this theoretical embodiment of evil is nevertheless a repository of wisdom and the seat of imagination in Chinese myth. So it was within this organisation equivocally full of brilliant and yet dangerous qualities. The Dragon had been repressed by St George since causing the original disaster and it was between these two elements that the major cause of conflict existed.

* *The Maiden Chained to a Rock* was represented by one of the most important subsidiaries of the company which was in the constricted position of having been without a chief executive for two years. But unlike the fable, the reason for this lay at the door of St George rather than the Dragon, the former having effectively taken away the Maiden's power and independence in order to prevent her from whoring about with the Dragon and ruining his reputation. One of the most important aspects of the organisation's subsequent therapy was the appointment of a managing director to this subsidiary so that the log-jam of internal dissent could be shifted.

* *Man's Best Friend.* The subsidiary concerned had a large administrative tail located away from London. Most of the people working there had served the organisation for many years, were totally loyal and trustworthy, felt pained and saddened by the internal wrangling and simply wanted to be allowed to get on with their jobs. Their attitude was that of a pet spaniel with soulful eyes who only needed the occasional pat of recognition for its life to be fulfilled, just as long as Master and Mistress stopped quarrelling too.

* *K-9, Man's Electronic Best Friend.*   The loyalty of this dedicated band was however shortly to be sorely tested by the introduction of a new computer with attendant acolytes who, it was feared, would usurp the position of the old stagers of the administration department and provide further cause for internal dissent.

Alas, many of these implications were too painful for the patient to accept at the time but after the passage of three or four years, and the retirement of the principals of this drama, the process of corporate psychosynthesis gently began to take place to the great relief and benefit of both the organisation and all who sailed in her.

In another parallel between the individual and the organisation, California management consultant Roger Harrison has restated our Rule of Three in organisational terms. He argues that each organisation has to display aspects of mind, heart and will in equal balance as a tripod of support. Heart and will but no mind is represented by the start-up organisatsion, the fledgling firm which does what it has to do because its people love their work but who once things get complicated are incapable of changing up a gear into the next stage of growth.

Heart and mind without will is the bumbling charitable or bureaucratic organisation, which never gets anywhere but carries on vapidly under its own momentum. This is a stage often reached in the period preceding a decline once the initial will of growth, success and excitement has evaporated. Mind and will with no heart is the ruthless power orientated organisation, the predatory takeover bidder and asset stripper whose methods and ideology are characteristic of Hitler's Third Reich.

Stress[9] – the Masculine and the Feminine Approach

Conflict and imbalance should not, however, be thought to apply only to wicked commercial organisations in the world of mammon. The most ferocious battles are often fought out in the gentle pastures of the caring professions and voluntary bodies. These and their members are vocationally driven by the forces of love and compassion, which are so strong and all-pervading that the shadow side beneath is absolutely suppressed. The shadow side of love is power, and to such people the ostentatious trappings of power are deeply offensive because they so fear the longing for it within themselves. It surfaces, however, in the vicious politics so frequently found inside these bodies which present so admirable a face (what for the individual, Jung called the persona) to the outside world.

As with the individual, so with the organisation. As with the organisation, so with the individual – unresolved internal conflict causes acute stress and forges links in the chain of ill-health and underperformance, leading to yet more stress. The Institute of Directors has stated that time off work because of stress-related illness has increased fivefold since the mid-1950s, and is costing hundreds of millions of pounds a year in lost output. The Health and Safety Executive report 'Mental Health at Work' stated that the increasing prevalence of stress was the root cause of 40% of all sick leave. City Health Care carried out a survey of 250 City of London high-flyers in late 1987 and found that stress, long hours, too much good living and too little exercise had led to the following –

raised blood pressure	18%
significant overweight	15%
diagnosed heart problems	10%
raised blood cholesterol levels	10%
impaired liver function	7%

'Executive Stress', a survey by Allied Dunbar, claims that most of the three million people who work in full time professional and managerial jobs in Britain suffer from stress, nearly a quarter of them being under pressure from deadlines and a further tenth from long hours and heavy workloads. 40% of executives complain of money worries and personal or family relationships, more than half of these using alcohol to try and solve the problem.

It is curious that a company will appoint a director or senior executive without giving a thought to the maintenance of that person as an asset. Even in a medium-sized company, it can cost the purchaser something like £500,000 over a ten-year period. Fixed assets of this value with a ten-year lifespan are automatically maintained, but it is only just being realised that people break down just like machines do and need to be maintained as well. Hence the rush to set up Employee Assistance Programmes now extant in 480 of the US Fortune 500 companies and rapidly gaining favour in this country.

Companies are now beginning to employ therapists to counsel both individuals and groups. For senior executives under stress the effects are often immediate and sometimes dramatic, and furthermore the innovation can be objectively tested in performance terms as producing long-term improvements in morale and corporate effectiveness. Counselling, therapy and analysis have also been found to make a positive and observable contribution to building the board team as has already been indicated.

According to Professor Cary Cooper who heads the stress unit at Manchester University's Institute of Science and Technology, the traditional male style of management contributes significantly to stress and thus actually prevents workers from producing their best. Compared to other countries, much of British management still tends towards the autocratic; and as a consequence stress at work costs the country between 5% and 10% of GNP through ill-health, disease and death.

'Stress at work is closely related to the amount of control people feel they have over their area of responsibility' he states, 'British managers – mostly men – are not in general too good at allowing their subordinates this kind of freedom because they are too sensitive about their own power.' He emphasises that in contrast to women managers they also tend to manage by punishment rather than by praise and that it is women in management who so often have the human skills that will be needed to steer British industry through the rapids of change ahead. 'Studies have shown that women are better at coping with change themselves and encouraging others to cope with it', Professor Cooper points out, but adds darkly that though more women than ever are leaving universities looking for a career in management, over 95% of company directors and 90% of managers are men.

Hence one in four of new businesses is now being set up by a woman[10]. In this capacity many women are being recognised as serious and extremely successful managers. When the share issue of Sophie Mirman's Sock Shop plc was 52 times over-subscribed on the Unlisted Securities Market, a prominent stockbroker commented that 'women rule the USM OK'. He cited Debbie Moore with her Pineapple Group in 1982; Anita Roddick's Body Shop (of which more later); Jennifer d'Abo of Ryman Group; and Irene Stein of Regina Health and Beauty Products. There are other well known names around too, such as Steve Shirley's previously mentioned FI Group and Maureen Smith's PR organisation The Communication Group. These women have managed to compete on equal terms with men and often outperformed them, not on a novelty basis but simply because they fulfil the new demands of management as well as those of the old ones that are still valid.

On the other hand David Clutterbuck and Marianne Devine can still argue convincingly in their book 'Business Women: Present and Future' that 'the map which constructs the world of work is one which has been drawn by men' – encapsulating the principal reason why, in so many industries, women still fail to reach senior management positions. They are entering junior management grades in growing numbers but are obliged to cope with career developments and terms of employment designed for male needs, and undergo severe stress through trying to balance the demands of work, family and community commitments. Hence the flood of entrepreneuses. In this they echo many inner directed men, who find that rather than beating their heads against a brick wall the best way of ensuring that they can work the way they want to is to start something up themselves.

Certainly the position of women in business is changing for the better, but it has a long way to go. Girls setting out on their careers are still discouraged by parents, teachers and career officers. They find it difficult to be accepted for an apprenticeship or training, and employers and unions put up barriers along the way to a permanent job. The Young Women's Christian Association conducted a survey based on three industries – engineering, construction and printing – and found discrimination at all levels and at all stages in the career process.

However there are some employers who do recognise that many women are better placed to get ahead by concentrating on cooperation and trust rather than confrontation and threat and by avoiding the misdirected flamboyance of macho self-expression. There is a growing acceptance that the worst aspects of the gung-ho outer directed style of management and business performance are both unhealthy and ineffective. As we have seen, they are found far less with companies or teams led by women; they are also found far less in the rapidly growing and successful cooperative sector, in the ever-increasing number of consultancy businesses and in companies where there have been buy-outs by employees. The feeling of personal and shared involvement in their work at all levels has transformed such organisations as The National Freight Corporation, already alluded to in earlier pages.

From Microcosm to Macrocosm

Meanwhile on the macro-scale a whole new inner directed perspective on the iron laws of economics has been initiated by TOES (The Other Economic Summit) and The New Economics Foundation.[11] Since 1983

TOES has regularly held conferences simultaneously with the annual Group of Seven economic summits proper, at which the great ones issue anodyne statements about the way the rich nations of the world plan to maintain their riches. The communiques produced by both sets of summits, both international in nature but with only the former including representatives from Third World countries, have been in stark contrast. How interesting it is, however, that at the 1988 summit the first steps were taken towards the relief of the international debt burden of the poorest nations, a proposal that had been put forward by TOES for long enough.

At the same time an ugly term 'soft-nomics' has emerged from Japan and is gaining currency among economists all over the world. This is a new set of economic assumptions which is based on people's growing need to be informed and to communicate on a scale, at a complexity and with a speed which makes small operations and local group solutions more efficient than cumbersome collectivist action. Small is thus beginning to be accepted as being more beautiful even in traditional economic terms, and the old centralised institutions and regulations are under threat.

Industrial countries have begun to recognise both their interdependence with the developing world, and its need to break the old ties of dependent economic colonialism and to establish a greater degree of self-sufficiency. It is no longer merely a question of our importing their raw materials and using them to manufacture industrial goods. To keep the global economy from stagnating we have to open our markets to Third World goods provided by their newly awakened secondary industrial sectors. It is only thus that we can in return export our tertiary and quaternary products of high-technology goods and services to this expanding market.

In recent years, too often it has been the poorest sections of the populations of these countries that have carried the heaviest burden of economic adjustment. Now the IMF and the World Bank are starting to work with their governments to help shelter the poorest against the more painful aspects of reform, while at the same time moving towards the overall goal of sustainable planetary growth.

With the appalling and mutually destructive international debt situation still hovering over us, there is greater general awareness that with nations as with people, we are all in this together. As New York governor Mario Cuomo expressed it 'You know that no man is an island. No woman, no village, no town, no state, no nation either. Today there is no purely national economy: there is a global economy. Only in an integrated comprehensive way can we deal with our cluster of economic problems – deficits, trade imbalances and debts – the lines interconnect everywhere on the map . . . Once the public understands that most of the world strives for peace, opposes terrorism and desires the benefits of trade, one further thing then becomes obvious – our need to deal with one another, to talk, argue, bargain and negotiate'.

Business Networking and Business Ethics

The writer has to declare two interests here, having been involved as a TOES steering committee member at an early stage in its development, and also as co-founder of the next example of the growth of holistic business practice, The Business Network.[12] Founded with a colleague, Edward Posey in 1982, The Business Network now has a national membership of around 400. Its meetings attract those who wish to participate in encouraging the human scale in business and its aims were originally expressed as follows:

* To guide business towards directions which are alternative and yet complementary to appropriate traditional principles; and encourage it to channel its human, financial and organisational resources into progressive social change, balancing the practical with the spiritual.

* To apply complementary principles to business philosophy and practice, with the purpose of fostering a holistic approach that brings not only material success but is also nourishing in the widest sense to all concerned.

* To be available as a mutually supportive group to help its members to humanise and harmonise their business and professional lives, providing a forum for discovery, experimentation, integrity and example.

* To create links with other spiritually oriented groups and to provide a practical counter-balance to what are often their very positive but diffused energies.

* Thus, to encourage the flow of ideas and concepts between traditional business and new thought by holding workshops, discussion meetings and debates, inviting speakers, conducting

research and publishing material relevant to the purpose of the Network.

Besides its British development, it has influenced the formation of sister networks in 13 other countries which form the International Business Network. It has also spawned a number of special interest groups such as The Business Samaritans who counsel individuals about problems at work on both an emotional and a practical basis; and groups of members who have researched and applied the Network's principles to computing, training, management, entrepreneurship and the relationship of business to peace.

Three of these special interest groups have actually hived off to become stand-alone organisations themselves. The first is New Initiative Ltd,[13] a consultancy which works with businesses in the development of their social programmes. Second is The Gaia Foundation,[13] a registered charity which relates the activities of business to the health and welfare of the planet. Finally, there is Financial Initiative Ltd[13] which has two major functions – it acts as an investment broker between ethical businesses and the individuals who wish to invest in them; and it advises potential investors on ethical unit trusts of which there has suddenly been a remarkable hatch.

Ethical investment, and indeed the whole subject of ethics in business, has been a hot topic for some time now. The largest unit trust, Friends Provident's Stewardship Fund, was founded in 1984 and with its concomitant insurance and pension funds stood at £120m four years later, well outperforming the corresponding FT indices in the process. By this time it had also attracted eight competitors into the field and more on the touchlines, where the emphasis was changing from a merely negative avoidance of companies involved in tobacco, alcohol, gambling, armaments or support for the South African regime, to a positive discrimination towards companies which benefit the environment. Most of the funds involved have committees of independent minders who act as both philosophical and performance-hungry watchdogs.

Meanwhile the rest of the commercial world is also responding to the pull of environmental concern.[14] Institutional investors are beginning to ask the companies in whose shares they have holdings what exactly is their impact on the environment, because they in turn have been asked the same question by their policy-holders, pensioners and unit-holders. For example, the Norwich Union, Refuge, Pearl, and the Church Commissioners have declared themselves as being highly concerned about the littering of the environment and its pollution by industrial organisations, and are now demanding answers to some pretty searching questions.

The Sunday Times 'Insight' campaign to clean up Britain's rivers has particularly attracted their support. They wrote to the polluters named by 'Insight' – among them ICI, RTZ, Coalite and Chemical, Coates Patons, British Coal, British Steel, Ciba Geigy, Unilever and Grand Metropolitan – to ask what they or their subsidiaries were going to do about their anti-social behaviour. Should their enquiries meet with a negative response, these and other large investors have made it clear that they may even be prepared to disinvest. Simultaneously, Sir Trevor Holdsworth, President of the Confederation of British Industries, urged member companies to take seriously the new environmental imperative – 'too many firms are keeping their heads down in the increasingly forlorn hope that the public will not be interested in their environmental impact'.

Ethics are demonstrably good business these days.[15] Green Pages[16] is a directory of opportunities in the environment business which is now reckoned to be a multi-million pound industry. Modelled on British Telecom's yellow version, it was launched in March 1988 and preaches the message that there is money in greenery. 9000 firms operate in just one sector of the market, that of pollution control technology, and 2 million Europeans work in the expanding environmental field. Green mail order, from The Whole Thing, was next, and then green marketing consultancy, from SustainAbility and Brand News. John Elkington, co-author with Tom Burke of 'The Green Capitalists' and one of the leading lights of the green entrepreneur movement, admits that to date green consumers like green investors have tended to take the negative view, boycotting CFC aerosol sprays, or firms selling furniture produced from trees indigenous to the tropical rain forests. Similarly, many businesses are still defensive on the issue, merely trying to avoid unacceptable practices, or to cover them up. But increasingly company directors are recognising the profit potential in products that are environmentally friendly.

He points out that there is a new positive consumer movement abroad, evidenced by the success of 'The Green Consumer Guide', an environmentalists' Which? that details the greenest buys in food, DIY, consumer goods, cars and even holidays.

Co-authored by him and Julia Hailes, the book sold 200,000 copies in the first six months and was in the top ten non-fiction best sellers for almost all that time. Together they also addressed a January 1989 conference, 'Attracting The Green Consumer', at which Environment Under Secretary Virginia Bottomley announced in a keynote address that the shopping behaviour of 30% of the population is now influenced by environmental factors. Such interest did the conference arouse the organisers had to change the venue to one providing five times the capacity of the original site.

Advertisers Lowe Howard-Spink divide green consumers into three camps. First there are the original radical greens who are anti-commerce and anti-profit motive (social resisters to us). Then there are the 'power greens', nimby pale green conservationists who care about the country-side close to their bijoux residences but worry little about wider issues (belongers and conspicuous consumers). Finally there are our self-explorers who genuinely care about all aspects of the environment, the mainstream customers whom the retailers are really trying to please nowadays. Mercury-free batteries, leadless petrol, packaging, water and food are their areas of concern; they see the movement as a whole and take on board all its implications, imbuing them with an almost spiritual quality that represents the holistic view.

For these, and indeed also for the social resisters and inner directed experimentalists, it is not possible to join the alternative movement in half measure. Trying to do so is rather like asking a builder to come and look at a broken tile on your roof, and then watching with mounting horror as he finds fault with everything else. 'You know what you've got 'ere', he cries, and the plumbing and the wiring have to be ripped out, there is dry rot in the basement and the chimney is cracked from top to bottom. All you thought you needed was a tile replaced, but no such luck. The mainte-nance of the house is an indivisible process.

Ethics[17] are not only about greenness, they are also at the heart of many of today's other management decisions. Consider for example the follow-ing –

* should a company invest in a developing country with a corrupt and despotic regime but whose people though badly governed desperately need the jobs?

* what action should a manager take if he suspects that his organisation may be breaking the law – when exactly is whistle-blowing justified?

* at what stage do safety levels become acceptable for a new product? The law may lay down minimum standards, but how long should testing continue if doubts remain after they have been met? And what happens when delay means that not only profits but jobs could be at stake?

* what responsibilities does a company have to its local communities, particularly if a given area is almost wholly dependent upon it? If the operation is shut down, what action should be taken to mitigate the effect on workers and community?

* To be competitive in overseas markets, it may be necessary to match practices of foreign firms which would normally be unethical at home. Does that mean that anything goes? If not, where should the line be drawn – particularly if jobs are at stake here too.

Many of these issues produce an unstable mixture of ethics and economics and involve awkward trade-offs. Managers generally muddle through them hoping for the best but we have reached the stage where there is need for proper research. The Institute of Business Ethics was formed for this purpose in 1987, with the aim of giving managers access to a body of knowledge, and of creating a climate in which organisations can become better informed to make good judgements in these fuzzy areas. In a January 1988 survey the Market Research Society sampled the population to gauge the perceived standards of honesty among various occupations. Top businessmen performed pretty lamentably with 17% regarding them as highly honest and 29% as highly dishonest. The Institute has entered the arena not a moment too soon.

Business in the Community – the Holistic View

Meanwhile the well known agency, Business in the Community,[18] has certainly raised awareness of the relationship between organisations and the communities in which they live, at any rate. BiC, which has already featured here, grew out of the 1980 Anglo-American conference on community involvement chaired by Tom King when he was Local Government minister. A working group was formed under Sir Alastair Pilkington, whose glassmakers had pioneered the movement in St Helens, and BiC was the result of its deliberations.

Enterprise agencies are BiC's main building blocks. When it was formed there were 23 of them compared to almost 300 by mid-1988. For small businesses these provide both a free independent counselling and training service; and links with each other and with banks, accountants, solicitors and other advisors and services. Money for each agency comes partly from local and central government and in rather higher proportion from among more than 4000 sponsors in the private sector. The agencies are credited with helping to create 50,000 jobs a year and saving another 25,000.

At the same time, the secondment process, where businesses lend the movement able executives free of charge, renders a two-way benefit both to the community and to management development. The secret here is an interconnective relationship – not top-down paternalistic largesse, but mutual involvement at the ultimate personal level. BiC also collaborates with a host of other organisations promoting economic regeneration in local communities, such as Action Resource Centre, The Industrial Society, Project Fullemploy, Livewire, Young Enterprise, The Prince's Youth Business Trust, Groundwork and Instant Muscle. These, in their various ways, constitute a band of what BiC's chief executive Stephen O'Brien calls 'social entrepreneurs' – the enablers who act as catalysts in the community to make things actually happen.

O'Brien would like to see a lot more of this, following the success of these models. 'My personal ambition is for every properly organised company in this country to have a thought-out policy for its involvement in the community. We aim to prove or otherwise that something can be done about a problem and then it is up to others to take that up.' Acting as pathfinder and prodding others to do likewise is Business in the Community's averred intent, unsurprisingly so, since it has Prince Charles as its president. We can reasonably expect to see some of the Prince's other ideas filtering through into the consciousness of business under its leadership. As Stephen O'Brien put it –

'Holistic is a word he uses often and in different contexts. I think the commercial world should be moving towards the important consideration of what a holistic business might be – one which has a sense of integration in its corporate philosophy. This should ideally balance the interests of the business and the company's interaction with society and the environment'.

We are right back on track once more. Research on the matter has already been initiated by another member of the BiC team, Eileen Conn, and an interested group of her fellow members of The Business Network. Reproduced hereunder is part of Eileen Conn's paper on the subject, 'An Outline of a Holistic Business Framework'.[19] What she asks is for the organisation to recognise its interrelatedness with the individual below and with society above it in the scale of things. She expresses this as creating a harmonious interchange between the 'inner life' and the 'outer life' of the business, which, once identified in the following terms, must be integrated in all its aspects so as to create the vision or mission of the organisation – Assagioli's 'recognition of the Higher Self'.

THE BUSINESS' INNER LIFE

The individuals in the business

A business cannot exist without human beings. For the business to be healthy in a holistic way, so too must the people in it. They must be developing a balanced interplay between their own inner and outer lives in body, emotions, mind and spirit – in some circles known as spiritual growth, in others as personal growth, and often described as personal transformation. An organisation comprised of individuals not aware of their inner lives and the interplay with their outer world will be an organisation which is unaware and unconscious too. Such an organisation will not be able to operate holistically.

At a minimum, there probably needs to be clear evidence that the individuals within the organisation:–

* identify with the organisation's mission;
* are concerned to integrate in a balanced way their work and personal lives;
* are consciously pursuing personal development.

The internal processes of the business

Just as with an individual, the inner life of the business has its physical, emotional, mental and spiritual dimensions. And there are as many, possibly more, ways of looking at the health of each of these for an organisation as there are for an individual. At the physical level there are the buildings, the furniture, the equipment, and all aspects of the working environment, all of which can have a role to play in how well the individuals in the organisation can operate. The culture of the business will also display

[247]

its emotional, mental, and spiritual natures. The processes of decision making play an important role in this; how much room individuals have to make their particular contribution and how much the process helps them to align their vision and purpose with that of the organisation.

A business which is self-aware will have internal processes which encourage the personal growth of the individuals in the organisation, and see this as an essential and integrated part of the inner life of the business. For example, the development of the business strategy needs to be related to the individuals' own development processes – otherwise the respective visions and missions will not remain aligned. Power distribution, management policies and style, reward policies, and decision making processes all need to reflect the need to provide scope for the individuals to develop and contribute, and to form well balanced groups within which to do so: such groups are an indispensable element of a holistic system's structure.

THE BUSINESS' OUTER LIFE

The business in society

The business' outer life comprises its relationships with other individuals and groups which comprise society. The main ones are:–

* **owners/shareholders/financial interests:**   The quality of the relationship between the financial interest and the business is critical for the right relationship. It needs to be a positive relationship. 'Ethical investing' tends to be negative or passive. The more that those who have a financial interest in the business are, in effect, part of the business, the more holistic the relationship.

* **traders/suppliers/distributors/competitors:**   The characteristics of the right relationship with these groups will include honesty and integrity in decisions and information, not abusing power, paying bills in time, honouring contracts in spirit as well as in letter, and acting so that other organisations can develop their holistic potential. Collaboration and cooperation will be the general style: not as either you or me, but as you *and* me.

[248]

* **customers/clients:** The customer/client must be viewed as a whole whether as an individual or as another organisation and must be treated with respect and dignity. Services must be honest and effective and the marketing, advertising and other information must be responsible, enabling and life-enhancing, not resting on stereotypes or encouraging dissension, greed or ill-health. The product must be relevant and socially beneficial.

* **public/community:** The business needs to have thought through its relationship with the public at large, as appropriate for its particular business, including the provision of information, and particularly with those parts of the community most directly affected by its operations. It needs to do this as an integral part of its business policies and activities and not as a marginal charitable activity.

* **institutions and other organisations:** There need to be right relationships with all other organised groups from government to voluntary agencies.

* **international groups:** There may be an international dimension in any one of the previous categories and it is important for the business to develop right relations internationally.

The business and the Planet

The Gaia hypothesis, that the Earth is itself a living organism, shifts us away from the current notion of the business as an exploiter and controller of the Earth's resources towards the notion of the business as part of the Earth's living process. To be holistic, then, the business' relations with the Planet must reflect the interdependence of everything in and on the Planet.

The key areas are:–

* **the effect on living species:** The business affects living species in two main ways – by using them in production and by affecting their environment. Any production process needs to enhance the well-being of living species or at least be neutral.

* **use of the Earth's materials:** All businesses use the Earth's

materials whether in the production process or in using goods made from them. If these are non-renewable materials, substitutes need to be sought and conservation practised. If they are renewable, they need to be properly managed. A holistic business will work to ensure that appropriate policies and programmes to achieve this are developed and implemented. This includes recycling and energy conservation measures, and precludes wasteful production processes and excessive packaging.

* **effect on the environment:** Processes should sustain the environment and avoid pollution or dereliction.

In a November 1988 lecture to the Business Network, Dr Willis Harman, President of the Institute of Noetic Sciences, described the task of business and business people as one of challenging the validity of the old order. 'In the past we have given power and legitimacy to institutions but once this is withdrawn, though they may struggle to hang on they cannot last. In the process of psychotherapy the client may initially play the victim and feel impotent. He may not want to change and actually hangs on to the role of being controlled. Then a perceptual change takes place and the client takes up an adversary position against injustices that have to be righted. Having gone through this phase he finally takes on the role of creator and creates the perception of things that can be done.'

'This can also be applied both to history and to the current state of affairs. Right now people, particularly in business, are getting together to change things by joining hands and helping them to change throughout the system. We are all culturally hypnotised to see reality in a certain way and it is only when we break this spell that we can see laterally that there are other ways of tackling our lives. Our present scientific and economic reality, so called, is in fact a hypnotic artefact; and unless we realise this, the solution of one problem will create others.'

'So it is no use tinkering with the greenhouse effect, change must be the result of altering the whole system; there is no solution short of re-inventing the world. We need to redefine development so that it is sustainable; we need to redefine employment – the economic links between people and society – so that work does not necessarily equal jobs; we need to redefine national security, which can no longer be secured by military strength; we need to redefine science, which leaves out such a lot of what is most important to people.'

Tough talking, and absolutely right in the long run. But the pure ultra-green philosophy can sometimes be self-destructive in the shorter term – Harman's 'adversary position' in action. Nobody is a hundred percent pure, and people who are travelling tentatively in a green or inner direction need carrot as well as stick. Progressively more and more businesses are moving forward in terms of both policy and action in all aspects of their operations which concern human beings and the planet as a whole. The way it happens is that they take note of and take on board the values of their employees who are themselves moving in this direction; and by doing so they effectively honour them as whole people rather than simply exploiting their work potential, which is all that has ever been thought of as appropriate in outer directed terms.

The lazy, grasping, or fearful will react negatively to this, of course. Cynicism is the last refuge of the slob. But until all human organisations are measured against such a holistic ideal they will continue to function as inadequately as they do now. It is not enough for Megalithic International to dish out 1% of annual gross profits to the local community in a lordly way if it is selling dangerous products to Brazil which are illegal here in Britain; to give its consumers a matchless service if it is screwing down its suppliers with late payments; or to give a generous boost to the pension fund if its working conditions are such that it would be something of a miracle if any of its employees ever reached retirement anyway.

An organisation that gives with one hand and snatches away with the other is the slave of old values and will find itself unrepresentative of our new millennium and shut out of its joys. Conscience money is going to be at a discount on the ethical currency exchanges of the future. Wool can no longer be pulled over eyes. Inner directeds may be green but they are certainly not green in the sense of being artlessly innocent.

But no business could possibly perform in such a manner, you may protest. Well actually that is no longer so. There are not very many large-scale models around as yet but there are a few, and here for a start are three examples. We began this whole journey with four straws in the wind. We end it with three bricks made from those and other straws. Very soon it will be time to build.

14

CODA AND FINALE

'Of all the lessons that have been learned about development, none is so unequivocally clear as this: projects defined and carried out without the active participation of the people they are intended to benefit rarely produce the expected results. They remain the projects of the outsiders, unsupported and unassimilated. Application of this lesson has been painfully slow. It contends with a misconceived notion of charity – that it is better to give than to receive. In fact it is better to *share*. It is complicated by forms of assistance that elevate the interests of donors above those of recipients. It is impeded by stereotypes of the Third World that provoke pity and generosity: pictures of helpless and suffering humanity. In fact, the poorest people are anything but helpless given the slightest opportunity to help themselves.'

(from 'For Whose Benefit?: report of the Standing Committee on External Affairs and International Trade on Canada's Official Development Assistance Policies and Programs)

The Body Shop

In a nutshell, not only do People Matter Most, but People Better Themselves Best. Enshrined in this interdependent betterment principle is the slogan 'Trade not Aid' that belongs to Anita Roddick,[1] founder of The Body Shop International plc. One of the stoutest supporters of The Business Network, she is on record as saying that it is here that she finds the inspiration of being among people with fellow feelings. Her Body Shop is a prime example of the holistic business of the future, in which all aspects of the organisations are orientated towards the same inner directed aim.

One of her company's annual reports had blazoned across the front of it the words 'Doing good is good for business'. Certainly it has been for her. Anita Roddick was named Business Woman of the Year in 1985, her company was Company of the Year in 1987 and in the New Year's Honours of 1988 she was awarded an OBE. She founded the company with her husband Gordon in 1976 with a £4,000 loan, and at the end of 1987 its turnover had reached £28.5m, generating pre-tax profits of more than £6m. She has 330 franchised branches in 33 countries and in Britain alone she had created over 3,000 jobs. She combines 60s idealism with 80s entrepreneurism and, to paraphrase J K Galbraith, contrives both to comfort the afflicted and afflict the comfortable. When she received the Company of the Year Award, her pin-striped audience wriggled guiltily as she slammed into big business for its inflexibility, pessimism and lack of social conscience.

She started her own organisation in Brighton, with the innovative but entirely commercial idea of selling natural cosmetics which were both ecologically sound and reasonably priced. Rule One was that natural products would take first priority and that neither animal products nor products tested on animals would be for sale. Since those early days she has crossed many frontiers and many cultures in the quest for her second ideal – profits with responsibility. Much of her time is spent in travelling – not only visiting outlying franchisees but also in exploring the natural beauty preparations of ethnic peoples throughout the world. What do Eskimo women do to try and keep their skins supple? How do they wash their hair in Nepal? How many different ways are there of using a coconut for cosmetic purposes?

'Trade not Aid' also entails a constant search for ways in which she can use manufactured Third World products in an unpatronising and non-exploitative manner. Thus Nepalese women, the real disadvantaged among one of the ten poorest nations of the world, are being trained to make the paper for The Body Shop packaging. As for another indicative Body Shop development, there is the history behind the company's 'Footsie' rollers; serrated wooden rollers for massaging tired Western feet which are manufactured by the young residents of an Indian orphanage.

These were first put out for quotation to a number of British suppliers. Taking the lowest, Anita Roddick went to Southern India and negotiated a similar price with the ex Jesuit priest who ran the Boys' Town in Tirumangalam. The boys were trained to turn them on a lathe, but instead of the usual Third World sweated labour set-up they were paid the equivalent of a First World price.

However, in order not to ruin the local economy and culture by swamping it with a group of highly affluent teenagers, for the time being the boys themselves have only been paid the going rate in the local labour market, the balance being held in trust for them until they leave the orphanage at 16 or so. At that time their share of the money is used to set up each of them in a trade – to buy a lathe for themselves or a loom, say, or a pair of oxen and a plough. Part of the money is also used to develop local craft workshops for village women – producing palm-leaf baskets, sisal shopping-bags, handmade paper products and silk from silkworms.

This sensitivity to situation and creativity in decision is characteristic of the company and indeed of the entire holistic management movement. But trade is not the only sense in which the business is based on an interdependent foundation. For Anita Roddick, it also involves 'taking care of the environment in which you work, the community in which you are a guest, the people you employ.' The Body Shop's entire operation has been consistently thought through and felt through; and here are some other examples of the integrated approach –

* 'If you've got 20 million people a week passing the shop, you have an avenue of education there'. Every year The Body Shop takes up a charitable cause in line with its own vision. In window displays and in the display of literature within the shops themselves, in 1987 they featured Greenpeace and in 1988 Friends of the Earth and Amnesty International.

* Fees for Roddick's numerous speaking engagements are put towards research on a pet project, START, in which St Stephen's Hospital, London is researching the treatment of skin diseases.

* The company's annual report is printed on recycled paper, and all 160 staff at the head office in Littlehampton, Sussex have two wastepaper bins under their desks. In the black bin goes all the paper that can be recycled and the white bin gets the rest. Warehouse staff also recycle cardboard boxes, and the whole exercise is expected to show a profit of £2,000 in its first year.

* With her fellow millionaire entrepreneur Richard Branson, Roddick launched the Virgin Health Care Foundation, whose first product is Mates, the cut-price condoms targeted to combat Aids. Neither The

Body Shop nor Virgin itself make a penny of profit from it – that goes to the Foundation to be used for an Aids education programme. In future, they plan to make a whole range of generic products that are cheaply and readily available, and to plough back the profits either into health education or some other form of health care.

* The Body Shop's rapidly growing turnover now enables it to exercise purchasing muscle with suppliers and to demand, for example, that the plastic bottles that contain its products are made of biodegradable material.

* Any applicant for a franchise is asked pretty early on in the interview how she plans for the outlet to be of service to the local community. Those that have no such plans get short shrift. Usually the schemes involve the company's own areas of expertise – for example free massages for residents of an old people's home, or free advice in economical beauty care for unemployed teenagers.

* Her attitude to money combines commerce with conscience, but she also sees it as a tool with which to create an organisation where there is a 'different attitude to business so that they go into work in a joyful way, and the only way I can do that is to make the job more resonant in its values'.

* Take, finally, her views on investment. 'Ethical investment can be such a sham. For example, some ethical investors won't invest in South Africa; but we *should* be investing in South Africa as long as we specifically channel that money as a means of giving the blacks empowerment'.

Anita Roddick looks after the back streets as well as the high streets. She has opened a shop in Brixton and is particularly concerned with the Easterhouse estate in Glasgow. 'You've got to treat these areas like the Third World; create trade and employment', she declares. 'The instigators of change have got to be business people. They've got the power to be listened to. All the aggression and excitement is now in business, in the City. Every time I give a lecture everybody feels sympathetic to the idea; then they say they can't do it because of the bureaucracy. But if every company took just one person to set up a social welfare department and see what they could do, that would be a fantastic start'.

The details of her own involvement in Easterhouse are illuminating and characteristic. The project she is creating here is a replicable model, a two-year blueprint for others to follow. To start the ball rolling she had a whip-round at a meeting of all her UK franchisees, and within a matter of minutes had raised £20,000 to create an adventure playground for the area. The basis was that the local kids would design it and state exactly what they wanted ('if they spend the £20,000 on balloons it's OK by us!'), and that the army would then help build it for nothing.

Secondly, she has planned a retail training scheme for young people in Easterhouse in conjunction with a local housing cooperative. Taking charge of one of a parade of shops, she intends to design it as a hairdresser's to the specification of the people who are going to work there and then train them to run it – the free training also being extended to retail employees and managers in the other shops. The purpose of these two first items of the programme was to make a strong visual impact on the locality, which would show that what The Body Shop was really doing was to help people become capable of improving their own condition.

Part three of the scheme was to employ Community Learning Initiatives,[2] a firm of consultants also involved in the other three projects, to train local people how to set up their own businesses or cooperatives. Finally, she has taken over a local factory which has been empty for years and converted it into a soap manufacturing plant. This involves job creation; training for local people – who will be given all the jobs there; establishing a quality, people-centred working environment; creating a trust fund to recycle 25% of the profits back for community use; inspiring similar projects elsewhere; and of course providing a high-quality, reliable product and service.

Some have questioned whether her schemes would not be still more laudable if they were hidden under a bushel, but this is off target. She is setting herself up as a role model for other businesses to copy, proving by her success that her ideas make sense – just as long as they are followed holistically and derived from the very DNA of the organisation. However, this can create misunderstandings among those who cannot share her vision and who translate everything into the old dead language. Take for example Maggie Drummond in *The Times* –

'I'm all for big business having a social conscience, which, practically speaking, means not doing things like ruining beauty spots and polluting rivers, and on the positive side handing over large sums of money to charities in return for a modest mention in a gala programme and the chance for the chairman's wife to meet the Princess of Wales. But when I walk into The Body Shop which is, for all its founder's social conscience, completely dedicated to the enhancement of self, is it necessary that I know how its new wood foot massagers are helping Third World employment or that by buying jojoba oil I'm helping to save the whales? . . . If they want to give, why don't they do just that – and quietly?'

Drummond complains that shopping there is emotionally exhausting and that she feels she is being sucked into a commercial gimmick, but unhappily she totally misses the point, the superabundant point, of Roddick's whole approach. It is only when real people come to personal terms with the issues and accept the imperative for individual involvement, that anything can move forward at all. Merely signing a cheque or dropping a coin into a tin without further thought is no longer enough. In the coming trans-industrial era of interdependence it is a matter of trade not aid in every sense. We must trade emotionally with other people of all sorts and conditions, and recognise that in the framework of our own personal contracts we should both give and receive full measure. This is true of individuals, of teams and of organisations – all the holons that go to make up society itself.

The Aquarian Agency[3]

Our second role model also adopts a totally non-traditional business approach to economic development, but here we move from retailing to technological and socio-economic breakthrough. The basis of this is an extremely elegant new method of producing fresh water from brine. But the holistic vision takes it far further to embrace the production of timber, fruit and vegetables in desert regions, marketing these and other locally derived products on the world market (trade not aid again), unemployment, educational and medical support, the protection of a local culture and the ecological enhancement of the world as a whole. To introduce it, here are comments from its chief executive Christopher Seebach –

'The only future hope for the industrial developed world to thrive at all is for it to create a new consumer market out of the Third World. Big money groups we have talked to are concerned about the increase in the carbon dioxide levels of the atmosphere and the consequences of the greenhouse effect, but as responsible money managers they feel they can't be philanthropic. Our new project represents a profitable investment to cure this problem, and one which is furthermore guaranteed by export markets. 'We can in the process grow trees in the desert, provide livelihoods and nutrition and introduce social care for local communities. Moreover, banks owed money by the countries concerned are thus in a better position to be repaid, while industry recognises the possibility of large-scale development projects in these places once again. The financial, industrial, technological and social aspects turn out to be mutually generative.'

Seebach was born in 1940 and spent 15 years in international management consultancy, followed by a lucrative stint as a commodity dealer with the Chicago Board of Trade. The money that he made from this activity he applied to help finance inventions in the agriculture, health and water purification sectors. One such was a solar heat pump.

The principle behind this invention is that under less than atmospheric pressure water boils at temperatures lower than 100°C. If a vacuum pump is used to raise water ten metres, the consequent decompression enables it to boil at 24°C or 77°F. When cooled again, this steam will condense and create its own vacuum. So once the priming pump has started up the system, under certain conditions the self-perpetuating main pump can carry on under its own steam. The steam will condense when it reaches a temperature 20°C less than its boiling point, so that these conditions are met where there is a body of water which is 24°C on the surface and 4°C more than ten metres lower down. Then the system will keep pumping indefinitely – and what is more provide spare power. In this form, the engine is only 4% efficient, but who cares, the power is free anyway.

With this under its belt, Aquarian suddenly became relevant to all countries with arid areas close to a tropical coastline – covering a great swathe of land that takes in much of the middle and southern latitudes. The first pilot scheme to be considered was situated in the Gulf of Aqaba at Wadi Araba in Jordan. However, to everybody's consternation, there was virtually no heat difference between the top and the bottom of the ocean at the proposed site. In answer, the team therefore designed a modified system incorporating a series of solar ponds which used layers of different densities of salt water. This produced a heat difference of 80°C and meant that it was possible to use the water five times rather than once, making the method not 4% but 30% efficient.

When condensed, this steam provides fresh water costing only $1 per 1,000 gallons, compared to the normal price of $7 in the region if it is mistakenly struck when drilling for oil – or up to $200 where there are oil-based geological systems and corrosion takes place as a result. Since the water is desalinated, no corrosion is involved, and the solar pond facility means that there is no longer any geographical limitation on the system – any brackish water can be used whether inland or at sea. Geographical coverage is enhanced by the fact that the increased power of the pump can easily move the water a distance 400 miles in any direction.

The germ of this creative process began to develop in 1981. By 1985 when the technological breakthrough had been made, large organisations from all over the world had joined The Aquarian Agency's consortium, with a cluster of individual professionals of all disciplines and from 40 different countries. There were 500 of these by 1988, plus many more who were experienced at grassroots level in the relevant fieldwork and in alternative and appropriate technologies. The organisation is geographically decentralised to the highest degree, but its sophisticated electronic communications are totally centralised, so that there is global compatibility of equipment; and the business proceeds through a constant process of networking and comparing electronic notes.

Back in 1985, Seebach and his team had only penetrated the implications of the technology, however. It took a further three year learning process to graft this technological knowledge onto the cultural, social and ecological realities of the site. They travelled the world to meet experts not only on technology but on funding, on the impact of development on primitive societies, on the nature of famine and its cure – and then wove them all together into a single practical philosophy.

For after the pure engineering problems had been solved, those they then had to answer were multiplex – the biology and ecology of creating a forest; the meteorological engineering – where would it rain if a large forest started growing in a particular place; the physical eco-systems that would need to be created and those that would need to be avoided – what type of undergrowth would be suitable for the soil and how to counter insect pests; and most important of all, the vital human eco-systems – how to ask local people what they wanted so as to find out 'where does it hurt', and then to come up with an answer that did not also destroy their culture.

In arriving at these answers, they harnessed their powers of insight, deliberately using their right brains to reach intuitive solutions based on contemplation, brainstorming and lateral thought – and then using their left brains to work back deductively and scientifically in pinpointing the method. They found of course that all these problems were interconnected. 'If you have enough information to ask the question, you can

[259]

generally answer the problem', says Seebach. 'We got everybody in the team to think this way as well – seeing the situation as a solution, assuming that all equipment, scientific support and money is available, and then working out how it could be done. Curiously, often the "solutions" had nothing to do with the original problems, but contributed to the general enhancement of the project instead. It seemed as if we were all being nudged in the right direction.'

The Aquarian Agency has proved economically that you can harvest trees in deserts with its system more cheaply than you can harvest rain forests. This therefore represents a reprieve for those vitally important environments, as well as a means of transforming the quality of life in areas of poverty and famine. Major money-funders, authorities and agencies are now becoming concerned about these areas of high poverty, realising that they are potentials for civil unrest and the destabilisation of governments, and of profound influence on commercial decisions as to whether or not to do business in a particular country.

Though at first cynical, the funding organisations therefore became fascinated as they discovered that the Aquarian approach was also strictly businesslike, and are now asking the agency to act as consultants in re-jigging their own schemes along positive environmental and social lines. Through this they have demonstrated that projects are more profitable and secure with a better chance of survival, if they are originally designed to accommodate countries' long term needs; and involve an extended commitment and a sense of continued cooperation.

The Seatec Jordan concept has proved itself to be economically, socially and ecologically valid, and since it also conforms to Islamic Law, has gained the backing of the Islamic Development Bank, who have agreed to finance projects in any Moslem country that first requests it. By mid-1989 five other countries in Asia, South America and the Middle East had also expressed interest in similar schemes. What the project is therefore doing is not only to create both geographical and cultural stability within an impoverished area, but to provide examples that can be copied in other arid parts of the world. It works on the principle that the only way for future generations to enjoy a whole and balanced planet is for our generation to engage in practical cooperation between different cultures on every level.

It is important to note here that this is not an activist or political organisation; it is providing rather than protesting and is engaging business as the driving force for social change. Furthermore, it is a servicing organisation with no manufacturing facilities of its own and few

[260]

overheads. It can therefore operate on a minute percentage of the gross figures involved, so that virtually all excess income will in effect be channelled into the creation of more products.

The financial mechanism for this is built round a Dutch-based non-profit organisation, The Aquarian Foundation, which acts as overall money manager. The Aquarian Agency itself charges a service fee for consultancy, takes commission for marketing the products and receives repayment for all outside costs. Taking the Seatec Jordan scheme as an example, the $200m involved will be raised through an international financial consortium, led by the Islamic Development Bank, in the shape of a 20 year loan on which no interest would be payable for the first two years. After five years, the project should generate enough income to cover the unpaid and current interest and to make the necessary loan repayments in addition. This scheme calls, incidentally, for a 90 hectare plant able to produce 7,000 hectares of trees.

Halfway through the third year, the plant will be capable of producing 5 million gallons of water a day. Every year after the fifth, in addition to repaying the loan and interest, it will generate enough income to build a new plant plus another 20 million trees every year – supporting 15,000 families – either on a nearby site or in a different part of the country. Given a cash flow of $10 per tree, cropped on a coppice basis so that 7% are thinned every year, this will mean $600m per annum by year twenty, creating assets of $7 billion. By year ten, the assets will have covered the original security one thousand fold.

Now, here the cruncher. These assets will eventually belong not to the Aquarian Agency but to the local community and government. This was the most innovative piece of social engineering involved. The local population are given the land and the water and then allowed to get on serving it properly. They are taught how to use the system, but not manipulated into anything that will induce too great a cultural shock. They are, in other words, empowered to take on something new at the pace and to the degree that they are able to accept.

Thus in the first instance villages closer to large cities can probably accept more technology than those further out in the backwoods. '99% of the job is education – and this especially applies to the women there', says Seebach. The cropping method must therefore be presented in a socially appropriate form.

For example, individuals will be shown that if they plant so many trees when a baby is born they can pay for his education; if they plant more then they will be provided for in their old age.

The plan is that each area will, besides deriving its main income from the trees, also create a whole new spectrum of agricultural and cottage industries as individual villages of 15,000 families grow their own crops – often on a permaculture basis under the tree cover. Thus the Seatec Jordan project will produce sawn wood, firewood, green fodder, green manure and charcoal for export and internal use. But the population itself will also be able to harvest its own citrus and banana crops, dates, mangoes, cherries, grapes, paprika, avocado, nuts, and so forth from medium sized trees, and such open-field irrigation and/or greenhoused crops as watermelons, peppers, cucumbers and tomatoes. In addition, a range of consumer goods will be produced from wood and agricultural by-products.

The plant itself is built to an aesthetically attractive design which embodies Islamic geometry and is therefore altogether appropriate to the area. It includes greenhouses for young trees and plant propagation, and an area for employee services – training, leisure and creches for example – all of which are totally unknown in existing development programmes. The system initially utilises biodegradeable growbags of trace minerals and water-retention materials so that the young forest can be irrigated by watering each tree only once a month. All these are unusual new ideas, but what is even more remarkable is the manner in which they have already been grafted so skilfully onto the existing culture. The fundamental premise is that the local people are not there to be exploited but are true partners – and indeed recognised as being more important than anyone else.

Transportation of the produce and goods of various kinds from one place to another will be effected via a system of lightweight 'canals', containing the new water and constructed in sections of a new form of fibreglass reinforced concrete that can be made from volcanic ash or any fine sand. The transport system is so designed that the people in all the different areas themselves become interdependent. As those from the interior trade goods with the more sophisticated villages nearer the plant itself, they will see ideas they want to take on board and a naturally interactive process of cultural evolution will gradually occur at its own pace.

Ultimately, the assets created by the timber will be available to finance the upgrading of the original canal system to a monorail one, powered by the electricity generated through the Seatec pools, which will move produce to distribution points from the sawmills and outlying agricultural areas. This will not need government subsidies to be profitable, since it can be used for cargo by night while the population itself uses it for passenger traffic by day. The income from the local produce will expand the project; the hedging (i.e. the pre-selling on world and local markets) of the timber will pay for the monorail; and the surplus will be channelled by the Foundation into new projects in other appropriate areas of the world.

The Aquarian Agency takes care of the whole of the outside world and provides a commercial infrastructure through which to sell the individual's produce, taking a small commission for so doing. The government of the country will actually be presented with the plant lock, stock and barrel after thirty years, and can either run it itself or continue to use Aquarian as a commercial partner. Over the previous period, The Aquarium Foundation will pay the government 'rent' in kind by supplying appropriate technology of all sorts to outlying villages, meanwhile also acting as a medium of education and support.

Consultancy – The Quiet Explosion

Not only is economic development the subject of a completely different holistic blueprint nowadays, so also is the art of business management.

Warren Bennis,[4] professor of management and organisation at the University of Southern California, defines four competencies that must be to some extent apparent in every true leader; characteristics that smack of a highly inner directed nature –

* management of attention: the communication of an extraordinary focus of commitment which attracts people to the leader

* management of meaning: the communication of the leader's vision, making his dreams apparent to others and aligning people with them

* management of trust: the main determinant of which is reliability and constancy

* management of self: knowing one's own skills and deploying them effectively – without which leaders can do more harm than good.

[263]

Part of this involves the capacity to make as many mistakes as possible and get them out of the way – and to encourage this in others. Failure, to the true leader, is not failure at all but simply the next step.

Bennis concludes that the combined effect of the management of all these aspects of leadership is one of empowerment, which is then made evident in four ways –

* people feel significant

* learning and competence matter

* people are part of the community

* work is exciting

To ensure this ideal in a world of change, the true leader must push himself or herself beyond traditional boundaries into daunting and hitherto uncharted territory – within. Within the chief's own self, and within the team he or she leads, there lie unimagined seams of the richest talent, ready for mining and smelting and moulding into the solid ingots of success. But this process of human discovery and extraction must, of course, start with the man or woman at the top –

> 'Initially, there has to be a top-down approach; it
> is essential for there to be dedicated support for this
> thing from whomever is in charge. It is not safe enough
> for others to risk it on their own.' (Ian Marks, Chairman,
> Trebor Group)

This is because here we are touching the hitherto unexplored areas of people's personalities, which for many are highly disturbing and vulnerable. Ian Marks again –

> 'We have to help people to open up, and this can be
> difficult at first. But you can't just engage with
> part of a person, with just the intellectual side, for
> example; the company only benefits to the fullest
> when the whole person is involved – integrated in
> body, mind, emotions and spirit. As employers, we're
> dealing with the complete individual, no less.'

Under the direction of human resources consultants Decision Development,[5] Trebor have conducted a number of courses – one might almost call them retreats – that have enabled senior managers to do exactly this. The process starts by helping them to cope with the increased health pressures that are now an inevitable part of effective business life, via a menu of physical techniques, exercises and experiments for them to choose from. At this bodily level, the thing involves learning about fitness, diet and relaxation – and the way in which these ostensible physical concerns have a direct impact on someone's mental state and capabilities.

> 'One starts with eliminating the bodily stress, which then leads up to eliminating the emotional stress, and finally each member of the team takes responsibility for himself or herself in the creation of the corporate vision. This is the necessary progression – mind, body, feelings, will. Given the right encouragement, everyone can cope with it – valuing their own uniqueness, then valuing the uniqueness of other members of the group, and finally valuing and reinforcing the team's overall uniqueness.

Marks's views echo that of Decision Development's own Lynn McGregor, who affirms –

> 'Managers must learn how to create a business environment where people can flourish spiritually, intellectually and emotionally. This is as important as running an organisation which is financially and technically sound. It involves understanding first oneself and then others; the recognition and use of the whole mind as opposed to the mere brain; and the knowledge and acceptance of a wider repertoire of ways of being.'

The first stage is often a series of personalised development programmes for each team member, working one-to-one with the consultant. One senior manager who found this experience unusual, but highly practical, was David Lyon, Managing Director of Bowater Group –

> 'There is a certain amount of distrust or fear among Englishmen about this kind of psychological thing, but I was curiously impressed by how accurate the analysis of my character turned out to be, after only three hours of talks with Decision Development. So I gave

all my top management a copy of my own profile, and then
sent them off one by one to have theirs done. They all
came back saying it was thoroughly worthwhile. Then I had
the profiles cross-referenced to show the team their
individual qualities and indicate how they could draw on
each other – not as a fetish, but quietly underlying the
whole fabric of the organisation.'

Here, then, taking the risk of openness has paid off – as it has with Geoff
Howard-Spink's executive team at his advertising agency, Lowe Howard-
Spink –

'I don't know what I expected, but it certainly helped a
group of people, all new to the problems of management,
to understand what they as individuals had naturally
within them *but didn't know they had*, to enable them to
take on a management role. It showed them their strengths
so that they could play to them and away from their
weaknesses.'

Moreover, as with both Bowater and Trebor, the process not only showed
people each others' strengths and weaknesses, but it also led to a far
greater understanding and self confidence among the team.

'It does something immense to your morale for others to
appreciate out loud what your strengths are, and that your
weaknesses are not abominable and destructive, but simply
the lack of something that another team member has got, so
not to worry . . . But as another result of this intense and
continuous interaction, now I can realise that if Max is
looking out of the window, he's thinking, not skiving.
And now as a group we can all realise that there's more to
communicating than what you *say* – it's what the other
person *hears*. It's your responsibility to make sure that
other people are hearing you right.'

Another convert to the methodology is entrepreneur Richard Curry,
managing director of his electrical equipment retailers, Merrow Sound
And Vision –

'My earlier personal assessment had confirmed what I
thought about myself, but also put it in a logical and
sequential way that I found most useful. When I started

Merrow, that experience led me to recognise that nobody's perfect but that a team can be, if built and developed right. As a result of putting my immediate colleagues through the same Decision Development hoops, now all of us recognise it. Now we have permission to say to each other – I don't like the way you do X, but I'm damned grateful that you're so good at doing Y.'

All this denotes a fairly unusual programme in management development terms – nothing less than the exercise of all aspects of the personality. But the wholly developed person is going to be the key to business success – indeed to every kind of success – in the remaining years of this century and beyond.

Decision Development is a consultancy only seven years old, and yet it has attracted a remarkable following among Britain's top companies. It is not alone. Over a similar period, a whole consultancy revolution has been quietly exploding under the seats of the mighty. There are scores, hundreds of little firms putting across the same kind of message, trickling down the truth over the unsuspecting heads of the pre-eminent. The Business Network alone has scores of members who are principals of these revolutionary consultancies, with specialisations ranging between teamwork management, performance training, negotiation skills, communication, leadership, awareness raising, organisational and personal change, inner growth, vision, higher purpose, creativity, overseas sponsorship, recruitment, search, selection and assessment. A dozen such are listed in the Appendix[6]. All have in common the same holistic approach; and a sample of the top organisations for which this has practical meaning is impressive forming as they do the collective client base of these consultancies, particularly since many of the following eighty of them employ more than one on the list –

Alcan	Blue Circle
Allied Dunbar	Boots
Allied Irish Bank	Bowater Scott Corporation
American Express	British Airways
Apple Computer	British Aerospace
Barclays Bank	British Gas
BASF	British Petroleum
BCCI	British Rail
BICC	British Telecom

BUPA
Cathay Pacific
Central TV
Commercial Union
Compaq
Corporation of Lloyd's
Courage
Courtaulds
Crown Life
Datapoint
Department of Employment
Department of Health and Social
  Security
Deloitte Haskins & Sells
DER
Digital Equipment Corporation
Eagle Star
LM Eriksson
Esso Petroleum
Family Planning Association
Haslemere Estates
Honeywell
The Hunger Project
IBM United Kingdom
ICL
Imagination
Imperial Chemical Industries
Jones Lang Wootton
Johnson & Johnson
Kleinwort Benson
Kraft Food
Eli Lilly

Marks & Spencer
Mars UK
McKinsey & Co
Milk Marketing Board
NCR
Nobel
Northern Dairies
Northumbrian Water Authority
The Post Office
Olivetti Group
Prudential Assurance
Rank Hovis McDougall Group
Rank Xerox
Reed International
Royal Marsden Hospital
Scott Bader Commonwealth
Shell
The Stock Exchange
Tandon
Taylor Woodrow
Texaco
J Walter Thompson
Thorn EMI
TSB
Trust House Forte
Unigate
Unipart
Wang UK
Woolwich Equitable Building
  Society
Arthur Young
Yorkshire Water Authority

The Guiding Principle

There are a number of features that distinguish these three examples of holistic business from the worthy but selectivity benevolent organisations that were outlined way back in Chapter 1. These are the same qualities that distinguish the inner directed and holistic individuals from the rest of the herd.

* they know that they are members of an integrated and interdependent system – embracing the individual, the team, the organisation, the society, the human species and the planet Earth

* they know as such that People Matter Most in all capacities; as employees, consumers, suppliers, associates, colleagues, creditors, debtors, shareholders, pensioners, the public as a whole, the citizens of the Third World, and finally the environment – the very person of Gaia herself

* they know that the needs of all these stakeholders must be considered – and also that they must be shown ways of working together for the common good through the agency of the organisation – so that the whole may truly become more than the sum of its parts

* they know that in this respect the effort and contribution of all must be appreciated whatever their tasks and attributes, and that the full potential of every human being can be realised within the framework of each of their differing personalities

* they know that the purpose of profit is to allow the organisation to grow to its optimum size and shape, to enable it to contribute both its money and its talents to the common benefit, and to empower others to do likewise by example and support

* they know that innovation and the use of new technology, new methods and new ideas are valuable and good as long as they are appropriate to the conditions

* they know in all this the dynamic principle of existence, whereby it is the lot of human beings to live in and through change and to harvest it as best they can

* they know, finally, that behind this whole vision there must always be a sense of spiritual involvement and an understanding of it as the very nature of the whole

There are those who know and those who don't want to know.
If the latter remain in the majority, and we prove so unimaginative,

cowardly and self-interested that we fail to tend the early growth of this small seedling, we will soon ourselves wither and die with it. But taken together, this knowledge constitutes the basis for the millennial society that is gradually beginning to unfold, not only in the worlds of business and work, but also in those of physics, biology, medicine, physiology, economics, and doubtless eventually in education, law, religion and politics as well. Its pioneers will have to be insistent, consistent and persistent,[7] but if they are they will predominate.

Something Else Is Going On.

ENVOI

Once upon a time and long ago, a weary soldier was marching along the road on the way to rejoin his unit. As night had begun to fall, he decided to take shelter in a small village. He knocked on the door of a cottage and an aged crone came out. 'Go away', you'll get nothing here', she quavered, 'we haven't had any food for days.' So he went next door and a bent old man came out. 'Go away, you'll get nothing here', he croaked, we haven't had any food for weeks.' So he went next door and a little boy came out. 'Go away, you'll get nothing here', he piped, 'Mother says we haven't had any food for months.' 'Ask your mother', said the soldier, 'if at least I can borrow her big black cooking pot.' This was agreeable at any rate, so the soldier carried the pot to the village green, filled it with water from the river, and put seven large stones in the bottom of it which he had picked from the river bed. Then he lit a fire under it. The villagers peeped out from behind their curtains in a fever of curiosity. Whatever was he doing? The little boy was the most feverishly curious of all, so plucking up his courage he walked over and stood beside the soldier and watched. 'Whatever are you doing?', he asked eventually. 'Making stone soup', replied the soldier. 'What, just with stones? That won't be very interesting! I'll get you a spoonful of salt and some herbs from the garden. He's making stone soup!', shouted the little boy so that the whole village could hear. 'That won't be very interesting!', quavered the aged crone, 'here are two old carrots you can put in if you like.' 'That won't be very interesting!', croaked the bent old man, 'here's some cabbage leaves and an onion you can put in as well if you like.' One by one all the villagers began putting their bits and pieces into the big black pot, a turnip here, a few potatoes there, a couple of leeks, a handful of dried beans, even an old chicken that hadn't laid an egg for as long as anyone could remember. 'Thank you very much', said the soldier, 'but there's far too much for me here, you'll all have to help me out.' 'Thank you very much', replied the villagers, 'indeed we will', and they happily shared every last morsel together. Everyone agreed that stone soup was the best soup they had ever tasted.

APPENDIX OF NOTES AND
REFERENCES

Chapter 1

1 'Capitalism Reveals an Acceptable Face', Francis Kinsman, *The Times*, 7/8/76.
2 For more of Sir John Harvey-Jones' business philosophy, see his 'Make It Happen: Reflections on Leadership'. Collins 1988.
3 'The New Agenda', Francis Kinsman, Spencer Stuart & Associates 1983.
4 See 'Business in Society – A New Initiative', New Initiative Ltd. 1984, available from New Initiative Ltd., 10 Well Walk, London NW3 1LD (01-435-5000).
5 See note 3 above.

Chapter 2

1 Disraeli's 'Two Nations' quotation is taken from his novel 'Sybil'.
2 Throughout this chapter and chapters 2–6 frequent reference is made and much acknowledgement must be given to the work of Taylor Nelson/ Applied Futures, formerly known as Taylor Nelson Monitor, which conducted the research on Social Value Groups in Britain up till 1987. In 1988, the subsidiary concerned negotiated a management buy-out with its parent group, and set up on its own as Applied Futures Ltd, (83/89 Kingsway, London WC2B 6SD: 01-242-0486), with Christine MacNulty as Managing Director, taking over the sole right to market and publish the concept of Social Value Groups (see also their report 'UK 2010', 1989). From 1989 onwards the social research involved in monitoring the relative proportions of these groups within British society was undertaken by NOP Ltd.
3 'Management and Motivation', Abraham Maslow, Prentice Hall 1952.
4 'The Nine American Life-styles: Who We Are and Where We Are Going', Arnold Mitchell, Macmillan 1983; summarised in *In Context*, Summer 1983.

5   'The Structure of Scientific Revolutions', Thomas S. Kuhn, University of Chicago Press 1970.

6   For an elaboration of this concept, and of much of chapters 2–6, see 'UK Social Change Through a Wide-Angle Lens', W. Kirk MacNulty, *Futures* August 1985.

7   'The Age of Unreason', Charles Handy, Century Hutchinson, 1989.

8   At a Wrekin Trust presentation at Bedford College, London 15/5/82.

9   'Age of Individual Dawning on the World', Brian Walden, *Sunday Times* 11/9/88.

10 At the World Futures Conference, Washington D.C., June 1975.

11 'Social Trends' is published annually by HMSO.

12 For a description of what these 'higher rungs' of Maslow's ladder might actually entail in a global context, see 'Future Vision In The Nuclear Age', Richard Slaughter, *Futures* February 1987.

Chapter 3

1   'IT Futures . . . It Can Work', National Economic Development Office 1987. Also 'Britain's New People Are Top of the World', Peter Large, *Guardian*, 7/2/86.

2   'New Cautionary Tales', Hilaire Belloc, 1930.

3   'The Wealth of Information', Tom Stonier, Methuen 1983.

Chapter 4

1   'Herculean: From Start to Finish', Cliff Temple, *Sunday Times* 4/10/87.

2   'Moral of the Fibre' Jane Thynne, *Sunday Times* 6/9/87.

3   'Hedgerow Cookery', Rosamund Richardson, Penguin 1980 (reprinting).

4   *The Sun's* 'Key to Life' series ran from 6/7/87 to 23/7/87; *The Sunday Times* 'Life-Plan' from 8/3/87 to 14/6/87.

5   'Brits and their Shrinks: What's Happened to the Good Old Stiff Upper Lip', *Observer* 13/3/88.

6   'Magic or Medicine', *Which?* October 1986, as reported in the spring 1987 newsletter of the Research Council for Complementary Medicine.

7   'Home Health Care: 1988 Mintel Special Report', as reported in 'More Favour Self-Medication', Jill Sherman, *The Times* 23/5/88.

8   'Tory Talent in the Shadow of Thatcher', Michael Jones, *Sunday Times* 26/2/89; 'Pioneering GPs Cut Drugs Bill', Jeremy Laurence, *Sunday Times* 19/3/89.

9   'Doctors Go To Class For Bedside Manner', Neville Hodgkinson, *Sunday Times* 4/10/87.

10 'Dahrendorf on Britain', Ralf Dahrendorf, *BBC 1* January 1983.

11 Quoted by Mrs. Steve Shirley at her Royal Society of Arts Presentation, 16/2/87.

12 See 'Networking in Organisations', Phillip Judkins, David West and John Drew, Gower 1985; 'The Telecommuters', Francis Kinsman, John Wiley & Sons 1987; 'Tomorrow's Workplace: The Manager's Guide to Teleworking', Francis Kinsman, British Telecom 1988.

13 'The Future of Work', Charles Handy, Basil Blackwall 1984; 'The Age of Unreason', Charles Handy, Century Hutchinson 1984; 'Getting to the Core of True Efficiency'', Charles Handy, *Sunday Times* 9/4/89.

14 'In Search of Excellence', Tom Peters, Harper and Row 1983.

15 'The Art of Japanese Management', Richard Pascale and Anthony Athos, Simon & Schuster 1981.

16 John Frank's consultancy described in the notes to Chapter 14.

Chapter 5

1 Danaan Parry's remark was made at a presentation to the Findhorn Community Conference 'From Organisation to Organism', October 16th 1987.

2 See note 4, Chapter 2.

3 See note 6, Chapter 2.

4 See note 2, Chapter 2.

5 Table 1 is reproduced by courtesy of Applied Futures Ltd.

6 Table 2 is reproduced by courtesy of Applied Futures Ltd.

Chapter 6

1 'A Clockwork Orange', Anthony Burgess, Heinemann 1962.

2 'The Questing Bushman of Buckingham Palace', Mick Brown, *Sunday Times* 12/4/87; 'A Prince's Concerns', Patience Collier, *The Times* 15/7/87; 'The Prince and the Healers', Jill Sherman, *The Times* 25/7/87; 'One Man's Lifelong Urge Towards the Apocalyptic', Catherine Bennett, *Sunday Times* 17/1/88; 'Death of a Friend', Simon Freeman and Alistair Scott, *Sunday Times* 13/3/88; 'The Prince of Remorse', Anthony Holden, *Sunday Times* 13/3/88; 'Charles the Misunderstood', Charles Jencks, *Sunday Times* 19/7/88; 'The Making of a Future King', Alan Hamilton, *The Times* 5/9/88; 'The Crusader Prince', Anthony Holden, *Sunday Times* 30/10/88; 'The Prince's Passion', Hugh Pearman, *Sunday Times* 30/10/88; 'A Marriage of Opposites', Anthony Holden, *Sunday Times* 6/11/88; 'Waiting to Reign', Anthony Holden, *Sunday Times* 13/11/88; 'The Student King', Denis Marrion, *Evening Standard* 14/11/88; 'Charles, The Galloping Philosopher', *Evening Standard* 21/2/89; 'Stopping This Disaster That Threatens Us All', *The Times* 7/3/89; 'Prince Attacks Policy on CFCs', *The Times* 7/3/89; 'Warning of Cosmic Horror to Come', *The Times* 23/3/89; 'Charles, A Biography', Anthony Holden, Weidenfeld and Nicholson 1988; 'The Real Charles', Alan Hamilton, Collins 1988; 'The Vision of Britain', Prince Charles, Doubleday 1989.

3   'Muck and Mystery', Libby Purves, *The Times* 17/1/89; 'Farms "Destroy Rivers"', Insight, *Sunday Times* 5/3/89; 'Farming's Green Light', Hannah Pearce, *Sunday Times* 12/3/89.

4   'Can the Theatrical Royal Get His New Act Together?', *Sunday Times* 24/1/88.

5   Norman Tebbit's comment was made in *Panorama*: 'Charles Prince of Conscience': *BBC 1* 11/4/88.

6   'Lagging on Unleaded', Robin Russell-Jones, *The Times* 24/2/89; 'Queen Urges Commonwealth to Think Green', Michael McCarthy, *The Times* 15/3/89; 'Duke Derides Claims of Man Conquering Nature', John Young, *The Times* 24/3/89.

7   'Do you Believe in Magic?', Anne Gottlieb, Times Books 1987; 'Storming Heaven', Jay Stevens, Atlantic Monthly Press 1987; 'Apostles of the New Age Movement', Mike Bygrave, *Sunday Times* 24/1/88.

8   'In a Class of Their Own', Judith Judd, *Observer* 6/9/87; 'Flexischool Opens for Learning', *The Times* 9/9/87; 'Town that's Under Sentence of Death', Michael Davie, *Observer* 1/11/87; 'Small is Educational', Diana Winsor, *Sunday Times* 4/10/88.

9   'We Simply Don't Know What We Are Killing', George Hill, *Sunday Times*, 30/9/87; 'Vanishing Planet', Bob Smyth, *The Times* 28/12/87; 'Farmers Criticise "Chocolate Box" Image of Countryside', Sam Kiley, *The Times* 30/12/87; 'A Harvest From The Rain Forest', *The Times*, 15/2/89; 'The World is Dying', *Sunday Times Magazine* 26/2/89.

10   'How to Save the Ozone Layer', Geoffrey Lean, *The Observer*, 20/9/87; 'Taking the Heat Off the Planet', Jane Bird, *Sunday Times* 23/10/88; 'Britain Joins Global Search for Culprit', Robert Matthews and Pearce Wright, *The Times* 27/10/88; 'World Effort is Way to Protect Ozone Layer', *The Times* 25/1/89; 'Historic Amazon Meeting: Summit in Bid to Save the Planet', Louise Byrne, *Sunday Times* 12/3/89; 'Hot News from the Pacific', Amit Roy, *Sunday Times* 12/2/89; 'A Word of Warning' George Hill and Pearce Wright, *The Times* 27/2/89; 'Total Ban on CFCs to Save Ozone Layer', Michael McCarthy and Michael Dynes, *The Times* 3/3/89; 'Ozone: UN Acts to Tighten Controls', Geoffrey Lean, *Observer* 5/3/89; 'Plugging the Hole in Our Sun-Roof', Fred Pearce, *Sunday Times* 5/3/89; 'Ozone Hole Found Above the Arctic', Richard Palmer and David Hughes, *Sunday Times* 5/3/89; '"Disaster Recipe" If Third World Uses CFCs', *The Times* 6/3/89.

11   'More Hard Wear than Hardware', Katharine Whitehorn, *Observer* 9/8/88.

12   'For Better and For Poorer', Caroline Phillips, *The Times* 21/8/87; 'Top Executives' Fringe Goodies Get Juicier Still', Geoffrey Golzen, *Sunday Times* 18/10/87; 'Why Staff Say No to the Big Job Move', Michel Synett, *Sunday Times* 18/10/87; 'More Executives Rebel Against Job Relocation', Ronald Faux, *The Times* 21/10/87; 'What is Business For?', Andrew Campbell, *Strategic Planning Society Newsletter*, October 1987; 'A Lateral View at the Top', Ann Hills, *The Times* 4/8/88.

13   *The Sunday Times Magazine* 4/10/87, 11/10/87, 18/10/87, 25/10/87, 1/11/87.

14   'My Hell – And Heaven', Peter Coleridge, *Observer* 20/3/88.

Chapter 7

1   'You're All Right, Perhaps, But What of Jack', Tony Blair, *The Times*
    1/7/87; 'Victorian Values', *The Times* 10/8/87; 'Prima Donna Inter Pares',
    Robert Harris, *Observer* 3/1/88; 'Ruled by the Roundheads', Conor Cruise
    O'Brian, *The Times* 3/2/88; 'Why I Can Never, Never Let Up', Brian
    Walden, *Sunday Times* 8/5/88; '"Thatcher's Children" Reject Rebel Parents'
    Ideas'. Richard Evans, *The Times* 11/5/88; 'On the Trail of the Warrior
    Queens', Victoria McKee, *The Times* 7/10/88; 'Beating Their Breastplates',
    Bel Mooney, *Sunday Times* 14/10/88; 'Thatcher's Bloodless Revolution:
    The Story So Far', Brian Deer, *Sunday Times* 6/11/88; 'Britons Enjoy
    Unprecedented Affluence and Materialism', *The Times* 3/1/89; 'Young
    Favour a Clean Living Style', *The Times* 27/2/89; 'Housewife Superstar',
    Robert Skidelsky, *The Sunday Times* 9/4/89; 'Victorian Values and
    Twentieth Century Condescention', Gertrude Himmelfarb, Centre for
    Policy Studies 1987; 'Boadicea's Chariot: The Warrior Queens', Antonia
    Fraser, Wiedenfeld 1988; 'British Social Attitudes', Roger Jowell et al,
    Social and Community Planning Research, Gower, 1988; 'One of us: A
    Biography of Margaret Thatcher', Hugo Young, Macmillan 1989.
2   Dr. Rupert Sheldrake's comment was made at a meeting of *Link-Up* in
    November 1987.
3   'Why Victorian Values Cannot Carry the NHS', Thomas Stuttaford, *The Times*,
    30/12/87; 'Maggie's Little Helpers', Noel Malcolm, *Observer Magazine*,
    19/2/88; 'Dark Deeds in the Great Bed of Ware', Simon Jenkins, *Sunday Times*
    26/23/89; 'Professionals under Attack', Jon Craig et al, *Sunday Times*
    13/3/89; 'White Collars Brandish Blue Books Too', Simon Jenkins, *Sunday
    Times* 27/3/88; 'Rumpoled!', Brian Deer, *Sunday Times* 29/1/89.
4   'British Aid to Third World at Record Low', Geoffrey Lean, *Observer*
    29/5/88.
5   'Mrs. Thatcher's Church', *The Times* 27/10/87; 'Church Angry at Move for
    British Moral Majority', Jon Craig, *Sunday Times* 13/3/88; 'From Archangel to
    Sybil Fawlty', Craig Brown, *The Times* 5/5/88; 'The Moral Defence', *The Times*
    23/5/88; 'Church Criticises Thatcher', Clifford Langley, *The Times* 1/6/88.
6   See note 2, Chapter 3.
7   'Pro-Life Lobby Turns Up the Heat', Tim Rayment, *Sunday Times* 1/11/87.
8   'School for Sabs Shows How to Outfox the Hunt', Hugh Clayton, *Sunday
    Times* 1/11/87; 'Animal Madhouse', Sam Kiley and Anne MacElvoy, *The
    Times* 24/2/89.
9   'A Front for the Front', Alan Franks, *The Times* 29/3/89.
10 'Never a Dull Day for a Story-Teller on Top of the World', *Sunday Times*,
    26/7/87.
11 'Branson Defends Clean-Up Campaign', Craig Seton, *The Times* 22/7/87;
    'What Richard Branson Learnt While Not Smoking Behind the Bicycle
    Sheds', Duncan Campbell, *Observer Colour Magazine* 1/11/87; 'Branson
    Plans Cut-Price Medical Supplies', Charles Langley 15/11/87; 'Branson

Blazes Virgin Trail of Soviet Enterprise', Christopher Walker, *The Times* 27/1/88; 'Richard Branson: The Inside Story', Mick Brown, Michael Joseph 1988.

Chapter 8

1   'Taking Over the World', Laurence Marks and Philip Kleinman, *Observer* 20/9/87; 'Saatchi Good Story', Melvyn Marckus, *Observer* 20/9/87; 'The Bank and The Banks', Melvyn Marckus, *Observer* 20/9/87; 'Birth of The Brothers', Ivan Fallon, *Sunday Times* 21/8/88; 'The Tory Sellers', Ivan Fallon, *Sunday Times* 28/8/88; 'Don't Write Off the Saatchis', Ivan Fallon, *Sunday Times* 26/3/89; 'The Saatchi Story', Philip Kleinmann, Weidenfeld and Nicholson 1987; 'The Rise and Rise of Saatchi and Saatchi', Ivan Fallon, Hutchinson 1988.
2   'Who's Afraid of the Tiger?', Brian James, *The Times*, 10/9/87.
3   'Citizen Maxwell', Tom Bower, *The Sunday Times*, 6/3/88; 'Maxwell: Tearaway Tycoon', Woodrow Wyatt, *The Times*, 12/3/88; 'Cap'n Bob's Beep-Beep', Piers Brendon, *Observer* 15/3/88; 'Citizen Kane Without His Rosebud', John Mortimer, *Sunday Times* 20/3/88; 'Libel Damages for Maxwell as Book Pulped', Howard Foster, *The Times* 25/3/88; 'Maxwell', Joe Haines, Macdonald 1988; 'Maxwell, The Outsider', Tom Bower, Aurum 1988; 'Maxwell: A Portrait of Power', Peter Thompson and Anthony Delano, Bantam 1988.
4   'Odd Jobs for City Refugees', Georgie Greig, *Sunday Times*, 25/10/87.
5   'Big Bang is Hit on the Knocker', Michael Davie, *Observer* 5/4/87; 'Flash Harry Meets the Embarrassed Capitalist', Jonathan Miller, *The Times* 27/3/87; 'The Greedy Feel Good While the Bell Tolls', Robert Chesshyre, *Observer* 21/8/87; 'The Secret of Undress', Matthew Parris, *Sunday Telegraph Magazine* 2/8/87; 'More Serious than Money', William Keegan, *Observer* 13/9/87; 'The Best and the Worst of Times', Barbara Amiel, *The Times* 30/10/87; 'A Wealthy Obsession', Alice Thomas Ellis, *The Times* 23/9/87.
6   Peregrine Worsthorne's letter to the Times was dated 12/6/87, and that of the Rev. Harry Williams 16/6/87.
7   'Elite Registrations' *Observer* 20/9/87; 'RU Al OK', *The Times* (Third Leader).
8   'Yuppies and Their Feats of Clay', Jane Thynne, *Sunday Times* 11/10/87.
9   'The Yuppie Millionaire's Guide to the Good Life', Charles Bremner, *The Times* 19/10/87; 'Gracious Living for Hire', Penny Perrick, *The Times* 29/2/88; 'Gentrification of the Carry-Out', Lis Leigh, *Sunday Times* 17/4/88.
10 'Chunk Chic', Bryan Appleyard, *The Times* 19/12/87.
11 'The New Eastenders', Ian Jack, *Observer* 12/4/87; 'Rock'n Railing with Cafe Society', Paul Pickering, *Sunday Times* 17/4/88.
12 'Seventeen But Going on Forty', Mick Brown, *Sunday Times* 15/11/87.

13 'Class and the Classroom', Peter Waymark, *The Times* 11/2/88.
14 'Tom Brown's Porsche Days', John Rae, *The Times* 31/7/87; 'Sick Transit – Yuckies Come Out', Carmel Fitzsimons, *Observer* 1/11/87.
15 'Kiddies Cosmetics', Sharon Churcher, *The Observer* 16/8/87; 'An American Dream', Carol Leonard, *The Times* 29/9/87; 'Toytown's New Tycoons', Victoria McKee, *The Times* 11/1/88; 'Consuming Fashions', Caroline McGhie, *Sunday Times* 13/11/88.
16 'Dog's Life', Carol Leonard, *The Times* 1/10/87.
17 'Bang, Crash, Wallop?', Peter Wilsher, *Sunday Times Magazine*; 'The Fall of Adam', Peter York and Michael Pye, *Observer*, 1/11/87; 'The 24-Year-Old Who Lost £3m', Richard Thomson, *The Times* 27/1/88.
18 'Captain Phillips is Allowed to Keep his Licence', *The Times* 1/10/87.
19 'Inheriting a Fortune – In Debts', Sally Brompton, *The Times* 29/9/87.
20 'Dunroamin' in the Elysian Fields', John Casey, *Sunday Times* 20/3/88; 'Nattering in Paradise', Daniel Meadows, Simon and Schuster 1988.
21 'Top Brass Fails to Impress Managers', Roland Rudd, *The Times* 14/3/88.
22 'Done Well, Thou Good and Faithful Servant', Phillipa Braidwood, *Sunday Times Magazine*.
23 'Eve Versus the Adams of the Church', Simon Jenkins, *Sunday Times* 6/9/87.
24 'Whitehall Watch', Peter Hennessy, *The Independent* 7/12/87; 'Times Diary', David Walker, *The Times* 21/2/89; 'Attack on Crude Regime at V & A', Peter Watson, *Observer* 9/9/89.
25 'Daddy's Army', Michael Yardley, *Sunday Telegraph Magazine* 25/10/87; 'Bully for Modern Moral Standards', Helen Mason, *Sunday Times* 8/11/87; 'Inhuman Rites', Andrew Lycett, *The Times* 9/11/87.
26 'War of the Word', Robin Lustig et al, *Observer* 19/2/89; 'Asian Pupils Are the School High Achievers', *Evening Standard* 21/2/89; 'A Blueprint for Disaster from the Best of Intentions', Barbara Amiel, *The Times* 24/2/89; 'Rushdie: The Censorship Begins', Geordie Craig and Amit Roy, *Sunday Times* 5/5/89.

Chapter 9

1 'Engineers Open Way for "Super-Union" Merger to Go Ahead', Roland Rudd, *The Times* 30/9/88.
2 'TUC Rethinks Capitalism', Paul Routledge, *Observer* 31/1/88; 'Share-owning Socialism', Alan Tuffin, *The Times* 22/2/88.
3 'The Dundee Debacle', *The Times* 19/3/88; 'How Stupidity Killed 1,000 New Car Jobs', Gavin Laird, *Sunday Times* 20/3/88; 'Extinct But it Won't Lie Down', Bernard Levin, *The Times* 24/3/88; 'Todd Quits Training Body', Paul Routledge, *Observer*, 29/5/88; 'Inflexible Potentate of the Left', *The Times* 1/9/88; 'Unions Vote to Boycott Training', *The Times* 8/9/88; 'The Quill Pen Versus Word Processors', Edward Pearce, *Sunday Times* 25/9/88;

'Rule of Ron's Gang of 64', Robert Kilroy-Silk, *The Times* 1/10/88; 'Give Him That Old-Time Religion, Any Day of the Filofax', *Sunday Times* 9/10/88.

4   'The Last Hot Metal Rascal', *Observer* 21/8/88; 'Mornin', Jameson Here: In Any Version You Like', Valerie Grove, *Sunday Times* 21/8/88.

5   'Why Our Clubman Like to Stay a Class Apart', Stephen Pile, *Sunday Times* 1/11/87; 'Hope for Workers Caught in a Trap', Brian Walden, *Sunday Times* 20/12/87.

6   'Bitches Who Shoot from the Lip', Brian MacArthur, *Sunday Times* 13/3/88.

7   'Clear the Rails of Prejudice, Demand Women', Richard Ellis, *Sunday Times* 13/3/88.

8   'Inner Cities Losing Out From Cradle to Grave', Thomson Prentice, *The Times* 23/7/87.

9   'Country Folk "In Urgent Need of Cheap Homes"', John Young, *The Times* 1/2/88.

10 'True Grit', Robert Chesshyre, *Observer* 6/9/87; 'The Return of a Native Reporter', Robert Chesshyre, Viking 1987.

11 'Assault on the Inner City', Peter Wilsher, *Sunday Times* 21/6/87; 'Mrs. Thatcher Journeys to Change the Social Landscape', Nicholas Wood, *The Times* 26/6/87; 'Partnerships that Build Cities', *The Times* 6/7/87.

12 'Happy Employees Vote Themselves a Fortune', Joe Joseph, *The Times* 22/2/88.

13 'Docklands to Get a Royal Flourish', Hugh Pearson, *Sunday Times* 4/10/87.

14 'Glasgow Reform: 1', Ronald Faux, *The Times* 21/9/87; 'Glasgow Reform: 2', Ronald Faux, *The Times* 22/9/87.

15 'All for the High Life', Pearson Phillips, *The Times*, 7/9/87.

16 'Age Old Problem', Barbara Amiel, *The Times* 29/1/88; 'The Home of the Zombies', *Observer* 13/3/88.

17 'Why Saturday is Murder in the Stands', Bill Burford, *Sunday Times* 7/5/87; 'Terraces Must Stand Up Against the Mindless Minority', *The Times*, 22/8/87; 'The European Hooligan Championship', Hugh McIlvanney, *The Observer* 22/11/87; 'Football Hooligans Lead International Violence Conspiracy', Ian Smith, *The Times* 4/12/87; 'Lack of Discipline Hardly the Fault of Referees', Stuart Jones, *The Times* 30/12/87; 'Hooligans Find the Security Loopholes', *Sunday Times* 29/5/88; 'British Vandals at the Gates of Europe, Simon Jenkins, *Sunday Times* 12/6/88; 'Social Violence Takes Time Off and Waits to Kick Again', Chris Lightbown, *Sunday Times* 16/10/88; 'Hooligans at Bay', *Evening Standard* 6/1/89; 'Football Awaits the Inevitable', Louise Taylor, *The Times* 18/1/89; 'Football Membership Scheme Under Attack', *The Times* 2/2/89; 'Soccer's Banana Army', Richard Littlejohn, *Evening Standard* 27/2/89.

18 'Steamer Mobs Bring a Vicious New Dimension to Street Crime', Geordie Greig and Andrew Hogg, *Sunday Times* 5/7/87; 'Riots That Go Unremarked', Robert Kilroy-Silk, *The Times* 22/8/87; 'When Parents are

the Victims of their Children', Andrea Waind, *Sunday Times* 13/3/88; 'Steamers Face a Hot Time', David Leppard, *Sunday Times* 21/2/88; 'Police Squads go on Armed Patrol', Jon Craig and David Leppard, *Sunday Times* 2/4/88; 'Local Groups are Urged to End Rise of Rural Violence', John Lewis, *The Times* 6/4/88; 'Climate of Violence', Tony Blair, *The Times* 12/4/88; 'Survey sees Well-Off Grow Violent', Steward Tendler, *The Times* 10/6/88; 'City Shamed by the Ugliness of its Pinstriped Yobs', Tim Walker *Observer* 9/10/88; '56 People Held in Acid House Raids', *The Times* 7/11/88; 'Reality of Ecstasy', *The Times* 7/11/88; 'Angels Prey on Fear of Violence', *Sunday Times* 29/1/89; 'Knife Gang Attacks and Robs Travellers on Late-Night Train', *The Times* 13/2/89; 'Vigilantes Fill Police Shoes and Stop Thefts', Jon Craig, *Sunday Times* 5/3/89.

19 'Broadwater Farm Riots Inspire Revival', Paul Eastham, *The Times* 31/7/87; 'Black Link to IRA', Arlen Harris, *Sunday Times*; 'Racism's Short Fuse', Matthew Carr, *Observer* 22/11/87.

Chapter 10

1 'How Thatcher Broke the Mould', Insight, *Sunday Times* 14/6/87; 'To Let: Vacant Plots in the Centre Ground', Michael Jones, *Sunday Times* 2/10/88; 'Our Exemplary Citizens', Robert Kilroy-Silk, *The Times* 14/10/88; 'Problems? I Can See No Problems', Michael Jones, *Sunday Times* 16/10/88; 'Tories Risk Stumbling on the Moral Ground', Brian Walden, *Sunday Times* 16/10/88; 'A New Pinkish Dawn Appears on the Horizon', Ben Pimlott, *Sunday Times* 6/11/88; 'By Disaster's Light, Our Ills Revealed', Martin Jacques, *Sunday Times* 26/11/89; 'A Grim Record', *Observer* 5/3/89; 'Stormy Summer Will Shake Out Cobwebs', Michael Jones, *Sunday Times* 5/3/89; Richard Ingrams' Column, *Observer* 5/3/89; 'Better Times for Kinnock', Robert Harris, *Sunday Times* 12/3/89; 'Mid-Term or Terminal?' Ronald Butt, *The Times* 16/3/89; 'She No Longer Walks on Water', Martin Jacques, *Sunday Times* 19/3/89.

2 'Thatcher Fears for Future of the Planet', Philip Johnston et al, *Daily Telegraph* 28/9/88; 'Tories Plan "Green" Bill', 'Geoffrey Lean, *Observer* 2/10/88; 'Rejoice: Now the Lady is for Greening'. *Observer* 2/10/88; 'A Reluctant Environmentalist', *The Independent* 13/10/88; 'Wolves in Green Clothing', Robert Kilroy-Silk, *The Times* 21/10/88; 'MPs Heading for Nuclear Bombshell', Robin McKie, *Observer* 5/2/89; 'The Rivers of Shame', *Sunday Times* 26/2/89; 'Tory "Green" Record Under Heavy Attack·by Labour', Nicholas Wood, *The Times* 27/2/89; 'Poisoning Our Rivers', *Evening Standard* 27/2/89; 'How Green is the Prime Minister?', Geoffrey Lean, *Observer* 5/3/89; 'Acid Rain Fumes Belch Through a Legal Loophole', John Rowland, *Sunday Times* 5/3/89; 'Thatcher Moved by Plea to Help Grandson's Generation', Michael McCarthy, *The Times* 8/3/89; 'Thatcher at Odds with Ridley on Ozone Stance', Pearce Wright et al, *The Times* 6/3/89;

'Thatcher Hits at Brazil on Forests', Michael McCarthy, *The Times* 8/3/89; 'British Hostility to EEC Wildlife Plan Under Fire', Michael McCarthy, *The Times* 28/3/89; 'Sewage Linked to Skin Disease in Fishermen', John Rowland and Richard Palmer, *Sunday Times* 9/4/89.

3   'We're in a 1920s Economy', Paul Hanoken, *Whole Earth Review*, Fall 1985; 'Faded 1929 Memories and the Prospect Now', Kenneth Fleet, *The Times* 23/10/87; 'The Wave that Crashed', Paul Barker, *Sunday Telegraph* 25/10/87; 'The Wave Principle', R.N. Elliott, Elliott 1938; 'Business Cycles', Joseph Schumpeter, NY, McGraw Hill 1939; L. Peter Cogan, 'The Rhythmic Cycles of Optimism and Pessimism', NY, William Frederick Press 1969; 'The Elliott Wave Principle', Robert Beckman, Tera 1976; 'Into the Upwave', Robert Beckman, Milestone 1988.

4   'May Week', H.C. Porter, *Cambridge No. 20* 1987.

5   'The Gurus Gored', Peter Brimelow, *The Times* 21/10/87; 'The Crash of 1987; *Observer* 5/10/87; 'Old Cycle Returns', Ivan Fallon, *Sunday Times* 25/10/87; 'Insanity of 1929 Repeats Itself', J.K. Galbraith, *Sunday Times* 25/10/87; 'The Seer Who Saw It Coming', Bryan Appleyard, *The Times* 26/10/87; 'Time to Count the Cost', Christopher Smallwood and John Cassidy, *Sunday Times* 1/11/87; 'To Hell and Back', Stella Shamoon, *Observer* 1/11/87; 'Crash of '87: Cause and Cures', Richard Coghlan, *The Times* 13/11/87; 'Cracks Show in Hong Kong', Jon Swain, *Sunday Times* 15/11/87; 'Meltdown for the Trading Houses', Stella Shamoon, *Observer* 24/1/88.

6   'Race for Eldorado', Brian Reading, *Sunday Times* 26/10/86; 'The Stock Market Paper Mountain', Nick Goodway, *Observer* 2/8/87; 'The Insider Scandals', Stella Shamoon, *Observer* 21/8/88; 'Why Bull Turned To Bear', William Keegan and Adrian Hamilton, *Observer* 25/10/87; 'Yuppies in the Firing Line', John Westwell, *Sunday Times* 6/12/87; 'Jobs Fall as City Dries-Up', David Brierly and Margaret Park, *Sunday Times* 24/1/88; 'Tripping up in the Dash for Growth', Brian Reading, *Sunday Times* 9/10/88; 'Edging Back From the Brink', John Jay, *Sunday Times* 18/10/88; 'Profits Hit as Lawson Juggles', Brian Reading, *Sunday Times* 6/11/88; 'Melt Down for Market-Makers', George Parker-Jarvis, *Observer* 4/12/88; 'The Big Sack', *The Times* 6/12/88; 'Death in the City', Kenneth Fleet, *The Times* 10/12/88; 'The Biggest Bang of All', Stella Shamoon, *Observer* 11/12/88; 'House Sales to Fall by One Million as Property Boom Ends', Richard Evans, *The Times* 26/1/89; 'Estate Agents Fear Shake-Out', Margaret Park, *Sunday Times* 29/1/89; 'The Share Rush', Stella Shamoon, *Observer* 5/2/89; 'Stumbling Back to Stop-Go', Brian Reading, *Sunday Times* 5/3/89; 'Inflation May Drive Interest Up', David Smith, *Sunday Times* 19/3/89; 'Interest Rates Rock Builders' Foundations', George Parker-Jervis, *Observer* 26/3/89.

7   'Our Endangered Earth', *Time Magazine* 2/1/89.

8   'Banking Crisis is Hard to Swallow', Irwin Stetzer, *Sunday Times* 31/1/88; 'America Still Holds the Key as Original Concerns Persist', Kenneth Fleet, *The Times* 13/2/88; 'Marshals Rein in the Cowboy Bankers', John Cassidy, *Sunday Times* 12/6/88; 'Wall Street Watchful as Trade Deficit Soars', John

Cassidy and Gareth David, *Sunday Times* 28/8/88; 'Can Leveraged Deals Weather Hard Times', Gareth David, *Sunday Times* 6/11/88; 'Recession Fear Looms on the Bush Horizon', Irwin Stelzer, *Sunday Times* 13/11/88; 'Reading the Reagan Legacy', Irwin Stelzer, *Sunday Times* 11/12/88; 'Bush Bucking Strong Protectionist Winds', Irwin Stelzer, *Sunday Times* 5/3/89; 'Pursuit of Happiness Outstrips America's Pioneer Spirit', Charles Bremner, *The Times* 8/3/89; 'Indecisive Bush in Danger of Catching the Carter Disease', John Cassidy and Mark Hosenball, *Sunday Times* 12/3/89; 'Jitters on Display as Dow Bows to Inflation', Mike Graham, *Sunday Times* 19/3/89.

9 'Praise to the King of all the Russians', Simon Jenkins, Sunday Times 11/12/88; 'Year of the Global Spring', Anthony Parsons, *The Times* 29/12/88; 'The Dawn of a New Age', Nigel Hawkes, *Observer* 5/3/89.

10 'Scam Threatens a Japanese Era', Brian Reading, *Sunday Times* 9/9/88; 'Investor Revolt as NTT Slumps', Peter McGill, *Observer* 26/3/89; 'Japan's New Empire', John Cassidy, *Sunday Times* 5/3/89.

11 'Poor Nations Need More Help', *The Times* 27/6/87; 'International Debt Sets Third World Dilemma', William Keegan, *Observer* 2/10/88; 'Debt Will Echo in the Bush White House', Irwin Stelzer, *Sunday Times* 13/11/88; 'Debt Threatens the Fragile Democracies of South America', Mac Margolis, *The Times*, 6/12/88; 'Raising Doubts Won't Lower Any Debts', Adrian Hamilton, *Observer* 9/4/89.

Chapter 11

1 'IT Futures . . . It Can Work', see note 1, Chapter 3.
2 'The Sane Alternative: A Choice of Futures', James Robertson, revised edn. 1983.

Chapter 12

1 Quoted in 'To Say or Not To Say', Katharine Whitehorn, *Observer* 13/3/88.
2 Sets of Quality Cards are available from Harley Miller, The Findorn Foundation, The Park, Forres IV36 0TZ (03093 0311).
3 Dr Steve Salter's paper 'Some Ideas to Stop World War III', explains the 'I Cut, You Choose' rule in further detail. Copies are available from him at The Department of Artificial Intelligence, Edinburgh University.
4 As quoted in 'Why The West Still Has Bad Dreams', Neil Ascherson, *Observer* 1/11/87.
5 'Psychosynthesis', Roberto Assagioli, Turnstone 1975.
6 'The Act of Creation', Arthur Koestler, Hutchinson 1976.
7 From 'Choruses From The Rock', T.S. Eliot.
8 From 'Jung and the Story of Our Time', Laurens Van Der Post, Hogarth Press 1976.

9   Max Planck's and Fritjof Capra's own quotations both came from 'The Turning Point', Fritjof Capra, Simon and Schuster 1982.
10 'Clairvoyant Reality', Laurence Le Shan, Turnstone Press 1980.
11 'The Gods Themselves', Isaac Asimov, Victor Gollancz 1972.
12 'A History of Western Philosophy', Bertrand Russell, George Allen and Unwin 1946.
13 'Popper', Brian Magee, Fontana 1973; 'The Open Society and Its Enemies', Karl Popper, Routledge and Kegan Paul 1945.
14 'The Man who Brought the Earth to Life', Bryan Appleyard, *Sunday Times Magazines* 6/11/88; 'Gaia', James Lovelock, Oxford University Press 1982; 'The Quest for Gaia', Kit Pedler, Souvenir 1979.
15 The 'Circular Statement' is available from Steve Smith Graphics, 16 Old Place Road, Norwich (0603 617981).
16 'To Say or Not To Say', see note 1 of this Chapter; 'Adoring Green', Katharine Whitehorn, *Observer* 1/5/88.

Chapter 13

1   From 'Little Gidding', T.S. Eliot.
2   In Search of Excellence', Tom Peters, Harper and Row 1983; but see also 'Megatrends', John Naisbitt, MacDonald 1984; and 'Reinventing the Corporation', John Naisbitt and Patricia Abardare, Warren Brooks 1985.
3   'Directors' Clarion Call', Edward Townsend, *The Times* 24/9/87; 'Minding Their Own Business', T.E. Utley, *The Times* 28/9/87.
4   See note 2, Chapter 1.
5   See note 15, Chapter 4.
6   'Gods of Management', Charles Handy, Pan 1985.
7   Sir Robert Haslam's and Mrs Steve Shirley's quotations came from interviews with the writer for Spencer Stuart & Associates' *Point of View No. 11* 1986.
8   'Management Teams: Why They Suceed or Fail', Meredith Belbin, Heineman 1981.
9   'The Employees are a Company's Biggest Asset, And They Must Always Come First', Coral Morgan-Thomas, *The Times* 19/3/87; 'Self Help Way to Cut Stress', Jill Sherman, *The Times* 17/6/87; 'Industry Counts the Costs of Stress', Edward Townsend, *The Times* 1/7/87; 'Women Bosses Would Reduce Stress at Work', John Spicer, *The Times* 6/1/88; 'Doctors Say Stress Causes 40% of Sick Leave in Companies', John Spicer, *The Times* 20/7/88; 'Executives Driven to Drink', Roland Rudd, *The Times* 20/2/89; 'Living with Stress', Cary Cooper, Penguin 1988.
10 Women Move into the Driving Seat', USM Review, *The Times* 11/5/87; 'Women Still on the Track Set by Men', Michel Syrett, *Sunday Times* 5/7/87; 'Bias Against Girls in "Male Job" Hunt', John Spicer, *The Times* 13/7/87; 'A Lovely Future Shaping up for Men', *The Times* 7/9/87; 'A Singular Sort of Future', Alice Thomas Ellis, *The Times* 9/9/87; 'Meek and

Mild – And Making Money', Liz Gill, *The Times* 30/9/87; 'Enter the Chore Lady', Penny Perrick, *The Times* 19/10/87; 'Something Small in the City', Jane Bidder, *The Times* 11/11/87; 'Business Women: Present and Future', David Clutterbuck and Marianne Devine, Macmillan 1987.

11 The Other Economic Summit and The New Economies Foundation are both at 88/94 Wentworth Street, London E1 7SE (01 377 5696); also in association, The Living Economy Network, School of Peace Studies, University of Bradford, Bradford, West Yorkshire BD7 1DP (0274 737143).

12 The Business Network, 18 Well Walk, London NW3 1LD (01 435 5000).

13 New Initiative Ltd. and the Gaia Foundation are also both at 18 Well Walk, London NW3 1LD (01 435 5000); Financial Initiative Ltd, Barchester House, 5a Brown Street, Salisbury, Wiltshire (0722 338900).

14 'Industry Sees Wisdom of Going Green', Sue Thomas, *Sunday Times* 22/1/89; 'Polluters are Called to Account', Insight, *Sunday Times* 19/3/89; 'City Calls for River Clean-Up', Insight, *Sunday Times* 19/3/89; 'British Steel Accused of Dumping Poisons', Insight, *Sunday Times* 2/4/89; 'How Firms Beat Law On Pollution – Campaign's Achievements', Insight, *Sunday Times* 9/4/89.

15 'Why the Greens are Growing', David Nicholson-Lord, *The Times* 21/3/88; 'Recycling a Message from the Earth's True Friend', Valerie Grove, *Sunday Times* 2/10/88; 'Odd, But the Autumn Has Turned Greener', Stephen Pile, *Sunday Times* 16/10/88; 'Firms Chase the Green Market', Wilfred Peters, *Sunday Times* 29/1/89; 'Green Consumers Voting with their Wallets', *The Times* 1/3/89; '2,000 People a Month Joining Green Groups', Michael McCarthy, *The Times* 6/4/89.

16 Green Pages and SustainAbility Ltd. are at 49 Princes Place, London W11 4QA (01 243 1277); Brand New Ltd. at same address but (01 221 2828); The Whole Thing, School Lane, Dunham Massey, Altringham, Cheshire WA14 5SZ (061 236 5116); 'The Green Consumer Guide ("How to Buy Products that *Don't* Cost The Earth")', John Elkington and Julia Hailes, Victor Gollancz, 1988.

17 'Company Philosophies and Codes of Business Ethics', Simon Webley, Institute of Business Ethics, 1988.

18 Business in The Community, 227A City Road, London EC1V 1LX (01 253 3716).

18 Eileen Conn's article first appeared in *The Business Network Newsletter* Summer 1988.

Chapter 14

1 'Profits are a Serious Business', Lesley Garner, *Daily Telegraph* 11/11/87; 'Philosophy and a Facial', Maggie Drummond, *The Times* 6/1/88; 'Paper Profits', *the Times* 29/3/88; 'Power of the Body Politic', Catherine Bennett, *Sunday Times* 6/3/88.

2 Community Learning Initiatives, 25 Forth Street, St Monans, Fife
  KY10 2AU (0333 7597) – a subsidiary of Creative Learning Consultants,
  The Barn, Nan Clark Lane, Mill Hill, London NW7 4HH (01 959 3372).
3 Aquarian Agency Ltd, 405 Kingston Road, SW20 (01 543 5956).
4 As quoted in the BCCI newsletter, Summer 1987.
5 Decision Development, 34 Courthorpe Road, London NW3 2LD
  (01 484 9938).
6 *The Alexander Corporation, 11 Heath Street, London NW3 6TP
  (01 794 0123)
  (Teamwork management, performance coaching and training)

'Are You Too Busy To Work Less – And Get More Done? . . . Anyone can
be coached to higher performance. Staff, at any level, will find they
possess untapped reserves of talent to help them resolve the problems that
have been holding them and the business back . . . our teamwork
managers will facilitate open, honest and productive communications by
using non-threatening techniques.

*The Coverdale Organisation Ltd, Dorland House, 14/16 Regent St,
London SW1Y 4PH (01 925 0099)
(Interactive skills training – teamwork, leadership, negotiation – 'our
business is to help others to succeed')

'Man must have meaning . . . Everyone has something to offer . . . The
will to improve resides ultimately with the individual . . . A group
cooperating to mutual benefit is more than a collection of individuals . . .
Being a manager does not mean doing the job yourself but helping others
to cooperate effectively in getting the job done . . .'
  'We sometimes come across people who think we dispense some kind of
black magic . . . It is commonplace in our work that we get instances of
applications coming not only from work but from someone's wife or
family. They are more tolerant or they have started to listen to their
children, or have taken on a new lease of energy. People report on
improvements they have made in the voluntary bodies to which they
belong . . .'

*Creative Learning Consultants, The Barn, Nan Clark Lane, London
NW7 4HH (01 959 3372)
('A creative people-based approach to social and economic development')

'Thinking, learning, creating – these are the three Rs of the new
information society; vision, concern and persistance are the basic ABC.'
  'The Creative Manager' [the title of the book by principal Roger Evans,
and Peter Russell whose details are also listed below] 'is someone who is
learning to think in a new way. He/she is open to learning as a continuous
process . . . sees that there is potential for learning in each moment . . .
recognises that the present times demand a creative response to change

. . . understands it requires of him increasing inner stability, a growing flexibility and a willingness to live with uncertainty . . . is aware that these attitudes are essential to a deeper understanding of the creative process.'

'We are concerned with reducing dependency and instead creating partnerships and mutually beneficial relationships, empowering people and groups of people to utilise their strengths, capabilities, talents and opportunities.'

*CTC Europe, 28 Woodman Close, Leighton Buzzard, Bedfordshire, LU7 89Y (0525 376685)
(Awareness raising and spiritual development as an aid to working effectiveness)

'Formulating organisation culture and business strategy; initiating the drive for change via the people that work there; permitting the recognition that people create their own reality; calming the fear that loss of burocratic control inevitably leads to chaos; insisting that vision is no longer an esoteric flippancy but a business must.'

*Fordwell Ltd, 24 Lynnette Avenue, London SW4 9HD (01 675 2901)
(Consultancy and training in change management)

'20 years in the fields of individual and organisational change; helping clients in blue-chip companies with change in culture, strategy, teamwork and life issues – including personal transformation for those who are interested.'

'Our experience has taught us that the capacity for change is what makes for successful business performance. Continuously renewing the extending capacity is at the centre of our work – which emphasises the essential linkages between individual, organisational and business development.'

*John Frank Associates, 49 Stanhope Gardens, Highgate, 6 5TT
(01 348 3174)

'Adding vision and clarity to people's working and personal lives; helping them towards individual and collective insights that are about the optimistic awareness of –

* their enormously powerful inner core
* their well of creative thinking
* the possibility of their true growth and development
* the business potential of the interpersonal process between themselves and others
* the means of establishing a 'group brain' for creative problem solving within teams'

*Kiddy and Company, 43 Queen Square, Bristol BS1 4QR (0272 215275)

(Business psychologists advising organisations on human resources issues – organisation change and devlopment, search and selection, assessment, management skills training and counselling)

'There are three themes to our approach. First we use our psychological expertise to help organisations achieve their commercial goals. Secondly we . . . draw on what is best in research and methodology, predicting the issues and themes of the next decade. Finally we see ourselves as challenging top management . . .'

*Natural Selection, Ely House, 37 Dover Street, London W1X 3RD (01 409 1343)
(Complete recruitment and promotion consultancy – 'Natural Selection implies the survival of the fittest')

'There is a myth that good people are hard to find: the fact is that good people are hard to keep. Our intention is to transform your recruitment position from one of scarcity to one of abundance.'

'We seek to answer the candidate's question – why should I want to work for this company? We therefore need to know, understand and appreciate this company's innermost soul.'

'Good fortune is a function of probability (but) spiritual salespeaople view luck as a manifestation of the divine . . . One technique often cited is that of affirmation. This merely involves the repetitive saying or writing a desired state; it's so simple that it is frequently dismissed out of hand.'

*New Initiative Ltd, 18 Well Walk, London NW3 1LD (01 435 5000)
(Linking organisations with overseas sponsorship projects)

'We act as a go-between for businesses wishing to sponsor effective schemes that will benefit communities in the Third World, and/or the natural eco-systems in these regions. This also involves increasing management awareness of the tremendous advantage to both sides when overseas subsidiaries become involved in these local projects, and of the importance of personal interest and commitment on the part of the organisation's own people at all levels. Apart from arranging and facilitating these schemes, we help to ensure the positive effects of external and internal public relations that flow from them.'

*PACE (Performance And Communication Enterprises) Ltd, Redvers House, 13 Fairmile, Henley-on-Thames, Oxon, RG9 2JR (0491 410112)
(The development of ability in communication and performance)

'The ability to manage personal performance; the ability to think in terms of practical outcomes and track progress towards them; the ability to establish rapport with a wide range of people; an acute focus and sensitivity to the situation of the moment and the flexibility and creativity to respond appropriately – all these abilities are often called intuitive. But

PACE's new modelling and training technology [of Neuro Linguistic Programming*]
provides practical means to develop them and to give senior managers and top sales, personnel and training professionals an added edge.'
[*'The understanding of body language in its relationship to thought and speech – the relationship between our neurology and the inborn and learned patterns which result in language.']

Peter Russell, 1 Erskine Road, London NW3 3AJ (01 722 7690)
(Business aspects of personal development, self-management and inner growth – via seminars/workshops and conference presentations)

'I work with a number of corporations who are looking for new ways of managing the future. This often focuses on the role which self-management plays in the development of individuals, organisations and society as a whole; on stress management, mindsets, the learning process and creative thinking. I am particularly interested in the long-term implications of social and technological innovation and the changes in human thinking that these could bring. Only by exploring and developing our inner potential, by gaining a much deeper understanding of the way we function, can we meet the challenges of the 21st century.'

Tom Thiss, c/o BCCI, 100 Leadenhall Street, London EC3A 3AD
(01 283 8566)
(Consultant in the fields of higher purpose, vision, creativity, integrity, imagination, quality and ecological awareness)

'One of the great paradoxes of our time is that despite our spectacular technological achievements we are today, more than ever before, dependent upon people. In a complex interdependent world, people make the difference. These who recognise this will have the edge in the 90s, a decade destined to become more human.'
'In order for this age to become more human we need to employ the spirit as well as the mind and the body. Long having been denied full expression in the business community, the spirit has begun to emerge. With our passion for control we have historically undervalued our human potential and thus denied ourselves the very thing we sought to gain – increased productivity. If energy is to be channelled toward productive ends it must first be released with the full power of its passion. Enlightened leaders are finding ways to do this today. The human spirit thrives on release, not control. The human spirit, no longer confined to play a covert role in business affairs, is moving into the mainstream.'
7   The quotation comes from Dr Francisco Kendel-Vegas, Ambassador for Venezuela in Britain.

INDEX

NOTE: This index includes no reference to the contents of the preface, nor of the appendix, nor of the list of companies in Chapter 14.